Janice Hart
29/06/2012
Romford

The Miegunyah Press

This is number fifty-six in the
second numbered series of the
Miegunyah Volumes
made possible by the
Miegunyah Fund
established by bequests
under the wills of
Sir Russell and Lady Grimwade.

'Miegunyah' was the home of
Mab and Russell Grimwade
from 1911 to 1955

A Celebration of
Australian Gardening

Gardenesque

RICHARD AITKEN

THE MIEGUNYAH PRESS

State Library
of Victoria

For JRA

THE MIEGUNYAH PRESS
An imprint of Melbourne University Publishing Ltd (MUP Ltd)
PO Box 1167, Carlton, Victoria 3053, Australia
mup-info@unimelb.edu.au
www.mup.com.au

Published in association with the State Library of Victoria, 328 Swanston Street, Melbourne, Victoria, 3000

First published 2004
Text © Richard Aitken 2004
Individual essays © Paul Fox, Anne Latreille and Michael Leunig, 2004
Images © State Library of Victoria, unless otherwise acknowledged
Design and typography © Melbourne University Publishing Ltd 2004

National Library of Australia Cataloguing-in-Publication entry

Aitken, Richard.
Gardenesque : A Celebration of Australian Gardening.

Bibliography.
Includes index.
ISBN 0 522 85127 4.

1. Gardening – Australia – History – Pictorial works. 2. Gardens – Australia – History – Pictorial works.
I. State Library of Victoria. II. Title.

635.0994

SPONSORS

The Australian Garden History Society
is a not-for-profit organisation that aims
to promote interest in cultural landscapes
and historic gardens and to encourage their
conservation as a component of Australia's heritage.
www.gardenhistorysociety.org.au

Every effort has been made to contact holders of copyright and to seek other relevant permissions.
If any omissions or errors are detected, the publishers invite relevant individuals or organisations to contact
them to ensure that appropriate acknowledgment can be made in any future editions of this book.

FOREWORD

The State Library of Victoria has a rich, and literally growing, collection of material relating to plants, gardening and landscape design. This is clearly demonstrated by the diversity of items that form the basis of this wonderful book—ranging from beautiful early nineteenth-century botanical works to computer-generated images of designed landscapes. Most of the works included in this book are rarely displayed, yet the great beauty of our Library is that they represent a public resource. I hope that the foresight of past generations in collecting these riches will enthuse present and future generations to follow their example.

This book was inspired by an exhibition proposal from Suzanne Hunt, who had previously been instrumental in the establishment of a Garden History Archive at the State Library of Victoria. Suzanne's passion for garden history, and for ensuring its preservation and accessibility, led her and her husband Robin very generously to support the curatorial development of the *Gardenesque* exhibition. The project—both in its published form and the exhibition—has also been generously supported by the Sunshine Foundation and the Australian Garden History Society (Victorian Branch).

This book and the exhibition form a complementary pairing. For those who are unable to visit the State Library of Victoria to view the exhibition, the book represents a delightful armchair guide. For this we have to thank our publishing partners, Melbourne University Publishing, through its prestigious Miegunyah Press imprint. We are particularly delighted to collaborate with MUP, and look forward to a continuation of such a fruitful partnership between two of Melbourne's great institutions.

The project has substantially benefited from the wide expertise found within the staff of the State Library of Victoria. It is one thing to have collections of outstanding richness, but without the dedication and knowledge of our staff, the exceptional potential of the collections as an educational resource would be greatly undervalued. I wish to thank all those who have assisted with the project. This has been a collaborative exercise, and one that demonstrates the versatility and potential of our institution.

I hope that you derive great pleasure from *Gardenesque*.

Anne-Marie Schwirtlich
CEO AND STATE LIBRARIAN
STATE LIBRARY OF VICTORIA

Part 12.

Price 1s. 6d.

April.

H. W. POTTS

Hand-Book of Australian Horticulture

By
H. A. James. F.R.H.S.
Gold Medallist
H.S. of N.S.W. 1891.

In Twelve
Monthly Parts

Illustrations By
Signor Guglielmo Autoriello.

SYDNEY.
TURNER & HENDERSON,
Publishers.

MELBOURNE
Melville, Mullen, & Slade.

ADELAIDE
W. C. Rigby.

BRISBANE.
Watson, Ferguson & Cº

HOBART
Walch & Son.

DUNEDIN
Wise Caffin & Cº

CONTENTS

PLATE 4

Fig.1.

Fig.2.

Fig.3.

Fig.4.

Published by J. Harding, 1810.

PREFACE

Suzanne Hunt

My fascination with the history of Australian gardens and gardening began not as a mid-life crisis but in response to a sea change forced upon me through ill health. As a social historian and curator, my professional interests focused upon the cultural aspirations of people's lives, and the material artefacts and archives derived from their endeavours. Unfortunately, recurring bouts of illness hastened my departure from work at Museum Victoria. Looking for a new interest, I decided to try my hand at landscaping on Victoria's Mornington Peninsula. After fifteen years, I've learnt the hard way about plants, soil management and the importance of scale to large country gardens. I've also discovered a creative avenue to channel my combined skills—researching the relatively unknown story of gardening in Australia. And what a passion it has become!

Nothing, of course, is ever as easy as it seems. The first difficulty I encountered during my quest was locating relevant archival material. Letters and pictures, for example, might contain descriptions or indicate attitudes towards gardening, but were often catalogued by donor or author, and not cross-referenced to gardening. To rectify this situation, and in collaboration with the State Library of Victoria, I assisted in the establishment of a Garden History Archive. Once fully established, relevant material in the Library—and future accessions and donations—will be automatically cross-referenced, easing the way for future researchers. My next quest was to raise the public profile of the Library's holdings and to encourage tertiary institutions to regard the study of gardens and gardening as a legitimate field of scholarship.

The concept of a major exhibition showcasing the State Library of Victoria's extensive collections was a logical next step. I hoped that it might promote the idea that garden history can be found in everyone's backyard—not just in large gardens of the rich and the famous. An exhibition would also act as a catalyst, encouraging future donations and stimulating interest amongst scholars to write and publish in this area.

One group, the Australian Garden History Society, has been at the forefront of identifying, researching and promoting the conservation of Australian gardens and gardening traditions. The Society was founded in 1980 and has forged strong links with state and territory heritage organisations. It was a co-publisher in 2002 of *The Oxford Companion to Australian Gardens*, an encyclopaedic volume that drew on the efforts of 220 contributors, many of them Society members and supporters. For those of you who hanker to learn more about our garden history, the Australian Garden History Society could be the first step on a road to discovery.

We have been fortunate that Richard Aitken, co-editor of *The Oxford Companion to Australian Gardens*, has accepted an offer to curate the *Gardenesque* exhibition, and to research and write this accompanying book. Richard brings a wealth of experience to the project as well as a quirky appreciation of the subject. He has been wonderfully supported by the staff of the State Library of Victoria, particularly Olga Tsara, assistant curator for the exhibition. This publication is also an outstanding tribute to the creative partnership newly forged between the State Library of Victoria and Melbourne University Publishing.

The history of gardening incorporates the story of everyday life in Australia. Cultivating a garden is an interaction between personal taste and the cultural aspirations of wider society. Economics and technology impact upon the types of gardens that can be created. Garden styles are influenced by trends in planting—for instance, in these water-conscious times there is a priority towards low-maintenance and dry-tolerant gardens. Teasing out these details is what makes this field of endeavour so interesting and exciting.

The relationship of Australians to their landscape has always been rich and complex. The way in which our designed landscapes have evolved is unfolded in this book, and also in the stimulating essays that speculate on the images and texts. The approach is at once personal and thought provoking. I hope that you enjoy your journey through this beautifully produced book and that it provides an enhanced understanding of the importance of safeguarding our garden heritage.

ACKNOWLEDGEMENTS

ANNE-Marie Schwirtlich acknowledged in her Foreword that a project such as *Gardenesque* is necessarily a complex, collaborative effort. As author of this book and as curator of the accompanying exhibition at the State Library of Victoria, it is a rewarding task to acknowledge my thanks to all those who have been involved, and to highlight those who have played a special part.

I am, first and foremost, grateful to Suzanne and Robin Hunt for the extraordinarily generous support they have shown for *Gardenesque*. This has permitted my engagement as curator, and also that of assistant curator Olga Tsara, and has given us the luxury of spreading the requisite exhibition-related tasks over an eighteen-month period. Suzanne's deep personal interest in the subject has also helped shape the project, especially in its focus on gardening as an integral part of Australia's social and cultural history. I am also grateful for the generous support of the project from the Sunshine Foundation and the Victorian Branch of the Australian Garden History Society. The interest and enthusiasm of Helen Page has been a crucial factor in the latter.

At Melbourne University Publishing, Louise Adler and her team have given the book their undivided attention. I am grateful to the Miegunyah Fund for their generous financial support, which has assisted in raising the quality of this publication to a standard that I dared not even contemplate at the outset. Editor Clare Coney and book designer Ruth Grüner have formed a wonderful complement to the MUP team.

At the State Library of Victoria, I have benefited from the support of many managers and other staff members. In particular, I would like to thank Dianne Reilly (La Trobe Librarian), Shane Carmody (Director, Collections and Services) and Andrew Hiskens (Manager, Public Programs) for their great interest in the project and for the manner in which they have facilitated support for it within the Library. Staff members of the Public Programs and Communications Divisions have been enthusiastic supporters of this project and I would especially like to acknowledge the assistance and interest of successive exhibitions managers, Edwina Portelli and Anat Meiri, curator Clare Williamson, and exhibition producer Kim Fletcher. Managers and staff members of the Australian Manuscripts, Maps, Rare Books, Pictures Collections and members of the Library's reference teams have all been generous in their support, as have those in the Conservation and Photography Departments. I am especially grateful to Des Cowley (Manager, Rare Printed Collections) for his advice and assistance, and to the skill of photographers Erica Lauthier and Peter Mappin, who have captured most of the images for this book.

On behalf of the publishers I acknowledge the cooperation of the following copyright holders and others who have given permission to publish images: Estate of Howard Arkley, ABC Enterprises, Barbara Barnes, Chris Barry, Georgina Binns, Ross Bird, Buda Historic Home and Garden (Castlemaine), Don Burke (CTC Productions Pty Ltd), Leigh Clapp, Professor Richard Clough, Craftsman Press, Helen Doyle, Lesley Frampton, David Glenn, Catherine Greenwood, Simon Griffiths Photography, Hamilton Art Gallery, Kristin Headlam, Frances Henke (Kelly), Ian Hill, IP Australia, Warren Kirk, Merryle Johnson, Ray Joyce Photography, Michael Leunig, Ruth Maddison, Bill Mollison, Monash University Library (Rare Books Collection), Monash University Museum of Art (MUMA), Colleen Morris, National Trust of Australia (Victoria), Peter Nicholson (Rubbery Figures Pty Ltd), James Northfield Heritage Art Trust, Nucolorvue Productions Pty Ltd, Harry Plumridge, Kalli Rolfe Contemporary Art, Room 4.1.3 (Vladimir Sitta and Richard Weller), Royal Botanic Gardens, Kew (London), Search Foundation, Southern Grampians Shire Council, John Spooner, State Records New South Wales, Richard Stringer, Howard Tanner, The University of Melbourne (Archives and Special Collections), John Viska, Jean Walker, City of Westminster Archives Centre (London), Glen Wilson, John Wolseley © Viscopy, and Zeeng Photography (Lynette Zeeng).

Many colleagues outside the State Library of Victoria have assisted with the shaping of this book and its text. In this regard, I am grateful to Elizabeth Anya-Petrivna, Richard Clough, Helen Doyle, Paul Fox, Anne Latreille, Colleen Morris, Peter Watts, and staff of the Koorie Heritage Trust. I am particularly grateful to Georgina Binns for her advice and patient support when she had every right to believe that 'the next book' was still some years away.

In conclusion it is a pleasant task to acknowledge the assistance of three people who have made this project especially rewarding and enjoyable. Tracy O'Shaughnessy, my commissioning editor at Melbourne University Publishing, has been a great advocate for *Gardenesque*. The clarity of her vision for this project, her attention to detail, and her ability to produce this book within improbably tight deadlines have been a revelation. Olga Tsara, assistant curator for *Gardenesque*, assisted in selecting the items presented here, drafted captions for several of the more recent images, oversaw preparation of the guide to sources, and has undertaken a host of tasks in connection with the related *Gardenesque* exhibition. Olga's expert knowledge of the State Library of Victoria's pictorial collections, and her advocacy of these collections, forms an integral part of the wonderful and often intangible spirit which imbues the State Library. Jane Rhodes, Exhibitions Assistant at the State Library of Victoria, has acted as production assistant for this book. Her practical idealism, infectious enthusiasm and seemingly effortless capacity for work have suffused the project.

I owe a great debt to all those who have played a part in this project, and in particular to the last three who have made *Gardenesque* such a special joy. With such a capable team *and* the key to the front door of the State Library, who could want for more?

INTRODUCTION

GARDENESQUE celebrates two centuries of gardening in Australia. Gardening is a very personal affair, and elusive to the precision sought by historians or ideologues. Ample evidence of this is demonstrated by the range of images presented here. Ask a hundred gardeners each to choose a hundred images, and there is unlikely to be much overlap. Such a consolidated collection might give a representative view of Australian gardening, but the choice here is a deliberately personal one.

My wide and somewhat quirky selection of items is a reaction against those with narrow minds and fixed views on the subject. The very idea of attempting to define gardening has no place here. The futility of this is aptly illustrated by past attempts to define historic gardens. The unwitting humour in English landscape architect Lawrence Fricker's definition of such gardens as 'an assemblage principally of vegetation, kept in a preferred state of ecological arrest by the craft of gardening' encapsulates the foolishness of such well-meaning precision.

Gardenesque includes one image to represent each year from 1801 to 2003, commencing with the earliest European garden-making in Victoria—by James Grant on Churchill Island—and ending with the unresolved debate over genetic engineering. These are book-ended by two images with transcendental qualities: an initial image by sketcher Henry Godfrey encapsulates the succession and cycles of Aboriginal environmental management while a final image—John Wolseley's 'After the Fire' (2004)—stands in the present and looks to the future with another timeless image, in this case depicting regeneration of vegetation after fire.

The last image also signifies the primary involvement of the State Library of Victoria in this book. Wolseley's lithograph was produced during a fellowship at the State Library, and his work exemplifies the institution's role as a creative centre for knowledge and ideas. The State Library of Victoria is also hosting a major exhibition during 2004–05 to showcase its collections in the field of gardening. This book is a record of the exhibition, and expands on its themes by the inclusion of essays as well as a guide to sources for further research.

The core of the book is a kaleidoscope of images and ideas, linked by a chronological progression. These images are given context by short captions, intended as brief dialogues between the reader and author to locate and embellish the chosen moments. Introductions mark the progression of the decades, highlighting major themes in each. But to begin, three essayists speculate on the assembled works and encourage readers to make their own voyage of discovery through the collection. Each of them speaks with an intensely personal voice and mode of expression and their essays—on volition, ideas and emotions—are as wide as the subject matter. The titles of the essays derive from categories devised by Peter Roget to facilitate the expression of ideas in his well-known *Thesaurus*; his basic divisions seem as relevant now as they did on their first publication in 1852.

Edna Walling's niece, Barbara Barnes, when responding to my queries about the inclusion of Walling items, was puzzled by the title *Gardenesque*. 'The term GARDENESQUE made me sit up a bit! Had to look up Macquarie to satisfy myself about that "esque" as an adjective suffix indicating style, names, or distinctive character and that it was not just some fancy made-up word!' This surprise is understandable, and is wholly in keeping with the spirit of the word. Writing in his own *Gardener's Magazine* in 1832, J. C. Loudon coined the term, commenting: 'Mere picturesque improvement is not enough in these enlightened times: it is necessary to understand that there is such a character of art as the gardenesque, as well as the picturesque. The very term gardenesque, perhaps, will startle some readers; but we are convinced nevertheless, that it is a term which will soon find a place in the language of rural art.' Despite a long absence from the gardener's vocabulary, it is my wish that *Gardenesque* revives the excitement imbued in its original usage, and reinforces the primacy of gardening in Australia's cultural history.

LANDSCAPE.
GARDENING.

VOLITION

Anne Latreille

WHY do I want to garden? Initially it is a combination of memories, experiment and experience.

I think back to the very beginning. The great height of the avenue of oak trees in my grandmother's large city garden is alluring. So is the leafy shade beneath the trees. The nurse spreads a rug there to accommodate afternoon tea and a tangle of toddlers, babies and rough-haired, long-legged Airedale terriers. Lying on that rug, I store away the memory. One day, I will want that same experience of sun, shadow, pets and conviviality in a space of my own.

There's a small hole inside the cypress hedge that runs beside the paddocks where our dairy cows graze. This becomes a retreat where my sisters and I play with dolls and get away from our parents. I hide there to smoke the cigarette I have filched from the shearer's packet of Craven 'A's, left on the kitchen table after morning 'smoko'. Since then I have often wanted to recreate the dusty, aromatic sense of enclosure that I remember inside that hedge.

My mother won't pay me any attention! Whenever I want her to play tennis she is busy in her garden, pruning the roses or weeding the violet patch where she picks huge bunches of unusually long-stemmed, jewel-like flowers of the deepest scent and hue. I decide that I will never want a garden, because looking after it takes up too much time. But I do wonder how it can be so completely absorbing.

Camellias grow on the sunny terrace outside the morning room of the villa where my grandmother moved after she left the big house with the avenue of oaks, and where I stay often as a teenager. She bred the camellias herself, and after breakfast she drifts outdoors to enjoy them. The contrast between the stooped old woman and the vitality of the shrubs, with their glossy green leaves and starry flowers, exemplifies all that is good about gardening— in particular, the freshness of new growth and the depth of experience that is needed to manage it.

The back garden of the house in upstate New York, where I spend a year at school, is a vista of grass and trees. Because there are no fences around the houses everyone's yard becomes a kind of communal open space. This is where we kill time after school and the ritual soda at the Sweet Shop, where we throw a football or play baseball, and where we enjoy evening meals on fine nights with whichever neighbours are at home. A garden doesn't

have to contain flowers, it can be a tapestry of greens. And it can be shared. City-dwellers in Australia, isolated behind their high fences, don't know what they're missing.

A tumbledown inner-suburban cottage, with timber shingles hiding beneath the corrugated iron roof, is my first house. As the months pass its garden, as neglected as the house, reveals a delightful symphony in pale pink. Scented winter-flowering *Luculia gratissima* gives way in spring to the pink/lilac flowers of two venerable Judas trees, then to pink-and-yellow lantana. In autumn the flower spikes of belladonna lilies, with dusky red sheaths and jaunty pink trumpets, spear up among the lantana. Creating an effect like this takes imagination, willingness to experiment, and patience. We salute the previous long-term owner, and are pleased we didn't alter the garden before letting the seasons elapse and seeing what it had to offer.

A mass of long rank grass, blackberries and two or three old trees fills the deep back garden of our next house, making it look like open country. It takes years to sort out! Knowing little about garden design, we make plenty of mistakes, some of which are remedied by seeking informed help. An expert in Australian plants and a landscape architect provide a well-furnished structure that has developed nicely over several decades. It is tempting to think that you can lay out your own garden, but it can be a relief to admit your deficiencies.

House renovations are a rite of passage in the early years of marriage. But rebuilding and extensions eventually give way to regular garden jobs like rubbish removal, cutting back plants, pulling so many weeds out of the lawn that my knees become calloused. The garden absorbs it all—barbecues, babies, children's birthdays, noisy games of backyard cricket and golf as well as the short-lived nightmare

of installing a swimming pool. Bringing up a family in a garden involves flexibility and, for the garden itself, a lot of give and take.

The garden eventually becomes a source of great pride and pleasure. Pruning, planting, altering, fiddling, titivating, admiring—its siren call is irresistible. How easy it is to embark on a five-minute task and come indoors two hours later! How satisfying to stand back and admire your handiwork! How exciting the arrival of a new catalogue from a favourite specialist nursery—and, years later, the sight of a healthy patch of perennials that has spread from the single plant you ordered! Instant plants in pots are all very well, but you also need to learn to wait in a garden. There are infinite rewards to be had from growing and nurturing.

We are asked to join Australia's Open Garden Scheme. Taking part is nerve-wracking, but the anxiety and expense of preparations is more than counterbalanced by the way the garden looks, and the heady experience on the day of sharing with others what you have created for yourself. As the visitors flock through the gate you feel besieged but also delighted, especially by the gardening lore you pick up from others who know far more than you. If ever you think there is nothing more to learn about gardening, then you are missing out.

A large and destructive dog joins the family. She demolishes the lawn, most of the mature shrubs and flowering plants in the back garden, and even the watering system. Again a flexible attitude is required. We give her the vegetable garden, which can be barricaded off, as a playpen. This is rejuvenated only after she dies twelve years later, when I discover anew how much tender loving care is needed to grow good quality vegetables. And how much water—with which I am not as profligate as I used to be.

We wake up one day to a new space in the sky. The old apple tree is reclining gracefully in the swimming pool, having given way so gently that even the person sleeping in an adjoining room has heard nothing in the night. Its golden-brown apples, an unidentified heritage variety, kept us in stewed fruit every autumn, its pink and white blossom was a springtime magnet for bees, and our loved little tabby cat camouflaged herself for years among its weatherbeaten grey branches. Eighteen months on, the gap is still unfilled. It is exciting to think about what to plant there. Never be in a hurry in a garden, which moves along at its own pace, in tune with the weather and the seasons.

There are planting successes. The variegated ajuga is spreading! This temperamental groundcover, with lime-cream dappled leaves and flowers of china blue, sulked for many years, but I decided not to move it because I knew where I wanted it to grow, at the foot of the crab-apple tree and spreading into the silvery gravel drive. Despite the drought, at last it is on the move. Sometimes you just have to cross your fingers and hang on.

And there are failures. I've unsuccessfully spent a fortune on stocking the sunny bed behind the stone wall near the swimming pool, where I see in my mind's eye a colourful blend of small, pretty Australian flowers. Nothing will thrive there. As a last resort I change the soil to a depth of half a metre. A new batch of plants grows famously for a while, then dies overnight like all the others. I dig up some indestructible dwarf agapanthus and succulents, and whack them in. Sometimes you just have to admit defeat.

More and more I use the garden for exercise.

Our new cat, who is a tomboy hoon, waits for me to emerge each morning, then cartwheels up and down the trees and through the shrubs. It's all a game, but as I rush after him I notice jobs to do, new growth to enjoy. This is a fun way of meeting the garden. There are few fresher places than a garden at first light, and if you've been busy in it the day before there is no keener joy than stepping outside to admire your handiwork.

A witness to highs and low, the garden is a backstop to our lives. From the tear-sodden burials of pets to the high jinks of twenty-first birthday parties, it sees them all. A garden has an innate constancy; it forgives inattention or temporary lack of interest and, reassuringly, it is always there. Its quiet peace, the restorative work of tending plants and tilling the soil, has helped many a person through a drama. As the seventeenth-century poet George Herbert wrote in 'The Flower': 'Who would have thought my shrivelled heart Could have recovered greenness? It was gone Quite underground . . .'.

Gardening is rejuvenating. It gets you bending, stretching and breathing deeply and it also feeds the soul by introducing you to fresh air, birdsong, light flickering off leaves, and the feel of soil beneath your fingernails.

I garden because of my memories, because of what I have learned through experience, and because I want to experiment. But most of all, I garden because I cannot help it. The garden allows me to switch off, it challenges me and makes me think, it lets my mind run free. It summons me outdoors in all weathers, and if I am not careful, it keeps me there. It is receptive, non-judgemental, inspiring. I cannot imagine a world without it.

ANNE LATREILLE *is a writer and editor whose work centres on gardens, landscapes, planning and the natural environment. She lives in Melbourne.*

IDEAS

you go into the garden.
It's a good place
to grow.

you pull out a little
weed; and some nasty
little worry leaves your
mind. How fascinating!

And there! A tiny
ant. So bright and
brave. It could be you.
Could it?

And look at that rose!
You are reminded of
your true love.
So beautiful... and
with sharp thorns.

Now contemplate the
compost heap. It's just
like your mind, your
memory, your history.
Breaking down but
getting richer.

Ah-ha! The trellis.
full of beans and peas.
You need a trellis
sometimes. We all need
a little support.

Oh dear. A stem has broken. Something has come to nothing. A hope is dashed.
But it's o.k. You will grow back. The sun will shine again.

But look at that beautiful, luxuriant fern. You are reminded of the book you want to write. Some sort of fabulous unfurling from an exotic part of your mind.

A bird sings and flits by. It scratches in the soil. Your heart is a bird. It flies up towards the sun.

The creeper needs cutting back. The petty worries, the nagging inhibitions, the nasty and the narrow. Those who drag you down. Cut yourself free.

Oh look at that! A new leaf! You can always turn over a new leaf. It will turn itself back again of course.

Ah yes, the garden, the fruits, the shoots, the blooms, the fragrance. The light and the shade. And you.... you are in love and growing...

Leunig

EMOTIONS
Paul Fox

THE human story begins in the Garden with the emotions expected of a best seller: divine anger, human sexual need and the disgrace of outcasts; it continues with the ordinary virtues of weeding, planting and pruning according to the seasons …

Let's begin with a super-human moment. The time and place? Eighteenth-century England. Here men's ambitions were as great as the acres they owned. While less fortunate people lost their common lands in an agrarian revolution, wealthy men transformed the newly acquired fields into landscaped gardens. In this story the landscape became a theatre; great acreages, stages; trees, lakes and follies, scenery; and grandees of the realm, actors who took their cue from the garden-producer. In this drama the gardener spoke sweet words to soothe, flatter and cajole the expansive patron who would own all nature. Spectators came from further afield. And the applause? None came from those who were forced to leave their fields to work in the new industrial towns or to emigrate to new lands.

In foreign lands, the desire to acquire new plants hatched enormous scheming among European intruders, who wished to grow rich and retire to the theatre of an English estate.

European political machinations to beggar China, and make an English cup of tea, saw tea plants sent out of China to be grown in Indian plantations.

Knowing this, how should we view the botanical illustrations found in Nathaniel Wallich's *Descriptions and figures of a select number of unpublished East Indian plants*? With all the wonder of seeing what was new to European eyes in 1831? With admiration for Wallich, whose energy in the pursuit of the rare and new plant was as immense as the subcontinent he collected? Or distaste borne of concern for the Indian artists who drew the illustrations to satisfy a man's passion for what was new to his European nature? (How these artists felt is not recorded in Wallich's taxonomic writings.)

If the discovery of plants had this darker side, it also created a new gardening fashion known as the gardenesque. It was a perfect style for cultivating newly discovered plants that arrived in England in increasing numbers from far-flung parts of the globe. In the nineteenth-century villa garden of the new middle class there was always room for one more plant from just one more country. Imagine the pleasure of seeing conifers from the Americas, Morocco, Lebanon, China and India growing in your garden, and knowing you possessed them all. This was a fail-safe way of satisfying the acquisitiveness of a mercantile class that claimed ownership of the whole world.

And in the colonies? What are we to make of the 1848 Melbourne garden of Bishop Perry, who hailed from an English mercantile background? My lord's garden has all the attributes of the gardenesque. Here Australia is imagined as an improved English garden where palms growing out of doors, rather than in glass houses, mock the cold English climate. This is very different to the view of Australia as an English parkland that was fashionable among sheep run holders at the time. Indeed, it is tempting to see the abundance of plants as evidence of the bishop having not only inherited God's kingdom, but also turned paradise into a middle-class domain.

In the colonial garden, other emotions were also at work. In Australia a patch of dirt provided a freedom lost forever in eighteenth-century England. Australians recouped the losses suffered by ordinary people during the British agrarian revolution by digging and planting the colonial earth. This has contributed to the feeling of the Australian garden. When ordinary Australians weed, plant and prune, they can create something different to the English gentleman's park and the acquisitive aesthetic of the villa garden.

Yet can planting a garden in a colony ever be done with innocence? Is there a calculated knowing in cultivating a place where Aboriginal people, who own the land, are portrayed as incapable of gardening a country where they have named all the plants? Like the biblical story, the colonial garden has its outcasts.

Perhaps this is nowhere more apparent than in the life of Chinese market gardener, Jong Ah Sing. His plan of his 1866 gold-fields' garden—where even the 'p-ss pot' has been drawn—reminds us that the garden at least gave a refuge, and a livelihood, to a man who lived at the edge of Christian society. Even

so, one wonders what he made of European gardens that included Chinese plants. Did their presence create the same longing for home as primroses did among English immigrants? Could a man who knew the value of manure to his economic survival ever afford to be this sentimental? Eventually Sing was committed to the Yarra Bend madhouse which was set amidst a landscaped park. Did this garden have its intended effect, and calm his nerves, or further heighten his sense of disorientation? On this point the historical record remains silent.

In the colony, civic horticulture bound people together. The public park, created first to improve the English industrial town, contributed to the democratisation of public space. Here everybody had the opportunity to see nature's spectacle, even if they couldn't afford a villa garden. Such a prospect fired colonists' passions: thousands of plants were grown from seed and sent from botanic gardens to every place under the colonial sun.

At a time when native forests and grasslands were being destroyed, the public garden became a prospect to imagine what the whole country might become.

In Australia, however, the elements often mock ambitions to garden new terrains. In response the garden attempts to ignore nature.

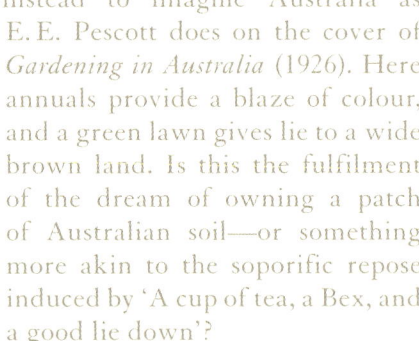

Consider the jejune garden bed in the shape of Australia celebrating the Federation of the six colonies in 1901. In all likelihood it would have been planted in the bright colours so beloved by Victorians (which today many consider distasteful). Yet the resulting carpet bed is no sunburnt country; instead it masks all the heartburn of Europeans who 'water those geraniums' in inhospitable places. In Australia where stoicism hides disappointment, planting and pruning according to the seasons is not only hard work but also an act of faith that you'll have something to show for all your effort of scratching the colonial earth.

Better instead to imagine Australia as E. E. Pescott does on the cover of *Gardening in Australia* (1926). Here annuals provide a blaze of colour, and a green lawn gives lie to a wide brown land. Is this the fulfilment of the dream of owning a patch of Australian soil—or something more akin to the soporific repose induced by 'A cup of tea, a Bex, and a good lie down'?

Seen from this perspective, the grand *allées*, intended picturesque lake, and conservation of timber-clad mountains of 1920s Canberra appear far too grand a setting for the Australian home with its flower-bed garden. If Canberra was an act of daring by avant-garde American designers, European modernity was hardly seen in the Australian garden. At this time,

the only modern machine for living was the rotary clothes' line. It was hidden in the backyard, where it masqueraded as an innocent whirligig of utility amidst the well-planned roads lined with trees, and the Arts and Crafts homes of the garden suburbs.

In 1956 a new machine appeared in the garden: the television. Something of its impact is captured by the 1961 image of a German immigrant family watching television in an unkempt suburban backyard planted only with a Hills hoist. Have they tuned into 'a show' to learn the art of Australian gardening?

When to plant northern-hemisphere bulbs for an antipodean spring and the first tomato seedlings (on Melbourne Cup weekend), and satisfy that most Australian desire: a weed-free lawn. Are they learning that gardening, mowing and reaping are part of being a 'good' Australian?

A decade later, if this family happened to turn on the television, much of the talk would have been about Australian native plants. This was a time when Australian flora was re-discovered and people delighted in what they found. So enthused did Australians become with having a bush prospect that even terrace owners threw commonsense to the wind and planted blue gums in pocket-handkerchief inner city gardens. In an era characterised by municipal engineers' aesthetic codes, some citizens awoke a nation to their country.

These bush designers provided inspiration for a new suburban aesthetic: the manicured garden suburb of the inter-war years gave way to suburbs where randomly planted gums towered above houses, and lawns were replaced by Australian shrubs set in leaf litter. Now honey-eaters and magpies flew in the Australian suburb, and Australians welcomed their arrival.

This reflected a confident, forward-looking nation. But soon nationalism took a backward glance, and discovered the past. The pioneer's cottage garden became de rigueur, and old-fashioned plants (thought to be beloved by early settlers) were planted in beds worthy of Victorian tastes. The more rigorous of these new pioneers made cough drops from hoarhound, grown in herb gardens even though it was a noxious weed. Other avid gardeners collected heritage roses, and learnt many a name of a French duchess whose pedigree contained no modern hybrid.

There is always a ghost in the Australian garden. In this era of modern pioneer gardening, English taste arrived in Australia in the guise of Sissinghurst, the country garden of gardening columnist and grand lady of horticulture, Vita Sackville-West. In the 1980s Sissinghurst's all-white garden reached celebrity status among Australian gardeners of taste, whose longing to realise its conceit was commensurate with the impossibility of obtaining it in the Australian climate. Yet effort is rewarded. Soon that coolest of flowers, the Iceberg rose, was to flower—and flower in many gardens across the land.

However, transplanting English gardening fashion never re-creates the original: that is the predicament of gardening in Australia.

Amidst all this hauteur and longing, the political cartoonist Peter Nicholson brings us down to earth. In 'Not in My Backyard' (1992) he reminds us the backyard is that most human and intensely personal of Australian spaces. In it Australians create, by the sweat of their brows, their own private paradise. Yet he chooses to locate politicians there. Why? Is Nicholson's cartoon a commentary on a new serpent appearing in paradise? In an age of popular television make-over shows, the backyard has become a site of conspicuous consumption and hard-headed property speculation. In this drama, does the politician, adept at understanding the ordinary, capitalise on the selfishness of a suburban people who see the nation in terms of their own backyard? Is this our fall from grace?

And are we poorer for the redemptive power of gardening being lost? In an age where emotion is represented in terms of the brain's electrical impulses and chemical balances (and imbalances), these sentiments may be nothing more than a human curse. Is this our next temptation?

PAUL FOX *is an honorary fellow of the Australian Centre, The University of Melbourne, and author of* Clearings: Six Colonial Gardeners and their Landscapes.

EUROPEAN IMAGINATION

(1800s–1810s)

New Holland defies our conclusions from comparisons,
mocks our studies, and shakes to their foundations the most firmly
established and most universally admitted of our scientific opinions.

François Péron, *A Voyage of Discovery to the Southern Hemisphere*,
London, 1809

THE temperate, sub-tropical and tropical splendours of colonial possessions fuelled the European imagination. Mirages of luxuriant landscapes, such as those depicted in Robert Thornton's *Temple of Flora* (1807), conjured visions of antipodean Edens where imperial rule might bring order to untamed wilderness. That this focus should fall in the late eighteenth century on the South Pacific *and* accompany momentous changes in horticulture and landscape design, profoundly influenced Australian gardening.

The European discovery of Australian plants coincided with a crucial phase in the history of horticulture. Technical advances meant that the glazed and heated protection necessary to grow Australian plants in the Northern Hemisphere was becoming more affordable and, as the nineteenth century progressed, a new class of suburban gardeners availed themselves of this horticultural luxury. Botanical classification of the riches garnered from voyages of exploration occupied botanists for decades, while the nursery trade enjoyed new commercial opportunities by exploiting the rarity of highly sought specimens. Novelty and display both figured prominently in Australian gardens.

Dramatic changes in landscape design also shaped the European imagination, which in turn moulded Australian gardening. 'Nature', as Brent Elliott recalls in *Victorian Gardens* (1986), had been long been held as the ideal that the gardener should follow. But what was nature, especially in a country such as England, where agricultural practices had altered the countryside from that known to its medieval inhabitants? Uvedale Price's *Essays on the Picturesque* (1794) had attempted to quantify absolute values that constituted the Picturesque, the Beautiful and the Sublime, although alternative approaches soon freed designers from the codified dictates of such theorists. Individual thoughts and associations were being expressed before long, leading to an almost bewildering stylistic choice for the nineteenth-century gardener.

The quest during the nineteenth century to elevate gardening from mere imitation to the more refined realm of art was an important adjunct to new aesthetic sensibilities. Instead of gardens imitating artists' depictions of nature, designers now aspired to make gardens works of art in themselves. Thus the term 'gardenesque' was coined, in imitation of 'picturesque'. The introduction into the garden of foreign plants was one obvious means of elevating art over imitative nature. New plants were sought from all parts of the globe. For Britain, the savant–botanist Joseph Banks identified the South African Cape, South America and Australia as priorities, complementing an established presence in India.

However, aesthetics initially counted for little as explorers and settlers made their first tentative gardens in strange new environments. The reality of these early gardens, and the landscape in which they were set, was conveyed in their logs and journals, and in the lightning sketches of botanists and shipboard artists. In particular, the image of productive landscapes—whether providentially bestowed or enhanced by cultivation—is one that recurs throughout the history of gardening.

Many contemporary images and ideas were, of course, tangential to Australia. Yet the cumulative impact of such investigations and publications formed a lode of botanical and horticultural knowledge for those who followed. In the mind's eye, the world was relentlessly shrinking.

Timelessness

Although painted in 1843, this view of Aboriginal women digging encapsulates a timeless succession of food production, common to Indigenous and transplanted cultures. Here, the bond between human needs and the land is immediate, intuitive and sustaining. For those who shared this bond, such ties with the land suffused all aspects of their endeavour—knowledge of bush foods was one part of a seamless environmental understanding. But the animated scene captured here by sketcher Henry Godfrey was soon overturned by the bewildering transformation of traditional Aboriginal lands by European cultivation.

Planting for 'Countrymen, Europeans or Savages' | 1801

The planting in 1801 of the first garden in the Port Phillip District of New South Wales—later to become the state of Victoria—recorded in the journal of Lieutenant James Grant is emblematic of early gardening in Australia. Finding fresh water and good soil on Churchill Island—which Grant named for the supplier of his seeds—his party cleared ground and erected a 'mansion-house' of logs. Grant planted seeds of fruits (apples, peaches, nectarines) and vegetables (wheat, Indian corn, peas, rice, potatoes, coffee). John Churchill, of Devon, had given the seeds with 'an injunction to plant them for the future benefit of our fellow-men, be they Countrymen, Europeans or Savages'.

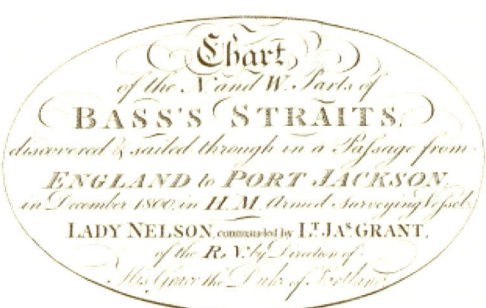

(124)

bour. The soundings were from 17 to 10, 6 and 2½ fathoms, the bottom muddy, but in the shoals sandy, which generally was the case when we stood over to the western side. Before leaving this place I will endeavour to account for it.

At half past five P.M. came to an anchor in six and a half fathoms of water, fine sand, and abreast of a sandy point, bearing W. three quarters of a mile, which I named Lady Nelson's Point, as a memorial of the vessel, as she was the first decked one that ever entered this port.

As the sun crossed the Equator this day to the northward, and heavy weather might be expected, I was glad to find a harbour that could afford us good shelter.

Mr. Barreillier went on shore with the second mate, and on their return they brought two ducks and a black swan which they had shot. They saw plenty of black swans, and red bills, an aquatic bird so called, whose back is black, the breast white, beak red, and feet not full webbed. It is an excellent eating fowl, much resembling in flavour a wild duck, and nearly of the same size.

On Sunday the 22d, or according to our sea account the 23d, it being past twelve o'clock at noon, I went with two of our crew in the smallest boat to search for a river or stream, described by Mr. Bass, at the head of the harbour, where fresh water was to be got. As a considerable track appeared to be perfectly dry at low water a short distance from the vessel across the harbour, with only small channels in some parts of it, I found it necessary to explore and sound the best passage, so as to have it always in our power, if possible, to get through the muddy flat. Pelicans and albatrosses in great numbers visit this flat, previous to its being left dry at low water, to pick up their food. In proceeding along the shore, I fell in with an island, pleasantly situated, and separated from the Main by a very

(125)

very narrow channel at low water, but even then sufficient for a boat to pass, though much larger when the tide is in. I passed through it and landed on the island towards the N. and W. It is of gradual ascent, well covered with trees of a considerable height, and much underwood. The situation of it was so pleasant, and the prospects round it so agreeable, that this, together with the richness of the soil, and the sheltered position of the spot, made me conceive the idea that it was excellently adapted for a garden. Having determined upon establishing a garden in this place, I thought it incumbent upon me to give the island the name of Churchill, after a generous and public spirited Gentleman, John Churchill, Esq. of Dawleish, in the county of Devon, who, on my leaving England, supplied me with a variety of seeds of useful vegetables, together with the stones of peaches, nectarines, and the pepins or kernels of several sorts of apples, with an injunction to plant them for the future benefit of our fellow-men, be they Countrymen, Europeans or Savages. I had, moreover, been furnished with many seeds for the like liberal purposes, by my friend Capt. Schank; but let me not omit the pepin of an apple, differing from all other fruit of the kind, in having rarely more than one pepin in each apple. I hope the name I gave with it in New Holland will not be forgotten (Lady Elizabeth Percy's Apple) should it happen to prove a common fruit of the country, as it was owing to her Ladyship's care and attention in preparing the pepins, that I was enabled to introduce it. Whatever is for the benefit of mankind cannot be of indifference, I therefore think I need make no apology to the feeling reader for this short digression.

From several good observations, I found Western Port to lie in lat. 38° 32' S. and that by the Chronometer its longitude was 146° 19' to the eastward of Greenwich.

I found in Churchill's Island several holes of large size, apparently

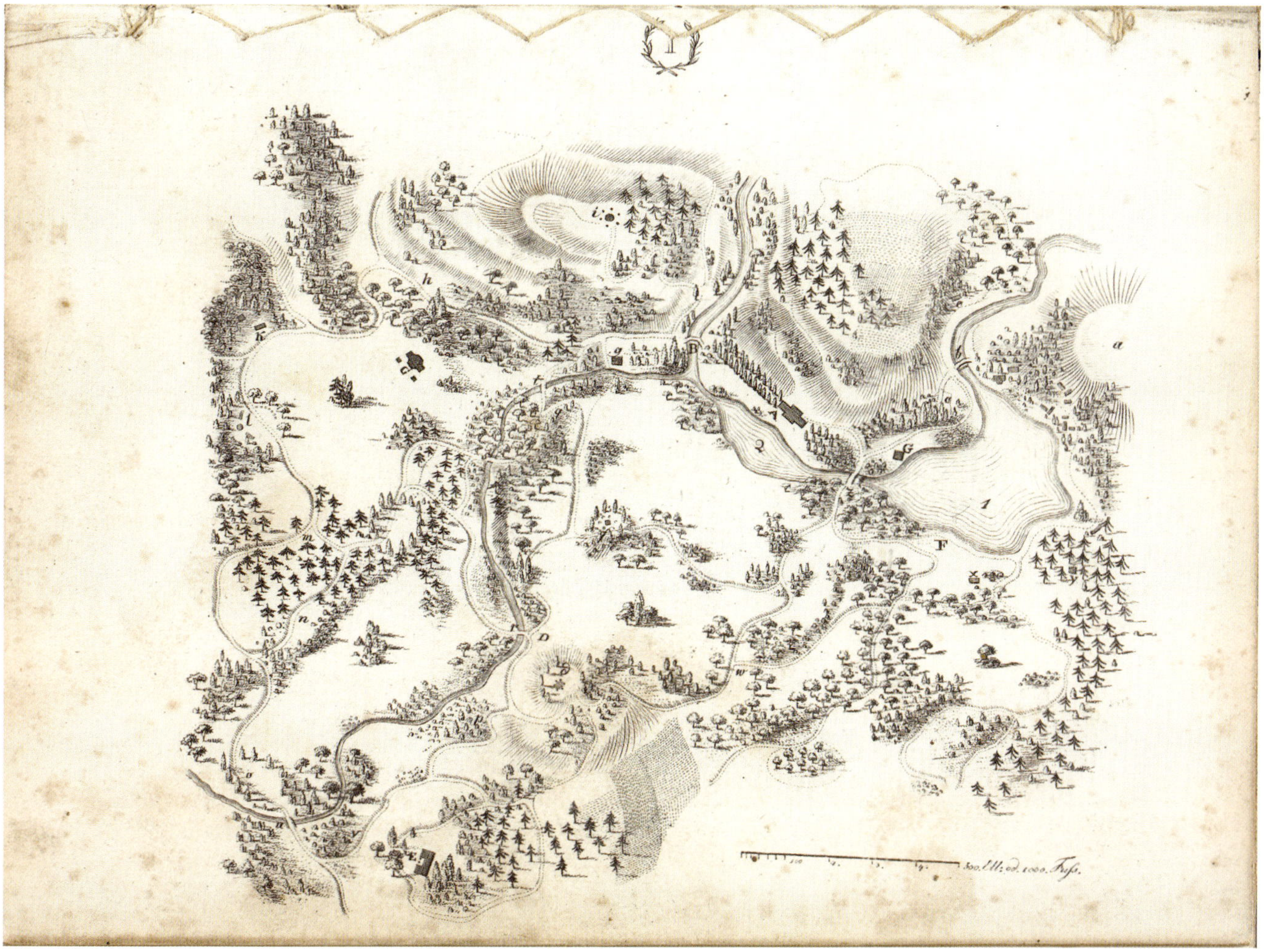

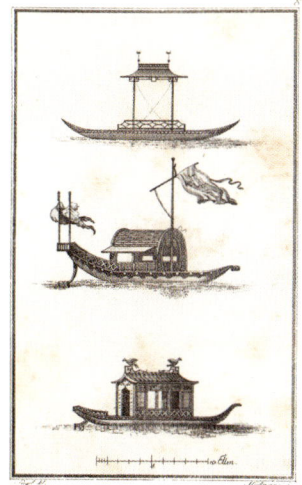

'Jardin anglo-chinoise' | 1802

The transfer of knowledge and ideas invests all gardens with rich meanings. Take, for instance, the journey of ideas represented in Chinese-inspired gardens. In this example, Mons Siegel's plan for a 'jardin anglo-chinoise' from *Descriptions Pittoresques de Jardins du Goût le Plus Moderne* (Leipzig, 1802) recalls Chinese garden-making based on venerated traditions. In the mid-eighteenth century, the studied asymmetry of Chinese gardens had been a model for English landscaping, and even given a sham name by its importers—'Sharawadgi'. Then, through sources such as *Descriptions Pittoresques*, the freedom of such designs became a model for French *jardins anglo-chinoises*. Even in the colonies, a diluted Chinese character could occasionally be discerned in our early garden architecture.

Sowing seeds
by the Yarra | 1803

James Fleming, transported from London for seven years for stealing clover seeds, arrived in Sydney in 1800. Employed by Governor King as a gardener at Parramatta, he was engaged during 1802–3 on the Colonial Schooner *Cumberland*. Under surveyor Charles Grimes, Fleming mapped vegetation and prepared a journal of the survey, which included Port Phillip Bay and the Yarra River. His observations, made with the observant eye of a gardener more than the detached precision of a botanist, saw potential for settlement, whereas Grimes was less optimistic. On 8 February 1803, at the Yarra Falls (later Dight's Falls), Fleming 'sowed some seeds by the natives' hut, where we slept'—presumably vegetables.

Novæ Hollandiæ Plantarum
Specimen | 1804

Jacques-Julien Houtou de Labillardière was one of the great French traveller-naturalists. In 1791–3, whilst accompanying Bruny d'Entrecasteaux in search of the explorer La Pérouse, who had disappeared after visiting Botany Bay in 1788, Labillardière made significant botanical collections. At a time when Britain and France were vying for supremacy in the South Pacific, the plants collected and named by Labillardière in his *Novæ Hollandiæ Plantarum Specimen* (Paris, 1804–6)—including *Epacris impressa* (Pink-flowered Heath), pictured here— gave his country a scientific advantage. The *Specimen*, virtually the first Flora of Australia, was made possible, however, only by the diplomatic intervention of British savant Sir Joseph Banks, who was instrumental in repatriating to France Labillardière's plant specimens, which had been confiscated in Java.

NOVÆ HOLLANDIÆ
PLANTARUM SPECIMEN.

AUCTORE JACOBO-JULIANO LABILLARDIÈRE,
INSTITUTI NATIONALIS SOCIO.

TOMUS PRIMUS.

PARISIIS,
EX TYPOGRAPHIA DOMINÆ HUZARD.
1804.

Browsing Line.

Observations on the Theory and Practice of Gardening | 1805

Humphry Repton's *Observations on the Theory and Practice of Gardening*
(London, 1803–5) was a major text for the new century. By this date Repton was Britain's
most celebrated landscape designer. Many of the *Observations* were taken from the distinctive
'Red Books'—so called from their red morocco leather bindings—which Repton prepared when
presenting designs to clients. He intended his new work to be 'a book of precepts . . . I wish to make
my appeal less to the eye than to the understanding'. Central to this was Repton's use of flaps, facilitating
an appreciation of his ideas and designs 'before' and 'after' improvement.

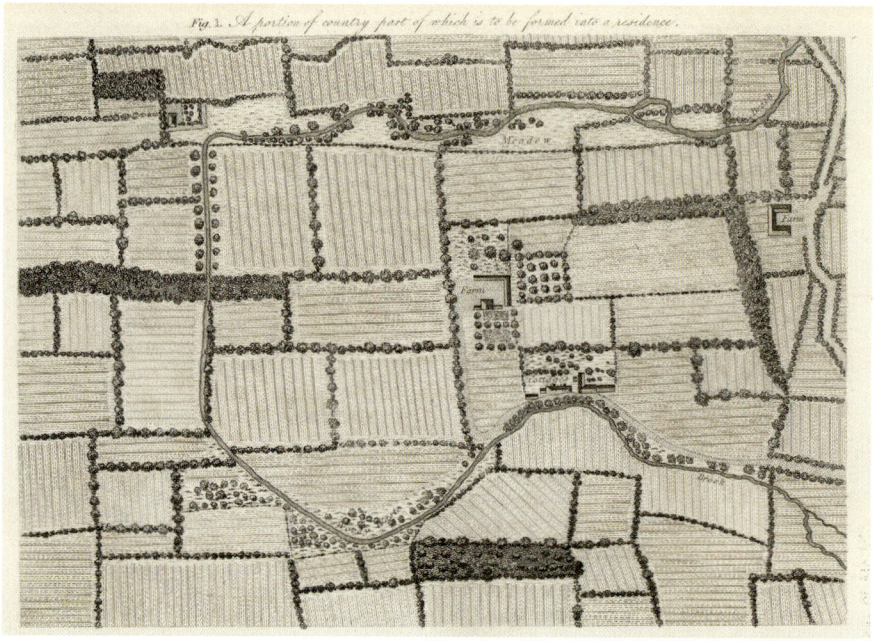

Fig. 1. A portion of country part of which is to be formed into a residence.

These plans from J.C. Loudon's *Treatise on Forming, Improving, and Managing Country Residences* (London, 1806) serve to introduce Australia's earliest professional landscape designer, Thomas Shepherd. Loudon's engravings successively depict a medieval arrangement of fields, and landscape designs of the seventeenth, eighteenth and early nineteenth centuries. They stand as a microcosm of

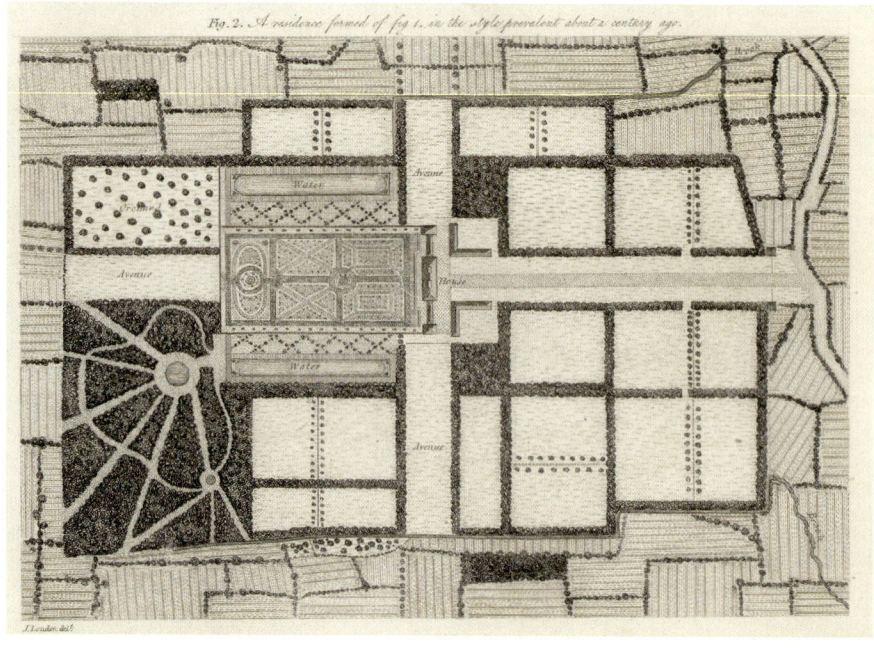

Fig. 2. A residence formed of fig. 1. in the style prevalent about a century ago.

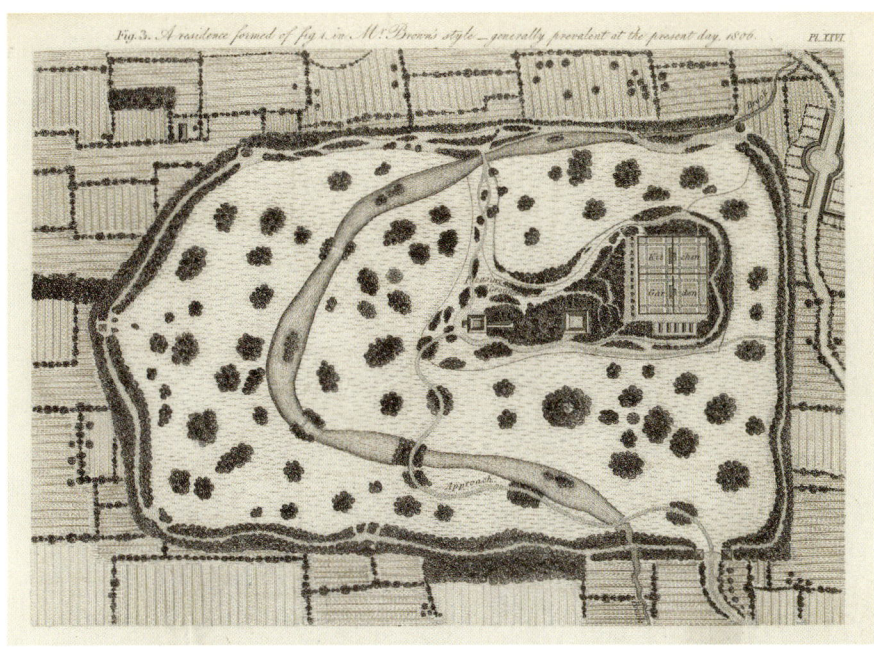

Fig. 3. A residence formed of fig. 1, in M.r Brown's style — generally prevalent at the present day. 1806.   Pl. XLVI.

Shepherd's career: British-born, trained under a disciple of the landscape master 'Capability' Brown and—especially through his *Lectures on Landscape Gardening in Australia* (Sydney, 1836)—a promoter of a natural style. Loudon's youthful 'characteristic or natural style', depicted in the last engraving, encapsulated Shepherd's preference for 'pleasing effects [and] . . . improved scenery'.

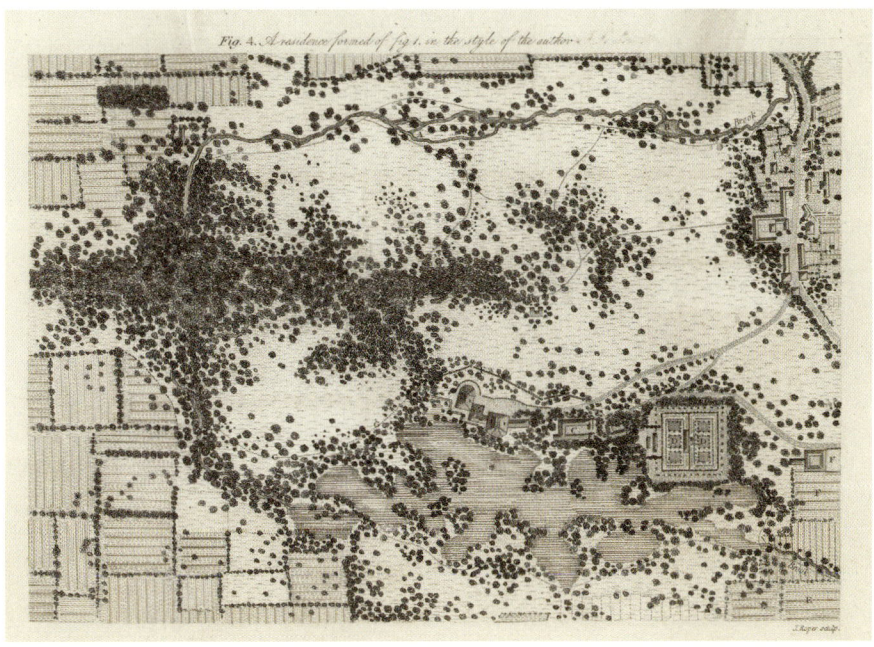

Fig. 4. A residence formed of fig. 1, in the style of the author.

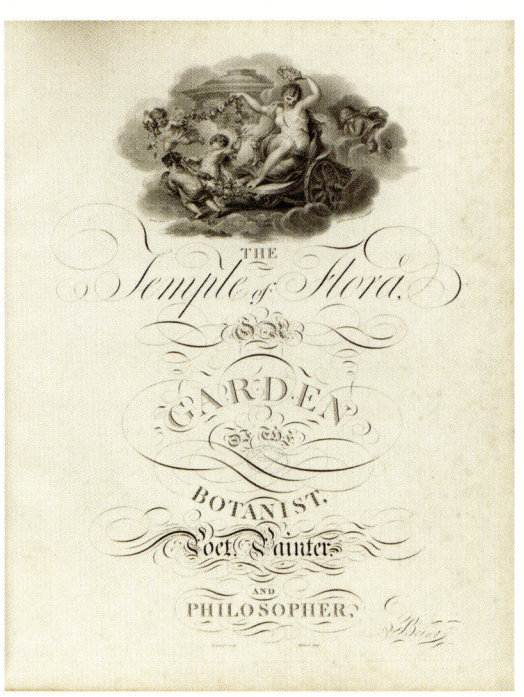

The Temple of Flora ⏐ 1807

The Temple of Flora is the third volume of Robert Thornton's massive and astonishing illustrated work *The New Sexual System of Linnaeus* (London, 1807). Inspired by Swedish botanist Carl Linnaeus, whose system of plant classification and nomenclature revolutionised plant science, the volumes range curiously from botanical didacticism to affectionate sentimentality. Breathtaking plates of closely observed plants in idealised geographic settings sit beside botanical dissections and quaint genre scenes. An arrow-wielding Cupid thus inspires plants with love, the petal-strewing Flora dispenses her favours on the earth, and both are joined by Aesculapius and Ceres to honour a bust of Linnaeus.

Remarks on Forest Scenery . . . relative chiefly to picturesque beauty ⏐ 1808

English clergyman William Gilpin travelled extensively through Britain, and his illustrated journals formed the basis of popular works on the Wye River (1782), Lake District (1786) and Scottish Highlands (1789) that almost single-handedly defined picturesque beauty. Gilpin translated his observations into a practical landscape manifesto, *Remarks on Forest Scenery* (1791), which analysed the contributions of individual trees, and their collective value as clumps, copses and forests. Many of the elite who travelled to the colonies in the early nineteenth century demonstrated picturesque tastes based on Gilpin's influence, kept alive through numerous revised editions of his works.

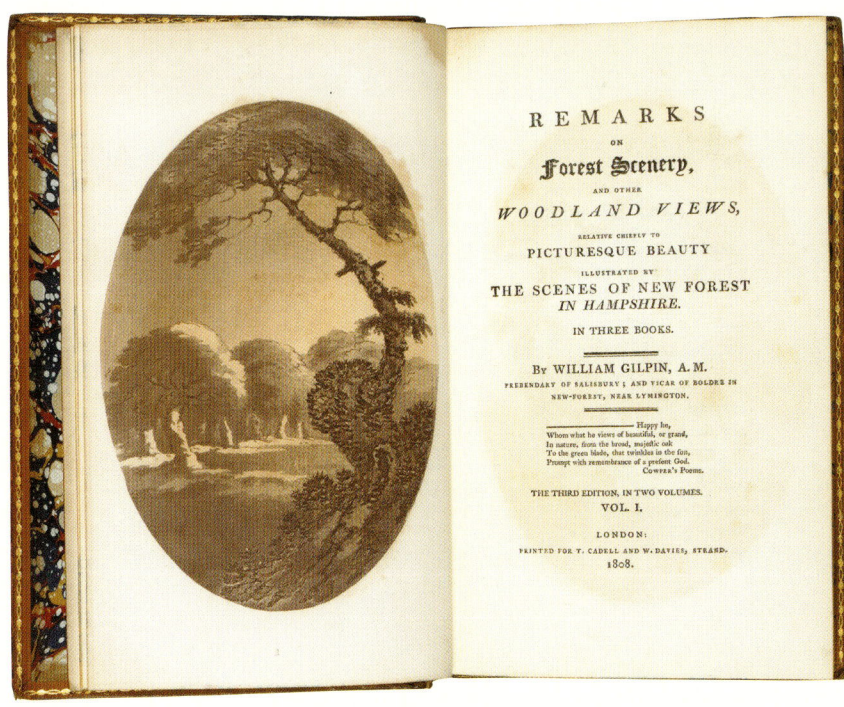

'Tyger-spotted Chinese Lily' | 1809

The European discovery of plants was a complex affair of politics. Competing colonial powers
jealously guarded recent territorial gains, while venerable nations maintained closed borders to all
but the most persistent enquirers. China in particular was a rich and tantalising horticultural storehouse
that held the West at bay. Publicity for exports was provided by a new type of publication, the illustrated
horticultural periodical, pioneered by William Curtis from 1787 with his *Botanical Magazine*. Here the
'Tyger-spotted Chinese Lily' (*Lilium tigrinum*, now *L. lancifolium*)—now a garden favourite—was
introduced to the horticultural world in 1809 as 'A splendid species which has not yet found a place
in any general system of vegetation'.

Florists' flowers | 1810

The growing of individual flowers, both for private admiration and open competition, was well suited to those of modest means. By the early nineteenth century the hobby was promoted by florists' societies and books such as James Maddock's *The Florist's Directory: A Treatise on the Culture of Flowers* (London, 1810). Eight plants dominated—auricula, polyanthus, hyacinth, anemone, tulip, ranunculus, carnation and pink. As these were capable of almost endless variation, Maddock (and later Thomas Hogg and George Glenny) defined an almost abstract set of properties governing shape, size and colour, so pervasive that even far-distant Australian enthusiasts used them in search of the perfect florists' flower.

PLATE VII.

Fig. 1. A plan of the surface of the west-end of the Hyacinth bed, on a scale of half an inch to a foot, as described, pages 26 to 28.

Fig. 2. A perspective view of a frame, or awning, to defend a bed, or stage of flowers, from the weather, with the cloth drawn up on one side. Pages 33 and 34.

a, One of the horizontal pullies (see Fig. 3.) screwed on the edge of the ridge-piece.

b, One of the perpendicular pullies (see Fig. 4.) screwed on the edges of the end rafters.

c, One end of a long wooden roller, fastened to the lower edges of the cloth, with which it is rolled up, or let down, by lines passing through the pullies.

d, One of the boards of the Carnation stage placed upon substantial supporters (as at e) the lower ends of which stand in reservoirs of water (as at f). Page 171.

Fig. 3. One of the horizontal pullies (a, Fig. 2.) Pages 34 and 171.

Fig. 4. One of the perpendicular ditto, (b, Fig. 2.)

Fig. 5. A transplanting instrument.

Fig. 6. A small hexagonal hand-glass.

Fig. 7. A rose of a watering pot.

Fig. 8. A small watering pot for Auriculas, &c.

INTRODUCTION.

— ◦◦◦◦◦ —

Sᴜᴄʜ is the force of natural habit throughout the universe, that even vegetables, natives of the warmer climes, between or near the tropics, cannot exist when transported to the more Northern latitudes, unless art steps forward to their assistance ; thence necessarily proceed the numerous glass erections throughout our Islands, under the denominations of Hot and Greenhouses, &c. &c.

The Exotic Gardener | 1811

The Exotic Gardener (Dublin, 1811) is amongst the earliest books about the growing of Australian plants in the Northern Hemisphere. Its author, John Cushing, was a departmental foreman with Lee and Kennedy, the celebrated London nursery proprietors who specialised in 'New Holland exotics'. Such plants would not thrive in northern latitudes, Cushing wrote, 'unless art steps forward to their assistance' through the agency of heated and glazed protection. Perhaps reflecting the numerous unproven methods of propagating Australian seeds in the book, its owner has impishly altered the 'Table of genera' at the end to read 'Table of general *humbug and nonsense*'.

Pomona Britannica | 1812

Pomona, the goddess of fruits and fruit trees, gave her name to a specialised type of book which described the fruits of a country— just as Flora had done with flowers. Of the many pomonas, George Brookshaw's magisterial *Pomona Britannica* (London, 1804–12) is perhaps the finest. Its large aquatint engravings display a breathtaking virtuosity and inventiveness. The need to record the best available varieties of fruit resonated strongly in the colonies, where fruit growing was an important task for gardeners. Works on fruit nomenclature and culture were keenly collected for public and private libraries alike, and pomology was an early focus for our agricultural and horticultural societies.

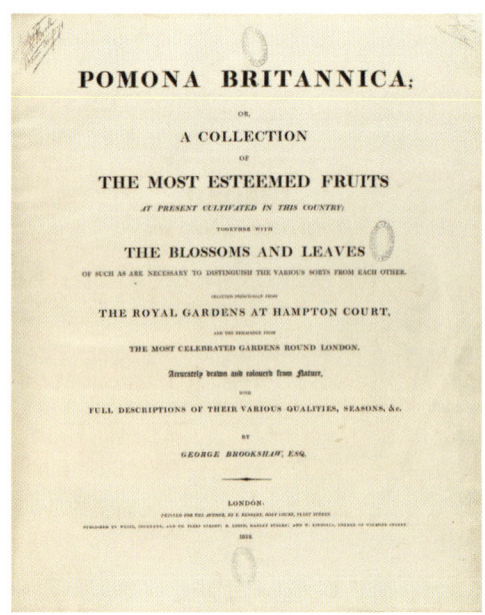

PLATE VI.
Painted & Published as the Act directs by the Author G. Brookshaw July 1st 1805.

Australian plants
at Malmaison | 1813

French interest in Australian botany grew with successive voyages of exploration, particularly those of Bruny d'Entrecasteaux (1791–3) and Nicolas Baudin (1800–3). Once seeds and specimens were safely returned to France, their horticultural potential was swiftly determined. The garden of the Empress Joséphine at Malmaison, the subject of Aimé Bonpland's exceedingly beautiful book *Description des Plantes Rares Cultivées à Malmaison et à Navarre* (Paris, 1813), was amongst the earliest and best known in Europe to feature Australian plants. Coloured engravings of the Australian flora, such as *Metrosideros glauca* (now *Callistemon glauca*) by the celebrated botanical artist P. J. Redouté, give the work a surpassing beauty.

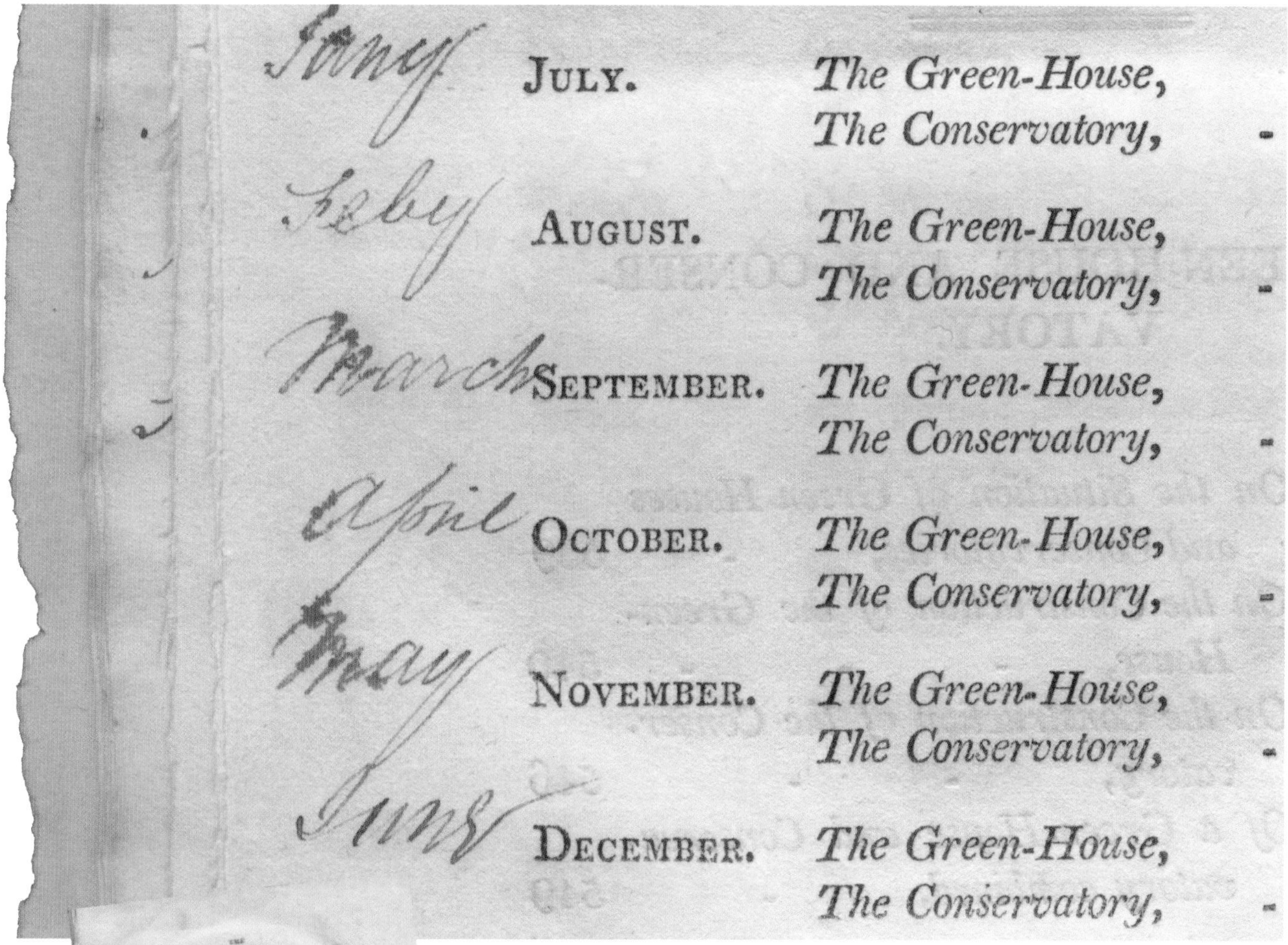

Jany JULY. *The Green-House,*
The Conservatory, —

Feby AUGUST. *The Green-House,*
The Conservatory, —

March SEPTEMBER. *The Green-House,*
The Conservatory, —

April OCTOBER. *The Green-House,*
The Conservatory, —

May NOVEMBER. *The Green-House,*
The Conservatory, —

June DECEMBER. *The Green-House,*
The Conservatory, —

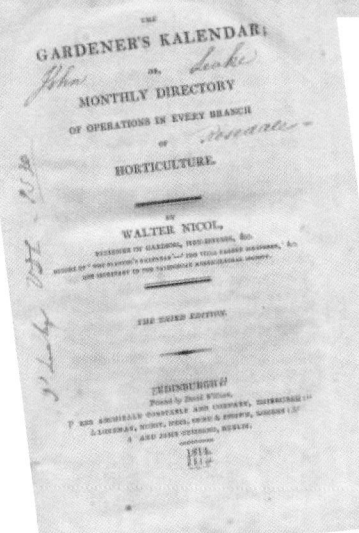

The Gardener's Kalendar | 1814

Scottish influence on Australian horticulture was informed
and enduring. Many gardens were created by wealth from
pastoralism, an industry also boosted by Scottish enterprise.
In Tasmania, for instance, pastoralist James Leake sought
guidance from Walter Nicol's book *The Gardener's Kalendar;
or, Monthly Directory of Operations in Every Branch of
Horticulture* (Edinburgh, 1814) to aid his garden-making
at Rosedale, near Campbell Town. With the dates altered
in ink throughout, to conform with seasons in the Southern
Hemisphere, Leake added a distinctive manuscript flourish
to this important Scottish treatise.

The Botanical Register | 1815

The *Botanical Register*, produced in London by Sydenham Edwards, followed the format pioneered by William Curtis of publicising new and rare plants in an illustrated periodical. Publication began in 1815 and early volumes featured numerous plants from New Holland. The Australian shrub *Pittosporum undulatum* (Waved-leaved or Sweet Pittosporum) had been introduced to Britain by Sir Joseph Banks in 1789. Edwards noted in 1815 that 'It is desirable on account of the great fragrance of the bloom, which is compared by some to that of Jasmine; to us it appears far stronger, but not so grateful [*sic*].' In this case, sadly, yesterday's novelty has become today's environmental weed.

Sydney Botanic Gardens | 1816

When Mrs Macquarie's Road was completed through the Sydney Domain in 1816, it formed the northern boundary of ground that had been cultivated for agriculture since 1788. This boundary, soon formalised by a masonry wall, henceforth sheltered the new plantings of Sydney Botanic Gardens from prevailing harbour breezes. Thus the site of the first Government Farm was rapidly transformed to become Australia's earliest acclimatisation and botanic garden. Emergent araucarias soon punctuated the horizon, while at ground level the grid of beds was quickly extended to form picturesque grounds.

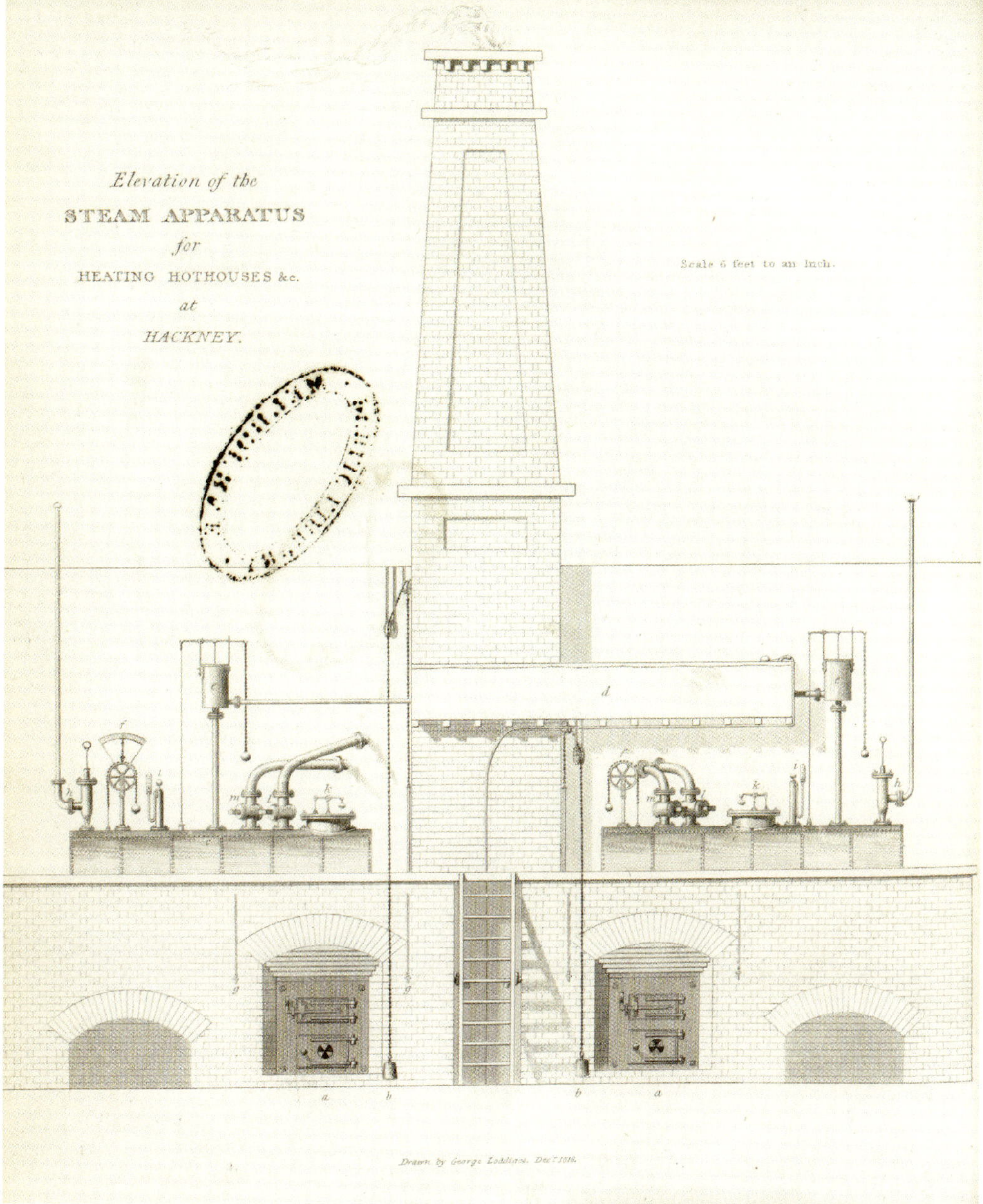

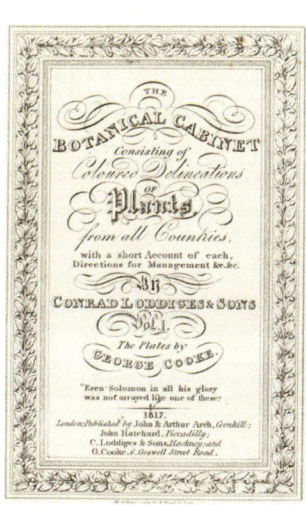

Elevation of the
STEAM APPARATUS
for
HEATING HOTHOUSES &c.
at
HACKNEY.

Scale 6 feet to an Inch.

Drawn by George Loddiges, Dec.r 1816.

The Botanical Cabinet | 1817

The London nursery of Conrad Loddiges & Sons rivalled most contemporary botanic gardens in the breadth of its collections of new and rare plants, as well as superior facilities for their growth and display. It was the Loddiges nursery that pioneered the use of glazed Wardian cases by successfully transporting plants to and from Australia in them. The first volume of Loddiges's *Botanical Cabinet* (1817) illustrated steam-heating apparatus used to maintain appropriate temperatures for tropical and semi-tropical plants. But this moist heat was to sound the death-knell for the popularity of Australian plants in the Northern Hemisphere, which thrived in the dry heat of increasingly obsolete heated walls and stove houses.

HISTOIRE NATURELLE

DES

ORANGERS

ORANGE DE NICE.
Arancio di Nizza.

Oranges and lemons, shaddocks and citrons | 1818

British books on fruit paid little attention to genera suited to tropical and semi-tropical climates, where most of the Empire's colonies were located. To counteract this imbalance, many in the colonies looked to works from France and Italy, whose Mediterranean coasts provided a more accurate model. Plant exchanges with the botanic garden at Marseilles, for instance, provided a much more logical source of plants than British botanic gardens. For those wishing to acclimatise citrus, works such as Risso & Poiteau's *Histoire Naturelle des Orangers* (Paris, 1818) described an astonishing diversity of potentially suitable varieties.

Plants of the
Indian tropics | 1819

By the late eighteenth century, Britain
controlled the Madras Presidency in India's
south-east, centred on the Coromandel coast.
Its tropical plants soon attracted the attention
of William Roxburgh, Scottish-born botanist
and superintendent of the (British) East India
Company's botanic garden at Calcutta.
Roxburgh's lavish three-volume *Plants of the
Coast of Coromandel* (London, 1795–1819) was
produced with the imprimatur of Sir Joseph
Banks, who presided with undisputed authority
over Britain's botanical empire. The plates
(including *Curcuma zerumbet*, pictured here),
drawn in India by local artists and hand-coloured
in Britain, combined to produce a work of
outstanding freshness and beauty.

ADAPTING TO
THE ANTIPODES
(1820s–1830s)

Quocunque aspicias hic paradoxus erit
(loosely translated as 'All things are backwards and unnatural')

Motto of the Tasmanian Society for the Promotion of Natural Science,
Agriculture, Statistics, &c. (Hobart Town, 1838–49)

JUST as the European imagination of Australia had involved a transposed image and a harsher reality *in situ*, so those adapting to the antipodes were confronted with an imagined metropolitan vision and a colonial reality. For British writer J.C. Loudon, countries in a 'wild state' required the firm ordered lines of a formal garden to implant artistry on the untamed wilderness.

In reality, the formal lines of Loudon were rarely adopted. Even driveways favoured the casual ease of the contour, and the antipodean *allée* envisaged by Loudon became a spine of shrubs and trees straggling through the paddocks. Even the colonial stream refused to behave, more often being amorphous or dry than firm and flowing. It was in towns and cities that formality came to the garden, where the ubiquitous grid of the surveyor provided hard-edged plots and yards. Here was the utilitarian beginning of the Australian backyard.

Other voices favoured a freer approach—terraces and dressed ground around the house but improved nature beyond them. Here the writings of Humphry Repton could be glimpsed. What other parallels can be drawn between Britain and Australia in the Regency period? George IV's love of Brighton, where as Regent he spent princely sums creating the Brighton Pavilion in the relaxed seaside atmosphere, had resonances for the colonial situation, relaxed through distance from central government. Fashionable society followed the Prince Regent, and striped verandahs, balconies and touches of rusticity became architectural hallmarks of the Regency style. Marine villas were well suited to this style, and the coastal nature of Australia's early European settlement saw a fortuitous chronological link between contemporary British fashion and the availability of freehold water frontage.

The rise of the *cottage orné* during the Regency period—whereby distasteful aspects of working-class cottages were conveniently removed and appealing aspects were appropriated, such as a linking of house and garden, often via a verandah and French doors—turned a humble shelter into an informal upper-middle-class pavilion. The necessity for portable or temporary buildings in the colonies lent itself to the casual cottage idiom of the Regency style; the royal representative living in a prefabricated cottage in Melbourne was surely the ultimate in informality.

The introduction of the ornamental flower garden around the residence and the use of ornamental shrubbery were design hallmarks of Regency gardens. The Regency interest in these was often combined in early colonial gardens with relaxed outdoor living, in a manner that is periodically raised as a hallmark of a 'distinctively Australian style'.

While Loudon's notion of taming wild landscapes by adopting formal geometric gardens met with a muted response from Australian garden owners and designers, the imposition of a formal survey grid locked this idea into the Australian mind. Ultimately vast acreages of land were mapped prior to detailed surveying, sale and subdivision within its rigid framework. Formality thus embraced the wider landscape and not just the garden.

The squared layout of early productive gardens was based on convenience rather than aesthetics, and had more in common with contemporary farm layouts than formal or geometric pleasure gardens. These vernacular, utilitarian origins have persisted in the vegetable patch and the grid planting of the orchard. Likewise in Australia's earliest botanic gardens, at Sydney and Hobart Town, the squared layouts reflected traditions of systematic botany and experimental plot rather than deep-seated aesthetic philosophies.

This period saw many horticultural advances—invention of the lawn mower and the trialling of tightly glazed Wardian cases for transhipment of plants, to name two of the best known. Many exotic plants were introduced to Australia, including Northern Hemisphere conifers, tropical plants from India and the East Indies, and garden favourites from Europe. Above all, horticultural advice was made more freely available through the advent of affordable gardening magazines and books.

Pocket libraries | 1820

Of necessity, many of the books brought to Australia by emigrant gardeners were pocket-sized. Charles Fraser, government botanist for New South Wales, had commenced his library at Sydney Botanic Gardens with C. H. Persoon's *Synopsis Plantarum* (Paris, 1805–7), for instance. Its two diminutive volumes were crammed with botanical knowledge in minute type, encapsulating contemporary knowledge for peripatetic possessors. Likewise, Christian Reichardt's *Land-und Garten-Schatz* (Erfurt, 1820), gave its emigrant German owner fundamental knowledge of herbs and medicinal gardens, as well as ornamental plants. Such herbals formed a vital resource in a society with limited access to professional medical care.

The American Gardener | 1821

William Cobbett's *The American Gardener* (1821) was published during a North American interlude by its outspoken author. Cobbett, the son of an English farmer, was a radical thinker who expressed his political views through writing of uncommon vividness and force. This copy is annotated 'Cobbett's Instructions about gardening will be as good for New South Wales as they are for America; the seasons—Spring, Summer,—Autumn, Winter—begin & end differently in the two countries.' Irrespective of seasonal differences, Cobbett's general views on horticulture brought the experience of an outspoken agrarian reformer to a new colonial audience, one gradually freeing itself from British shackles.

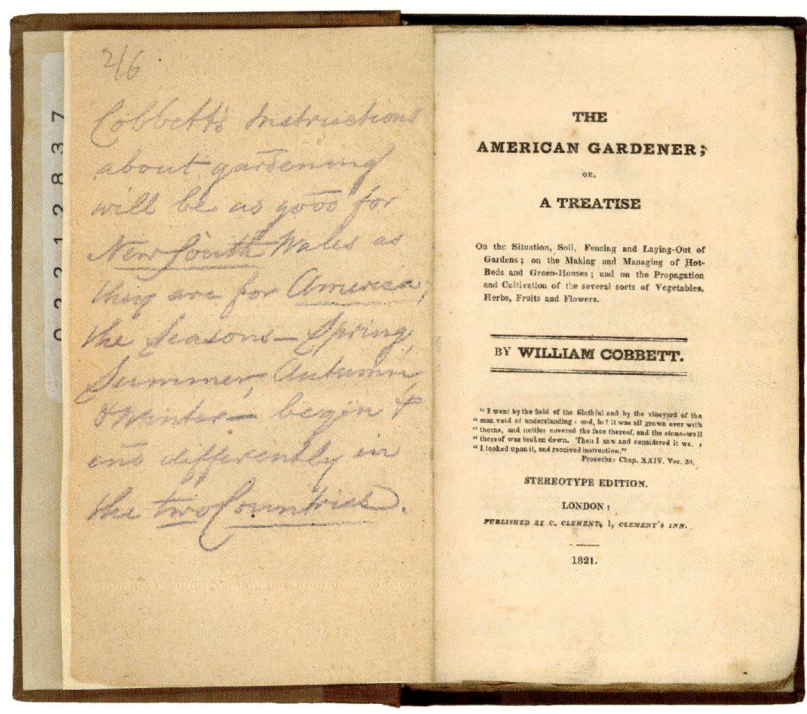

Plate 4

FRONTISPIECE TO THE FLORISTS MANUAL.

Eng.ᵈ by H.W.Timms

Published May 20.1822 by Henry Colburn & C.º Conduit Street

Gay flower-gardens | 1822

When Maria Jackson published *The Florist's Manual* (London, 1822), she explained to her sister-florists that it was aimed at 'procuring a GAY *Flower-Garden*'. Jackson confined herself to those 'gratifications' derived from the visual, olfactory, and saporific senses, very properly excluding the grosser charms of plants. Flower gardens and ornamental shrubberies were at their zenith. Jackson's design of a 'mingled flower-garden' was one of several beguiling images of contemporary bedding practices. This 'much desired object' had its complexities, including the tricky but adroitly handled matter of laying a small gay parterre before a parlour window.

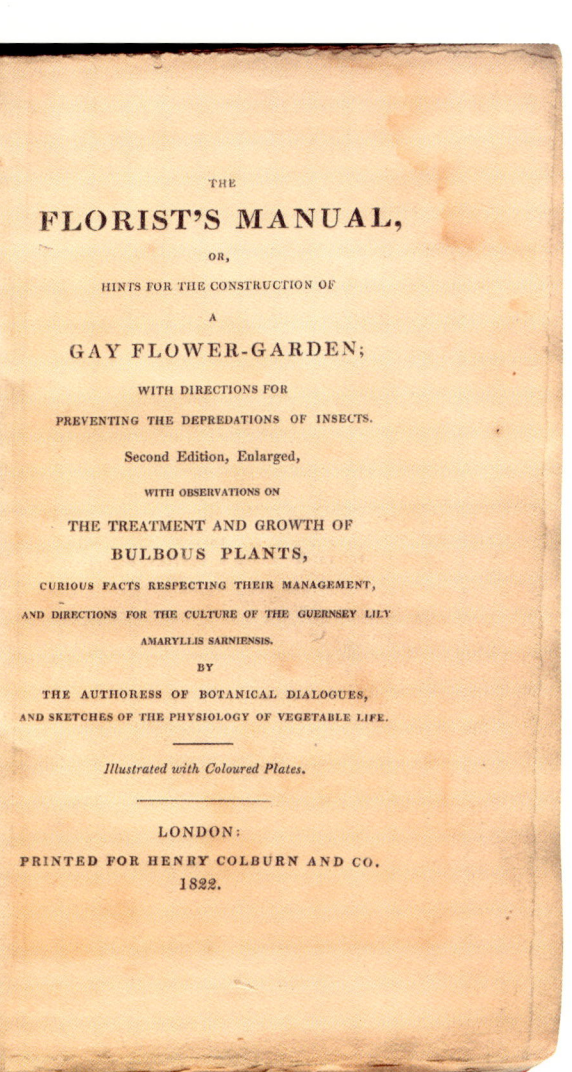

THE

FLORIST'S MANUAL,

OR,

HINTS FOR THE CONSTRUCTION OF

A

GAY FLOWER-GARDEN;

WITH DIRECTIONS FOR

PREVENTING THE DEPREDATIONS OF INSECTS.

Second Edition, Enlarged,

WITH OBSERVATIONS ON

THE TREATMENT AND GROWTH OF

BULBOUS PLANTS,

CURIOUS FACTS RESPECTING THEIR MANAGEMENT,

AND DIRECTIONS FOR THE CULTURE OF THE GUERNSEY LILY

AMARYLLIS SARNIENSIS.

BY

THE AUTHORESS OF BOTANICAL DIALOGUES,

AND SKETCHES OF THE PHYSIOLOGY OF VEGETABLE LIFE.

Illustrated with Coloured Plates.

LONDON:

PRINTED FOR HENRY COLBURN AND CO.

1822.

Sylva Florifera | 1823

Much is made of flower and vegetable gardens, but during the early nineteenth century the ornamental shrubbery rose to prominence. The shrubbery could link house and lawn, and screen 'disagreeable' views. Henry Phillips made an important contribution with his book *Sylva Florifera* (London, 1823). Two rival systems were then in vogue: the mixed or mingled shrubbery—employing alternating single species—and the grouped manner of massed plantings. Drawing on William Gilpin's *Remarks on Forest Scenery* (1808), Phillips favoured the grouped manner, especially as it could include the exotic plants that were becoming available in increasing numbers. The garden of Government House, Sydney, incorporated an early example of this style.

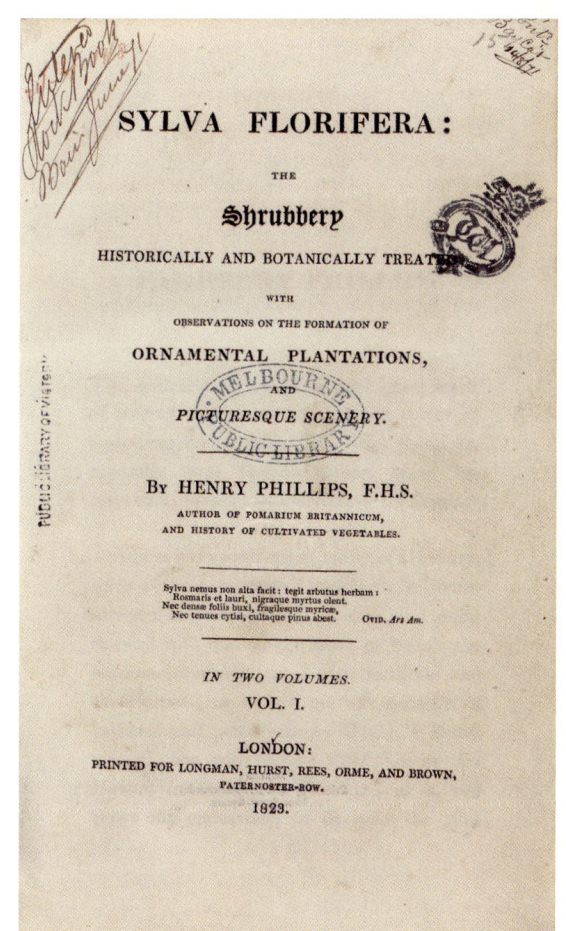

Australasian Pocket Almanack | 1824

The earliest garden guides published in Australia were contained in yearly almanacs, commencing with George Howe's *New South Wales Pocket Almanac and Remembrancer* (Sydney, 1806). Almanacs evolved in Australia from a reliance on horoscopes to become pocket-sized compendiums of useful knowledge. Befitting almanacs' calendrical layout, their garden advice was usually monthly or seasonal. Local horticultural experience was preferred but overseas publications were sometimes utilised. The *Australasian Pocket Almanack* (Sydney, 1824), for example, contained extracts from William Cobbett's *The American Gardener* (1821); 'The Colonial Gardener cannot but profit by this selection' claimed the editor, although elsewhere errors were incorporated—pines (pineapples) were confused with pines (conifers), for instance.

Botano-Theology | 1825

Many religions have profound spiritual links
with nature. In established Christianity,
the human anatomy was regarded as the first
and most convincing proof of a 'divine Author
of Nature', especially the ends 'for which they
[humans] are manifestly adapted—to volition,
to intellectual exertion and enjoyment'.
The vegetable and animal kingdoms were
closely allied and also considered 'a manifest
part of a universally concatenated system,
[that] presents unquestionable traces of the great
Intelligence which has planned and constructed
the whole'. John Shute Duncan's anonymously
authored book *Botano-Theology* (Oxford, 1825)
drew on established writings in a quest to find
theological meaning in the natural world.

BOTANO-THEOLOGY,

AN

ARRANGED COMPENDIUM,

CHIEFLY FROM

SMITH, KEITH, AND THOMSON.

By
John Shute Duncan, Fellow of New College

There is neither speech nor language: but their voices are heard among them.
Their sound is gone out into all lands: and their words into the ends of the world. PSALM XIX.

Ὁ μὲν δὴ Θεος, ὥσπερ ὁ παλαιος λογος ἀρχην τε και τελευτην και μεσα των οντων ἁπαντων εχων, εὐθεια περαινει. ARISTOT. Περι Κοσμου.

Herbarum ... potentia approbat nihil a rerum natura sine áliqua occultiore causa gigni. PLIN. NAT. HIST. LIB. XXII.

Of these matters no satisfactory account can be given by any mechanical hypothesis, or any other way, without taking in the superintendance of the great Creator and Ruler of the world. DERHAM, PHYSICO-THEOLOGY, VOL. II. p. 161.

By investigation the following points are always gained, in favour of doctrines even the most generally acknowledged, (supposing them to be true,) viz. stability and impression......If one train of thinking be more desirable than another, it is that which regards the phenomena of nature with a constant reference to a supreme intelligent Author. PALEY, CHAP. XXVII.

OXFORD:

SOLD BY J. PARKER, OXFORD:
J. MURRAY; AND C. AND J. RIVINGTON, LONDON.
MDCCCXXV.

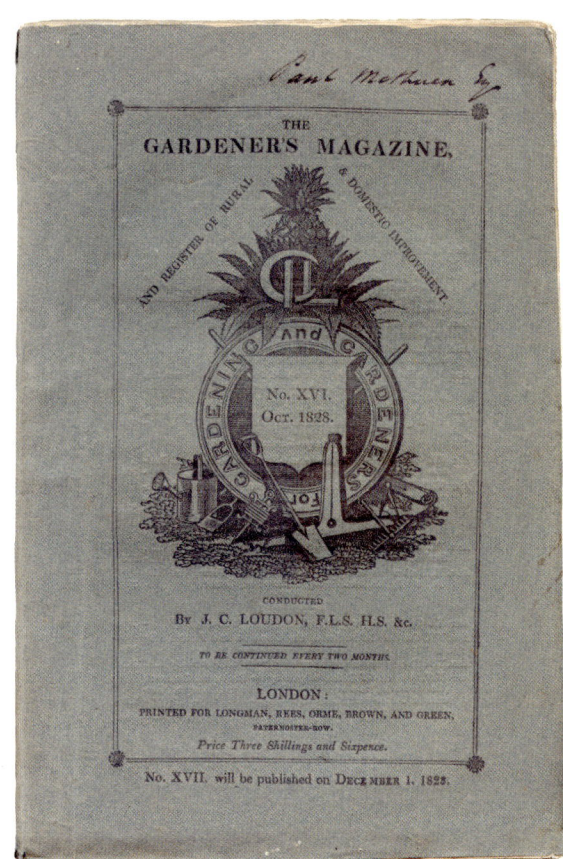

Loudon's Gardener's Magazine | 1826

John Claudius Loudon typified Scottish industriousness. His prodigious output of books, encyclopaedias and journals revolutionised early nineteenth-century horticulture and gardening, both in Britain and the colonies. The first issue of his *Gardener's Magazine* (1826) was a revelation. Its closely set pages and economical wood engravings produced a journal vastly different from the expensive botanical periodicals of Curtis, Edwards and Loddiges. Loudon's didactic tone leapt from the pages, admiring and admonishing in equal measure. In this, the prototype gardening magazine, Loudon coined the word 'gardenesque', using it to describe a style that distinguished gardens as works of art rather than imitations of nature.

which will thrive in the open air in Britain. Mere picturesque improvement is not enough in these enlightened times: it is necessary to understand that there is such a character of art as the gardenesque, as well as the picturesque. The very term gardenesque, perhaps, will startle some readers; but we are convinced, nevertheless, that it is a term which will soon find a place in the language of rural art. Landscape-gardening, it will be allowed, is, to a certain extent, an art of imi-

Flora Australasica | 1827

The earliest book to deal exclusively with Australian plants was *A Specimen of the Botany of New Holland* (London, 1793–95) by James Edward Smith, founder of the Linnaean Society. A generation later, Robert Sweet compiled *Flora Australasica*, published in parts during 1827–8. Sweet, a Fellow of the Linnaean Society, had previously compiled several botanical works including *The Botanical Cultivator* (London, 1821), which provided advice on cultivating hothouse and greenhouse plants. Sweet's *Flora* illustrated many of Australia's best-known and horticulturally desirable plants (such as *Dryandra longifolia*, pictured here) which might be grown in Britain by those with the wealth to maintain appropriate horticultural buildings.

43

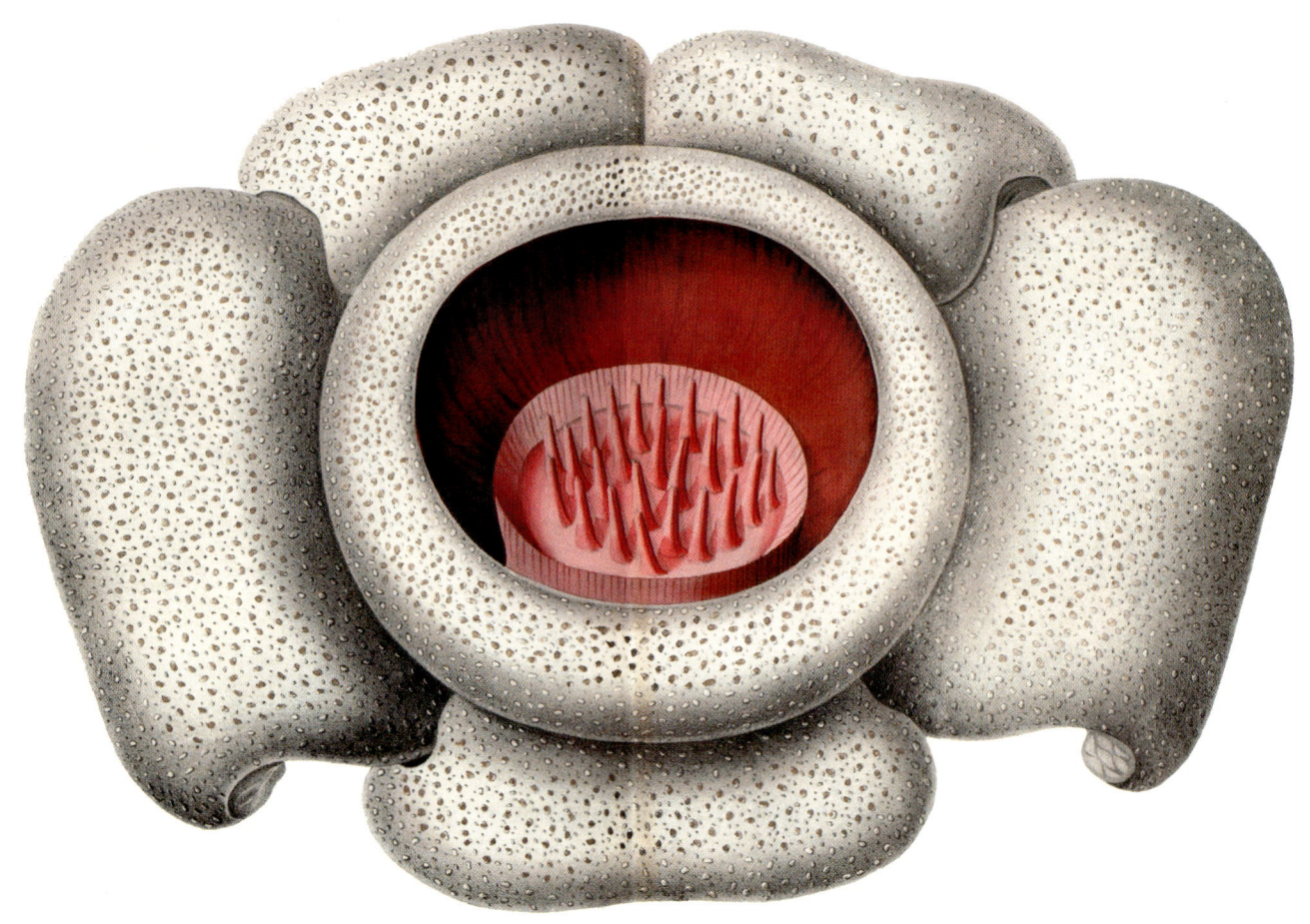

RAFFLESIA PATMA.

'The smell of tainted beef' | 1828

The European discovery of *Rafflesia arnoldii*, the world's largest known flower, encapsulates
a nineteenth-century love of the bizarre. Discovered in 1818 by Joseph Arnold, an assistant to Sir
Stamford Raffles, Governor of the (British) East India Company's establishment at Sumatra, the
metre-wide flower aroused enormous interest. The plant—now exceedingly rare in the wild—was
pollinated by flies. Reporting the find to Sir Joseph Banks, Arnold wrote, '[it] was truly astonishing.
My first impulse was to cut it up . . . It had precisely the smell of tainted beef.' This illustration, from
Karl Ludwig Blume's *Flora Javae* (Brussels, 1828), perfectly captures the flower's putrid fascination.

The sunk wall or ha-ha | 1829

Killymoon, overlooking the Break o'Day River floodplain near St Mary's, Tasmania, was built for pastoralist Frederick Lewis von Steiglitz on land acquired in 1829. Irish in its inspiration, the dressed ground of the terrace was set high above the surrounding countryside. The bollarded retaining wall drew inspiration from contemporary designs for sunk walls, permitting an uninterrupted view over the countryside while simultaneously restricting the movement of stock. Often known as a ha-ha, the sunk wall was later put to more forbidding use in lunatic asylums, giving patients and the public alike unrestricted views, but securing one from the other.

Machine for mowing lawns | 1830

For a generation reliant on scythes or grazing stock, the invention of the lawn mower struck a revolutionary blow in the horticultural conquest of grass. Edwin Budding's 1830 patent demonstrated the salient points of the new machine—namely an arrangement of toothed wheels and pinions that propelled a barrel encased with spiral cutting blades. The machine's smooth action produced an elegant sward and propelled the rise of lawn as a garden feature, rather than a mere background for floral decoration or shrubbery.

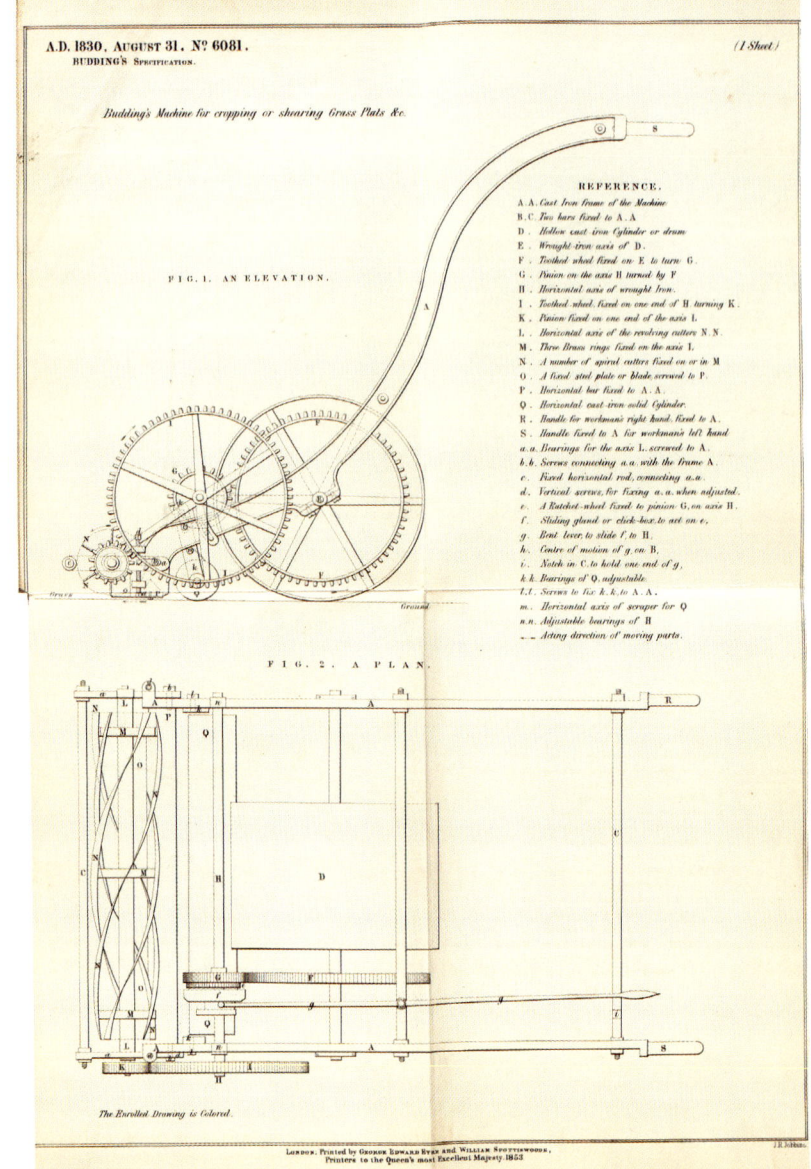

Plantae Asiaticae Rariores | 1831

The proximity of northern Australia and Asia, and their shared tropical climate, ensured that many spectacular Asian flowering plants including crinums found their way into Australian gardens. A key figure in this horticultural exchange was Nathaniel Wallich, author of *Plantae Asiaticae Rariores; or Descriptions and figures of a select number of unpublished East Indian plants* (London, 1830–2). Wallich, a Danish-born botanist and surgeon, enjoyed a period of acclaim during his superintendency (1817–41) of the long-established botanic garden at Calcutta, a key institution in global plant and seed exchanges.

Crinum Herbertianum

Pinus Canariensis.

The colonial pinetum | 1832

The araucarias, conifers of ancient Gondwanan origins indigenous to the north-eastern coast of Australia and the Pacific islands, achieved early popularity in colonial gardens. Species such as *Araucaria hetrophylla* (Norfolk Island Pine) and *A. bidwillii* (Bunya Pine) became popular specimen trees. Many other conifers, particularly pines, were also planted during the early nineteenth century and Aylmer Bourke Lambert's *A Description of the Genus Pinus* (London, 1832) was one of several works that aided their popularity. With their bold evergreen forms and rapid growth, conifers were soon favoured for parks, gardens, windbreaks and a dedicated new compartment—the pinetum.

Park-like Panshanger | 1833

Australian horticulture has been immeasurably advanced by dynastic families. In the nursery trade, the names of Brunning, Creswell, Hackett, Shepherd and Yates have spanned three or more generations. Amongst garden owners, Archer, Macarthur and McLeay are prominent. The Archer family arrived in Van Diemen's Land in 1817 and by 1833 Thomas Archer and his sons had established significant gardens at Woolmers, Brickenden and Panshanger (photographed here by Ray Joyce). As the family's biographer notes, their homesteads form a 'memorial to their sagacity and taste'. The park-like expanses of Panshanger were the equal of any colonial estate, but the open grassy setting also recalls other, much longer dynasties of local Aboriginal groups, who sagaciously managed this environment with fire.

Edward Henty's journal | 1834

The primary place of gardening in the process of colonisation is documented in the journal of Edward Henty, pioneer of the Portland Bay District. Refused a land grant in Van Diemen's Land, Henty and his party arrived at Portland Bay in November 1834: 'We landed 13 Heifers, 4 Working Bullocks, 5 Sows in Pig, 2 Turkeys, 2 Guinea Fowl, 6 Dogs, Seeds, Plants, 1 Whale boat, 4 Men, H[enry] Camfield & Myself'. Within a week Henty noted that the men were employed making a hut, with 'Camfield & self digging a piece of Ground for Garden', one of Victoria's earliest records of garden-making.

Colonial capriccio | 1835

W. F. E. Liardet's painting 'J. P. Fawkner's first house' provides an intriguing juxtaposition of the events of 1835. His view—painted from memory in 1875—shows John Pascoe Fawkner's Melbourne cottage being erected, with log sawyers cutting the last planks. In the foreground John Batman negotiates his treaty with Aboriginal Elders for the 'purchase' of Melbourne, while the 'wild white man' William Buckley has returned to European civilisation after living with Wathawurrung people for 32 years. None of these events occurred at precisely the same time or in the same place, yet they form a microcosm of contemporary sensibility: Buckley's experience of Aboriginal environmental management, Batman's commercial eye for the land, and Fawkner's restless assessment of its capabilities.

Every Man his Own Gardener | 1836

Thomas Shepherd's *Lectures on the Horticulture of New South Wales* (Sydney, 1835) is generally agreed to be the earliest Australian gardening book. His *Lectures on Landscape Gardening in Australia* (Sydney, 1836) and Daniel Bunce's *Manual of Practical Gardening* (Hobart Town, 1838) followed soon after. Publishers in London were eager to capture new markets and often teamed with colonial publishers. Thus Abercrombie and Mawe's well-known book *Every Man his Own Gardener* was released in 1836 with the imprint of James and Samuel Augustus Tegg of Sydney, alongside that of publishing houses in London, Glasgow and Dublin. Any lack of Australian relevance was hastily ignored.

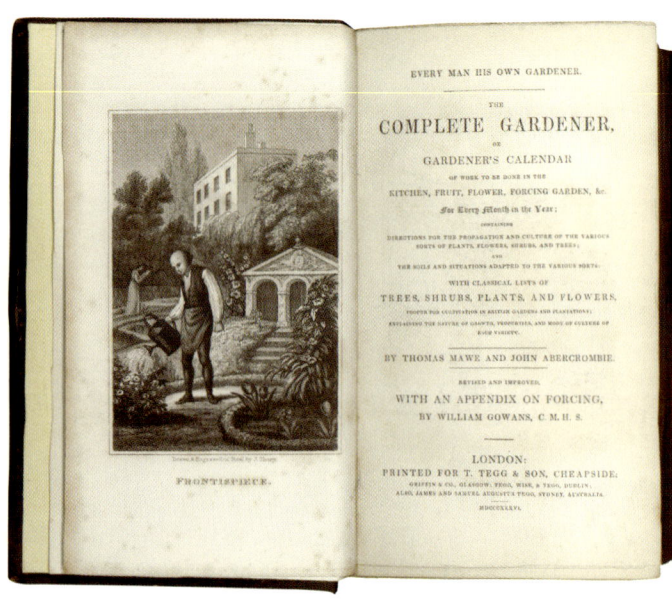

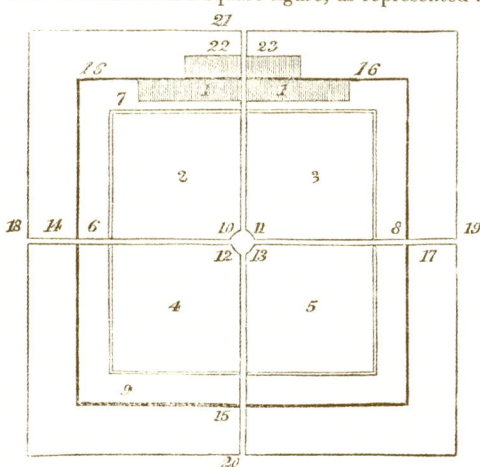

Walled gardens | 1837

The protection afforded by walled gardens—so necessary in Britain—was rarely required or provided in Australia. Walled kitchen and picking gardens were generally located in older established properties in Van Diemen's Land and New South Wales. Beaufront, erected in 1837 at Ross in the Tasmanian Midlands, retains a fine example of a walled garden, along with early orchard trees, grateful for its shelter. Shade rather than costly impervious protection from wind assumed a far greater priority in colonial gardens, and—rather by default—a hedge or fence with climbers more usually fulfilled a dual role in providing such shelter.

Various forms for the culinary garden have been suggested, particularly for that part which is to be surrounded by walls. Some have recommended a square figure, as represented here:

1. 1. *Hot-houses.* 2. 3. 4. 5. *Quarters.* 6. 7. 8. 9. *Borders.* 10. 11. 12. 13. *Walks.* 14. 15. 16. 17. *Walls.* 18. 19. 20. 21. *Outer Boundary.* 22. 23. *Back Sheds.*

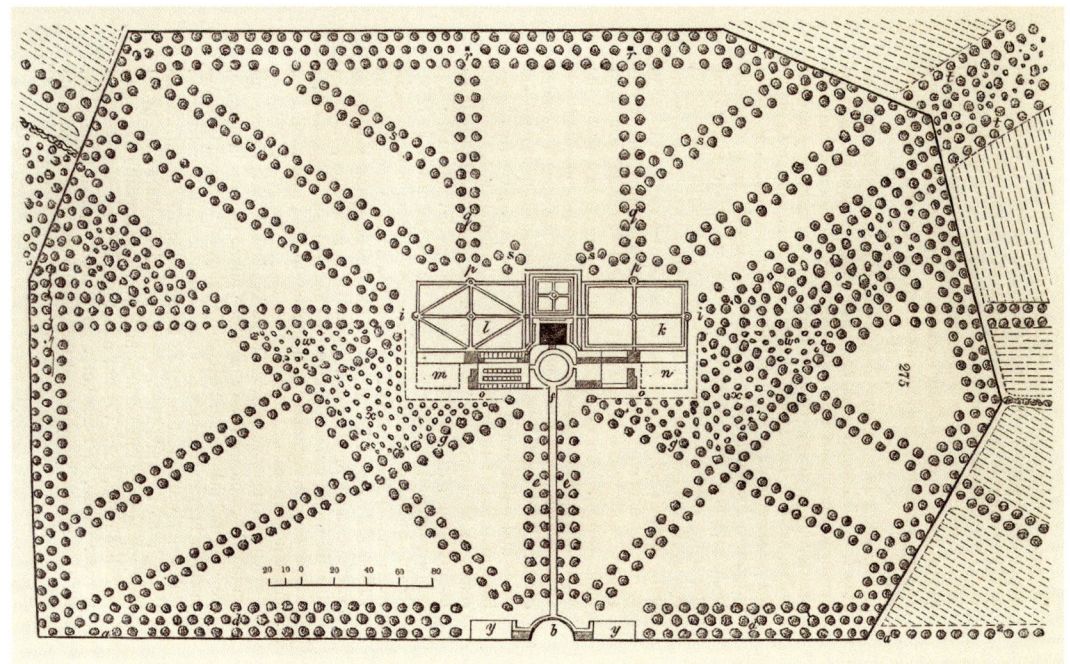

Garden for a country in a 'wild state' | 1838

The notion of the Australian landscape as having rough or untamed qualities led to the formal school of landscape design being promoted as appropriate. In his book *The Suburban Gardener and Villa Companion* (London, 1838), John Claudius Loudon recommended the geometric style for countries 'in a wild state'. His plan was based on a strongly held philosophy that gardens should be recognisable as works of art, and not mistaken for wild nature. He cited contrast and the 'obvious expression of art and refinement' to support his plan. Unstated was a powerful message about imposing physical and psychological order on newly acquired and unfamiliar landscapes.

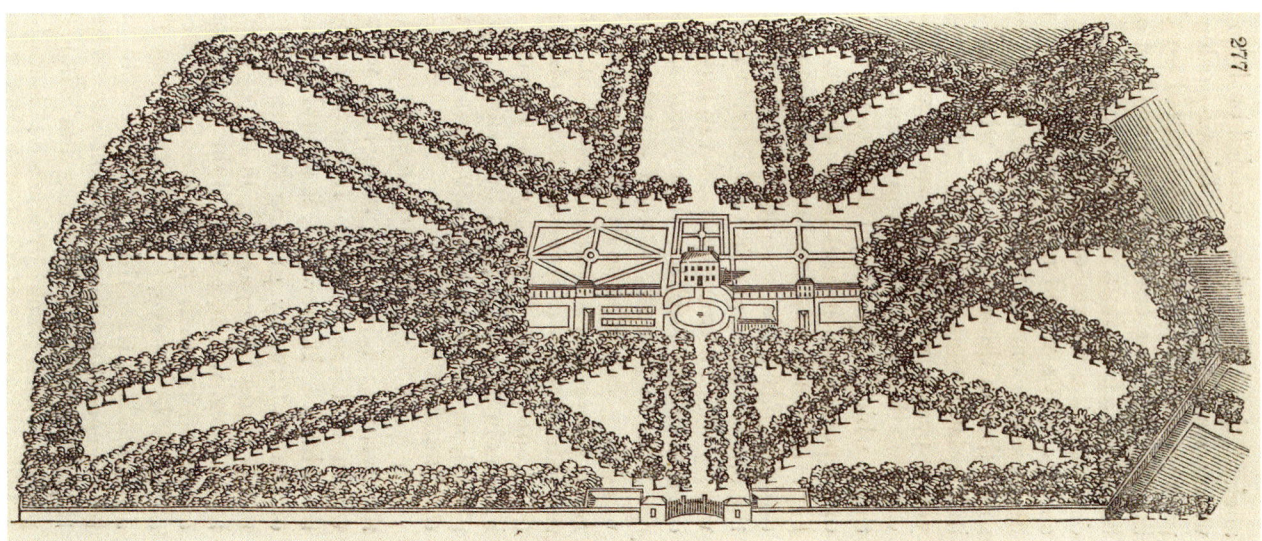

Backyard beginnings
| 1839

The backyard, so long a staple feature of Australia's domestic gardens, seems quintessentially a suburban phenomenon.
Yet townships developed before suburbs and so it is to town gardens that we must look for local origins of the backyard. This rare and charming auction plan of 1839 depicts a residential property in the centre of Melbourne. The city was in its infancy, with sufficient space to permit even this modest cottage to enjoy a substantial 'Garden Ground' at the rear. Occupied only by a privy, even at this early date the back garden seems alive with promise and tranquillity, away from the bustle of Lonsdale Street.

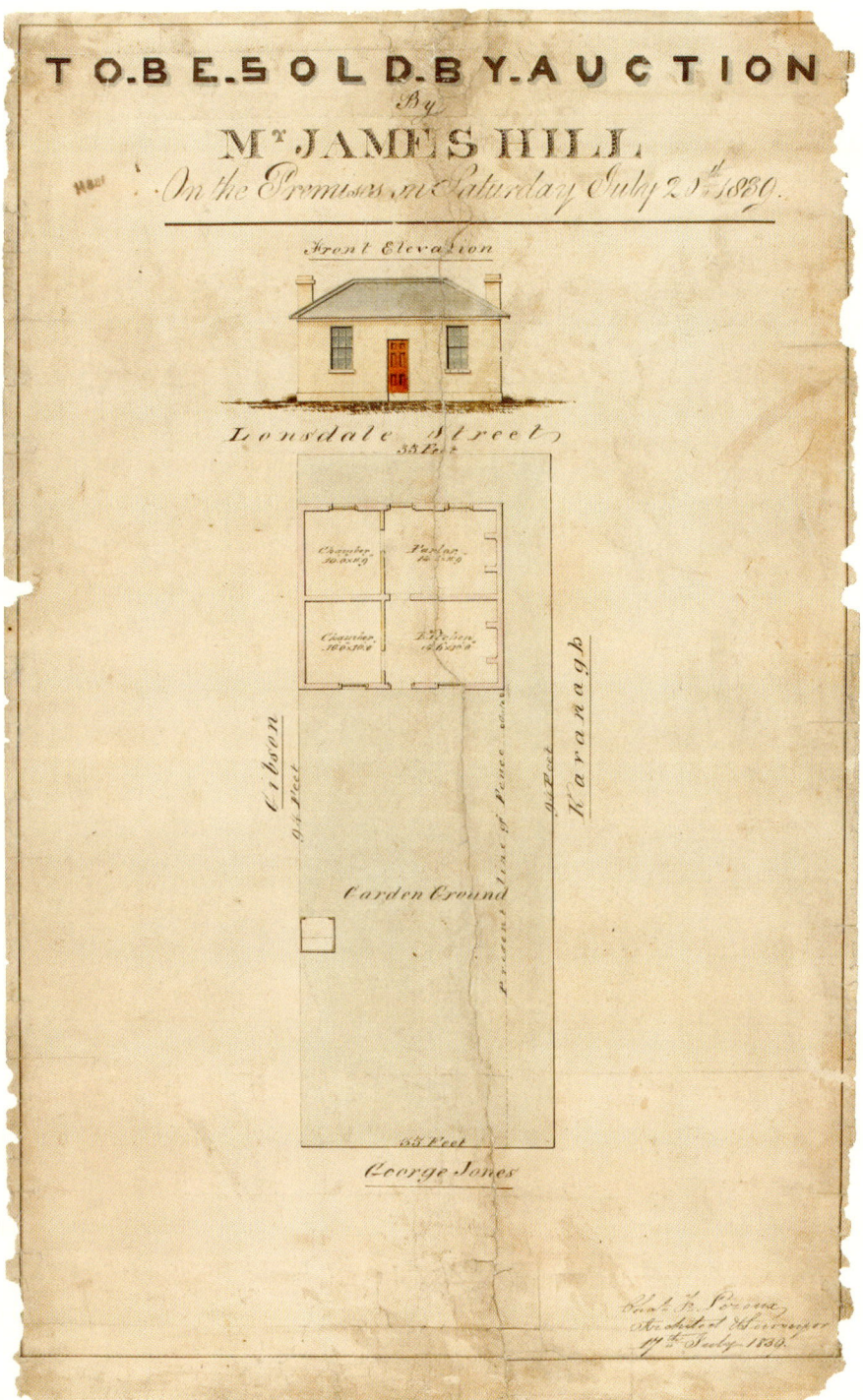

THE EMIGRANT
GARDENER
(1840s–1850s)

*The Australian colonies at the present time are said to be greatly in need
of useful agricultural and domestic servants . . . And who knows but a Lee,
a Repton, or a Loudon, may be forwarded amongst them, who may arrange the
flora, or ornament the landscape, and improve the whole horticultural aspect
of that distant, yet promising land?*

Gardeners' and Farmers' Journal, London, 10 June 1848

GARDENING and horticulture in Australia during the 1840s and 1850s was undertaken largely by a migrant workforce. Those who designed, laid out and maintained gardens wereoverwhelmingly trained in Britain, with Scotland providing a disproportionate share. Many of these gardeners had trained in large establishments—Chatsworth in Devonshire; Dalkeith, south of Edinburgh; and the Crystal Palace Gardens in London—where a strict hierarchy governed working life. Those with aptitude rose steadily through the ranks of apprentice, journeyman, under-gardener, and ultimately to head gardener, a position of considerable status. Those who tired of regimentation drifted, often finding work as agricultural labourers.

Yet agricultural labour was keenly sought in the Australian colonies, and many emigrant gardeners started their career with back-breaking toil under the sun. Few gardens comparable in extent or sophistication to those at 'home' existed in the colonies at this time. Those that did soon attracted gardeners of a high calibre, whose letters and comments— keenly reported in the British press—stressed the need for stamina, perseverance and low initial expectations. With hard work, though, an enhanced situation in Australia was sufficient incentive for many emigrants.

The gold rushes of the early 1850s attracted a much wider pool of emigrants, and many a gardener or nursery proprietor commenced their working life in Australia digging for gold. Their reward was usually found some years later when they returned to their former profession, now able to capitalise on an expanding market for their services and wares. Pastoral wealth had led the way, but now in town and country a growing middle class sought the refinement offered by horticulture and landscape gardening.

The establishment of horticultural societies gave the emigrant gardener an outlet for displays of skill through competitions, but also an opportunity for a free interchange of knowledge and ideas. For those of the pinnacle of the professions—and also those whose wealth permitted them to participate in gardening as 'amateurs'—the major horticultural societies provided an elite horticultural circle in which to mix. For improvers, the various gardeners' mutual improvement societies strove with earnest endeavour to educate and advance the welfare of their members. The two seldom mixed at an official level—proposals to merge were invariably doomed—although many gardeners were members of both kinds of society and lengthy newspaper reporting of their meetings kept the public abreast of horticultural developments.

The post gold-rush period saw the rapid growth of seed merchants and the nursery trade. Whereas imported lots of plants, often disposed of by auction, had been the norm in the early nineteenth century, now wholesale and retail outlets proliferated. Their printed catalogues conveyed the wealth of exotic plants pouring into the country and form an indispensable record of early plant availability and preferences. Botanic gardens, too, were becoming major centres for plant acclimatisation and distribution, often at odds with the commercial nursery industry but immeasurably enriching public parks and gardens with new plants. The stage was set for the creation of some of Australia's finest nineteenth-century gardens.

Date of arrival.	Donors.	Ships.	Boxes. Closed.	Open.	No. of sorts.	Remarks.
1836.		Brought forward,......	18	27		
Oct. 15.	19. The Right Hon'ble Earl Auckland, from N. S. Wales, ...	H. M. Ship Rattlesnake, ...	2	0	8	Part of a fine collection.
Novr. 6.	20. Royal Botanic Garden, Bourbon,	Gabrielle, ...	1	0	23	Partly alive.
„ 13.	21. C. Learmouth, Esq., Hobart Town,........................	Perthshire, ...	0	1		All the plants dead.
„ 30.	22. Messrs. C. Loddiges and Sons,	Windsor, ...	2	0	39	Very fine.

Hon'ble Company's Botanic Garden, Calcutta | 1840

The botanic garden established by the East India Company at Calcutta was one of the most important botanical outposts of the British Empire. Superintendent Nathaniel Wallich established a prodigious exchange program and, with a botanist's eye for detail, his *Report of Superintendent of Hon'ble Company's Botanic Garden, Calcutta* (1840) devotes 70 pages to a detailed list of plants and seeds sent out and received during 1836–40. His list of Australian contacts—including Allan Cunningham, Alexander McLeay and John Bidwill—is impressive, and belies the commonly held belief that Australian botanic gardens were solely dependent on England (and, by inference, Kew Gardens) for plant and seed exchanges.

Labouring with no illusions | 1841

The journal of Daniel Halfpenny, compiled with economy and directness, encapsulates the life of an emigrant agricultural labourer in the Port Phillip District. Arriving in Melbourne in December 1840, Halfpenny recorded: 'Engaged on Board the ship for 3 months for 15£ wages not to commence to arrival on the station.' Duties for his master at Pastoria (near Kyneton) were simple: 'I was employed as useful man about his hut & garden'. Halfpenny's garden work commenced in June 1841, and the earliest of his snatched journal entries concern the seasonal routine of digging ground for potatoes and killing snakes.

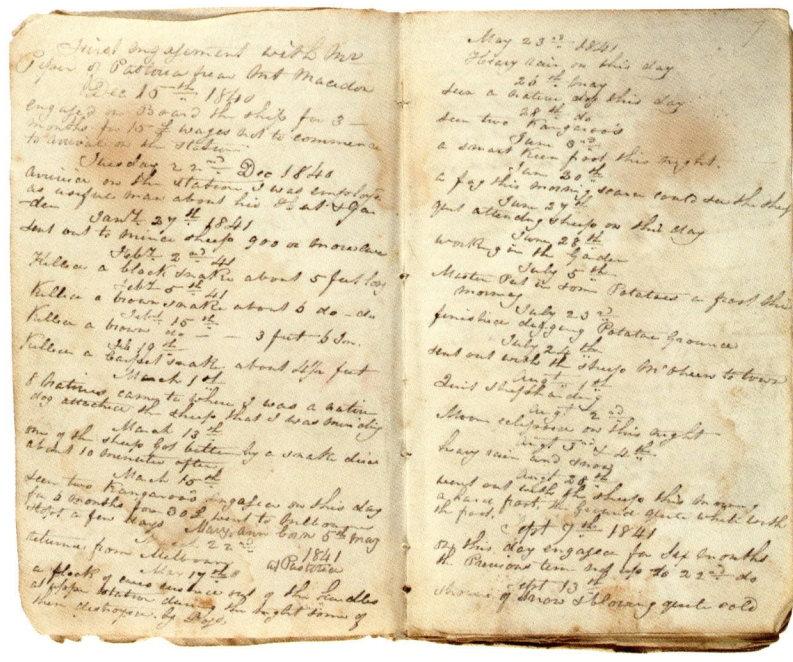

he digs, but finds it hot

'He digs, but finds it hot' | 1842

The cheerful humour of the Australian bush, often a foil for hours of toil, shines through Edward Wilson's naive but engaging sketches. This witty pairing depicting the fruits of labour—merely two of many images contained in a sketchbook—provides a tantalising glimpse of Wilson's commentary on early colonial life. 'He digs, but finds it hot' is an honest reflection on labour in the field and garden. The rejoinder, in which our hero '. . . refreshes himself with a little water-melon', is perhaps suffused with heat-inflicted delusions of a promised land, where spoons are larger than spades and the produce is bountiful.

And refreshes himself with a little water-melon.

The eye of the beholder | 1843

The Regent's Park Gardener's Society, which published its first book of essays in 1843, represented the energetic world of mid-nineteenth century British horticulture. This group had as a mentor Robert Marnock, director of the Royal Botanic Society's garden, which was in the Inner Circle of Regent's Park. The garden displayed the wealth of new plants then being brought into cultivation. Early botanical exploration generally perceived exotic vegetation with European potential in mind. Thus the Australian flora was at first valued in British horticulture for its exoticism. The juxtaposition of *Banksia* cone and vase on Marnock's mantelpiece made this point with casual eloquence.

Superintendent La Trobe's house | 1844

This watercolour by W. F. E. Liardet, painted in 1875 from his memory of Jolimont, perhaps unconsciously highlights details of the flower garden. The thought of Superintendent La Trobe simultaneously tending his flower garden and mentally rehearsing matters of state is a beguiling one. In 1844 La Trobe wrote to English friends: 'Pray send us occasionally a few of the rarer seeds; I particularly wish you would slip into your letters a pinch of pelargonium seed, of the finer varieties, which grow marvellously well here—Tell some of our friends to send us English field flowers seed & you may send us a box of Bulbs. Cape bulbs we have in abundance.'

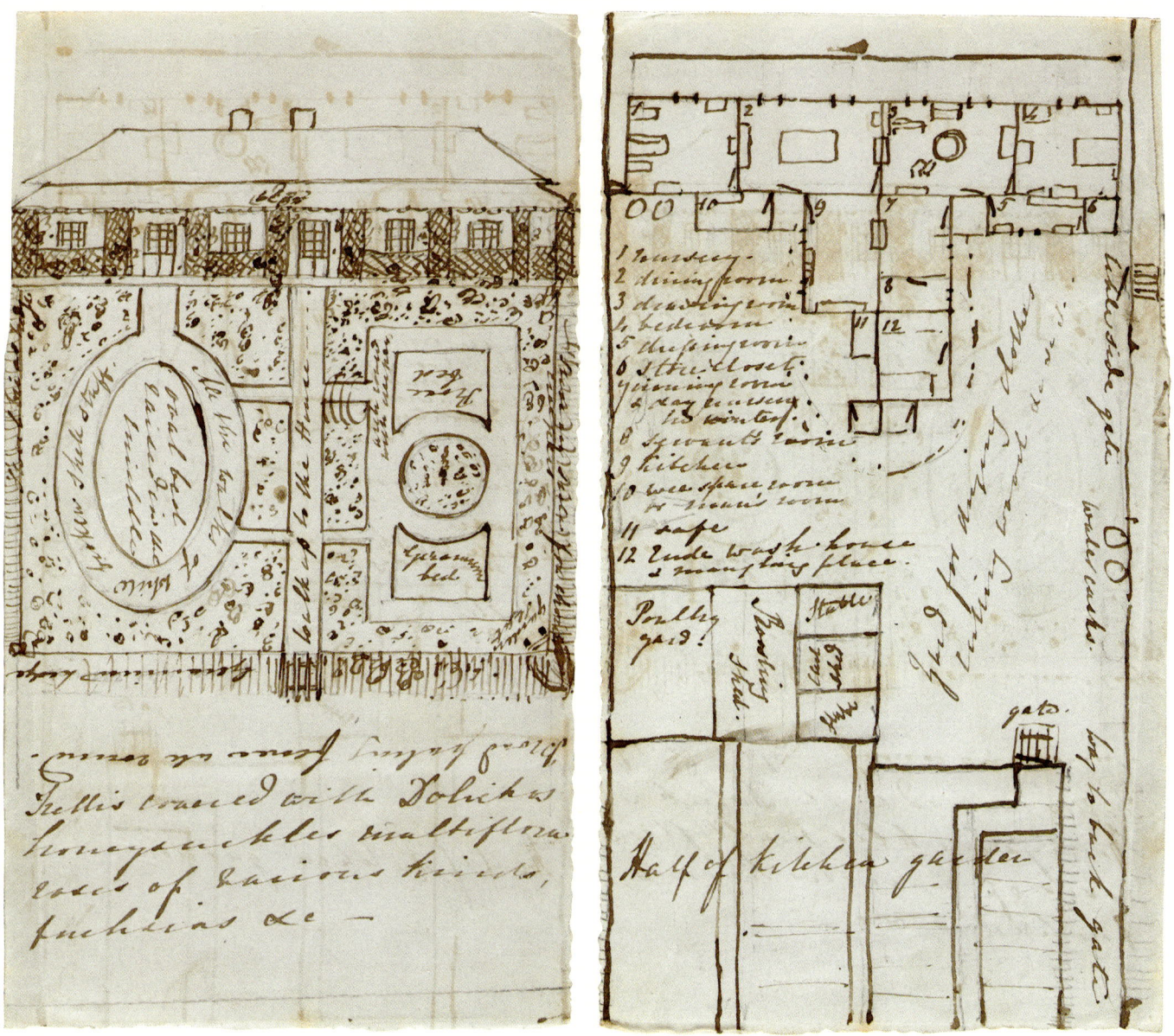

The suburban front garden | 1845

Letters to family and friends 'at home' provide many intimate glimpses of early colonial gardens. Here Sarah Bunbury describes her front garden in Williamstown, one of Melbourne's earliest bayside suburbs. The broad paling fence, hedged with geraniums, frames a square yard with paths of crushed white shells. The trellised verandah is covered with honeysuckle, fuchsia, 'multiflora roses of all kinds', and the drought-resistant Australian pea vine, *Dolichos lignosus*. A gap in the verandah balustrade, opposite the drawing room, leads to a raised oval bed, while the sequestered nursery and dining room overlook squared beds of roses and geraniums that are approached through an archway on the main path.

Beer gardening at the Crown & Anchor | 1846

The role of the hotel as a social hub is well demonstrated by this illuminated address from the Long Ditton United Gardeners and Land Stewards' Society, recognising meritorious service by Frederick Plumridge. The Crown & Anchor Hotel, Long Ditton—in Surrey, in England's south—was a convenient and convivial meeting place. The numerous societies established around this time by gardeners paralleled a wider interest in self-improvement, seen most clearly in the establishment of mechanics institutes. When Plumridge arrived in Port Phillip in 1849, the social and educational models invoked by this address were in a formative phase in the colonies.

Pears, poplars and picotees | 1847

Melbourne pioneer John Pascoe Fawkner is associated with the establishment of the nursery trade in Van Diemen's Land and the Port Phillip District as an importer and promoter. Amongst Fawkner's surviving papers are numerous invoices, plant lists, letters and business records that attest to his horticultural enterprise. This 1847 invoice for plants and seeds, shipped from Liverpool, combines commercial quantities of 'forest trees' with a select collection of individual fruit, shrub and flower varieties. The inclusion of 500 yards of one and a half-inch mesh suggests that Fawkner was supplying owners of new gardens with much-needed netting for the protection of precious garden plots.

Bishop Perry's residence | 1848

Prior to the completion in 1853 of Bishopscourt in East Melbourne, Anglican Bishop Charles Perry and his family lived in a small cottage on the Jolimont estate. Writing in 1848, Perry's wife, Frances, described their new house and garden: 'The flower-garden is of a moderate size, and there is a small kitchen-garden beyond; and beyond that the Government Paddock . . . There is a verandah round three sides and a half of the house, and altogether it looks very pretty.' In Liardet's watercolour, Bishop Perry enjoys the front garden from the contemplative distance of the verandah, perhaps hoping irksome gardening tasks might be undertaken by divine intervention.

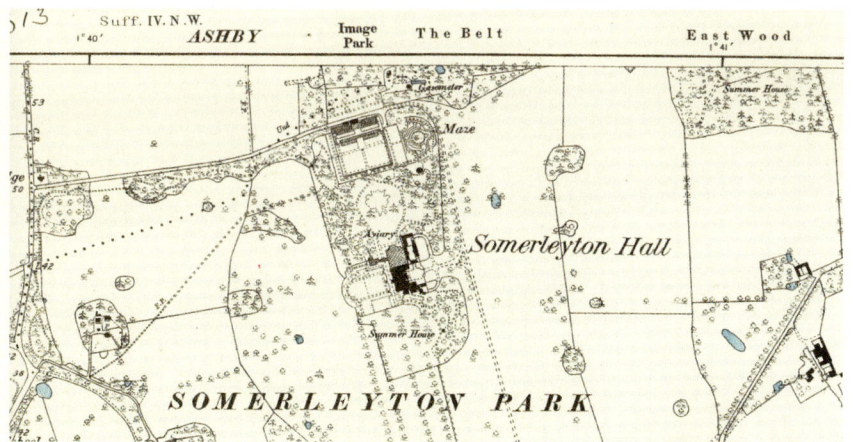

Somerleyton Hall, Suffolk | 1849

As a boy, George Brunning trained at Somerleyton Hall, Suffolk, where by 1849 the celebrated garden designer W. A. Nesfield had redesigned the garden. Brunning arrived in Australia in 1853 and soon established the well-known nursery business bearing his name. Maps such as these detailed Ordnance Survey plans, commenced in the early nineteenth century, provide vital evidence of the physical environment of Britain, birthplace and training ground of many emigrant gardeners.

The native garden | 1850

The writings of Daniel Bunce ensure his place as a horticultural pioneer. Having run nurseries in Hobart Town and Melbourne, and botanised with Leichhardt in the Australian interior, Bunce drew on extensive experience. His *Australian Manual of Horticulture* (Melbourne, 1850) was the earliest gardening book published in Victoria. The vegetable garden, orchard and flower garden all received month-by-month instructions. The flowers he highlighted—roses, fuchsias, dahlias, carnations, geraniums and South African bulbs— give an indication of contemporary favourites, in part based on ease of propagation and cultivation. Bunce's helpful remarks on transplanting native shrubs may come as a surprise to those who assumed this horticultural appreciation to be a late twentieth-century phenomenon.

Water lily dreaming | 1851

The discovery of the Victoria Lily in British Guiana by Robert Schomburgk in 1837 fuelled a horticultural frenzy. Flowering the lily required considerable expertise and expense, with success at Chatsworth in 1849 prompting outpourings of admiration and wonder. In the colonies there was keen rivalry between botanic gardens during the 1860s to emulate this. Ferdinand Mueller in Melbourne flowered the plant first, but Richard Schomburgk (brother of the discoverer) in Adelaide had the most sustained success. George Lawson's charming book *The Royal Water-lily of South America* (Edinburgh, 1851) captured this contemporary enthusiasm. The proliferation of library stamps— perhaps in emulation of the lilies— suggests a more prankish enthusiasm.

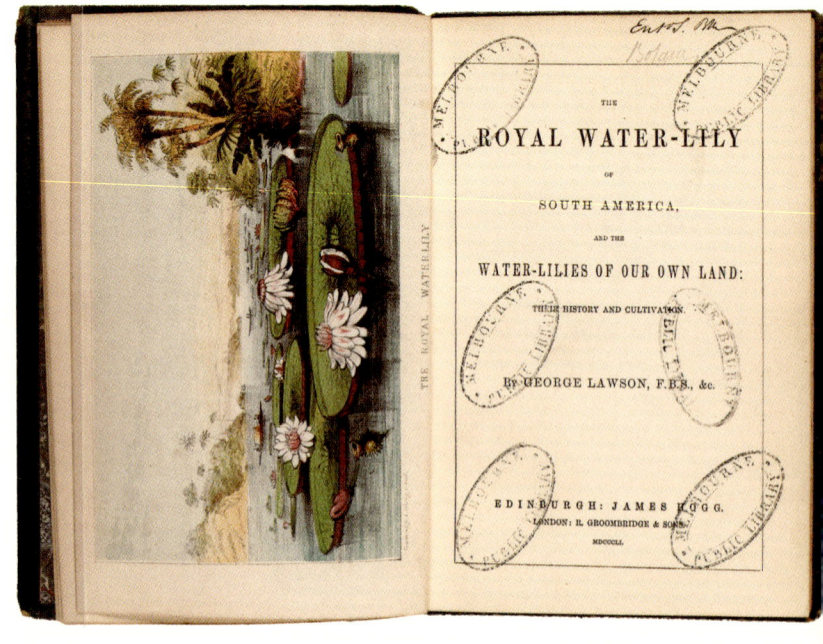

64

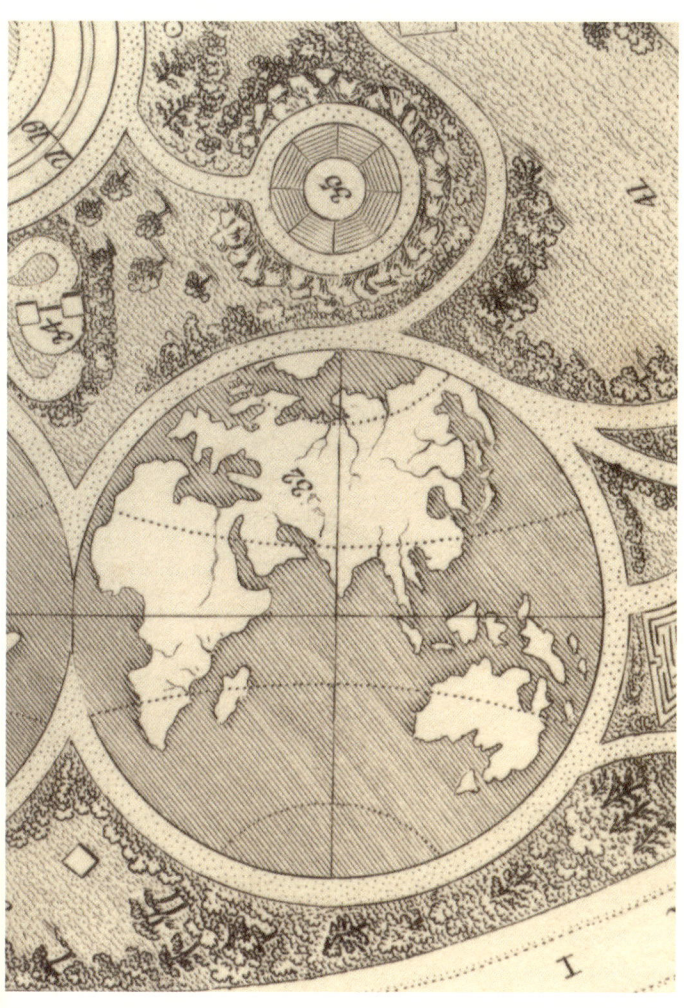

Botanic nationalism | 1852

When Charles H. J. Smith arrived in Australia in 1855 he was the most experienced emigrant landscape gardener and garden architect in the country. His book *Parks and Pleasure Grounds; or, Practical Notes on Country Residences, Villas, Public Parks and Gardens* (London, 1852), which he presented to the Melbourne Public Library, summarised his long career in Scotland. His remarks on public gardens were particularly apposite for a rapidly developing colony. In advocating botanic gardens to represent each country, 'and even to convey an expression of its external physiognomy', Smith presaged by half a century the enthusiasm of federated Australia for celebratory garden beds in the shape of the continent.

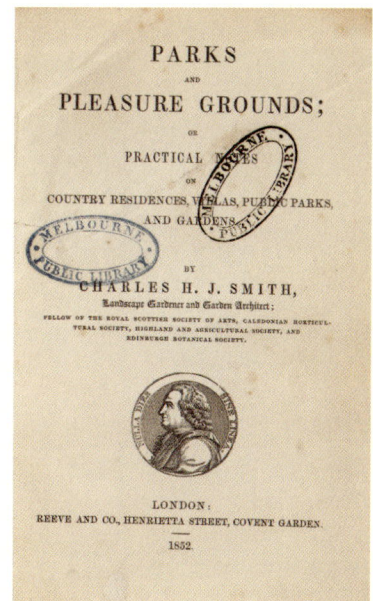

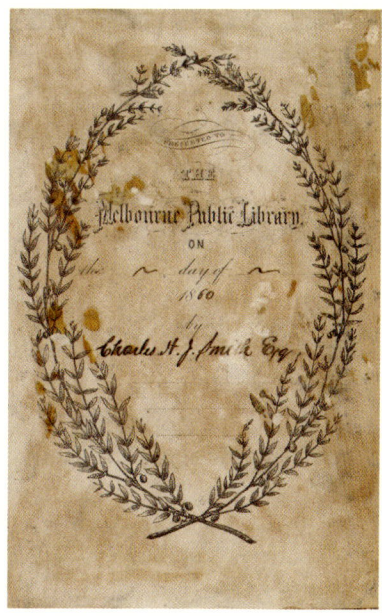

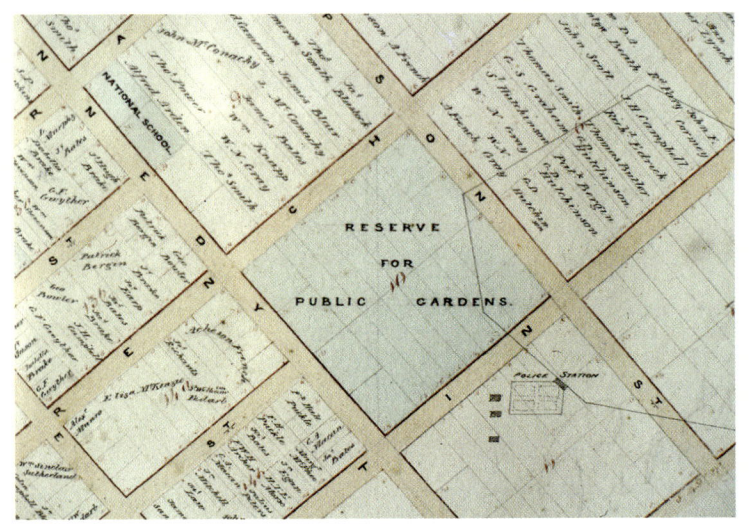

The grid plan | 1853

The adoption of grid plans for Australian townships—exemplified by the early town planning of Governor Macquarie—imposed a formal designed landscape, but within this much variation flourished. The potential of parkland townships in South Australia and streamside esplanades in Tasmania's townships sat at one extreme. More often—as at Hamilton (1853), in Victoria's Western District—public gardens were merely allocated space within the grid. Yet this formal framework seemed to work in a manner opposite to those who promoted it, and informal garden designs became the norm. There were many factors at work here, but perhaps this was an early example of nationalism in Australian gardens, a reaction against constraint, an early expression of larrikin flair.

The Colonial Gardener | 1854

Brunning's Australian Gardener is the oldest continuously published Australian gardening book, in print for almost 150 years. The first edition, a modest 24-page pamphlet entitled *The Colonial Gardener*, was published in Melbourne in 1854 by Smith, Adamson and Co., one of the city's earliest seed and plant merchants. Limited initially to fruit and vegetables, its advice was soon extended to cover the flower garden and its name changed to reflect a national scope. The Brunning family purchased the rights to the book in the 1880s, ensuring its continuous publication until the mid-twentieth century, when the title was taken over by a commercial publisher.

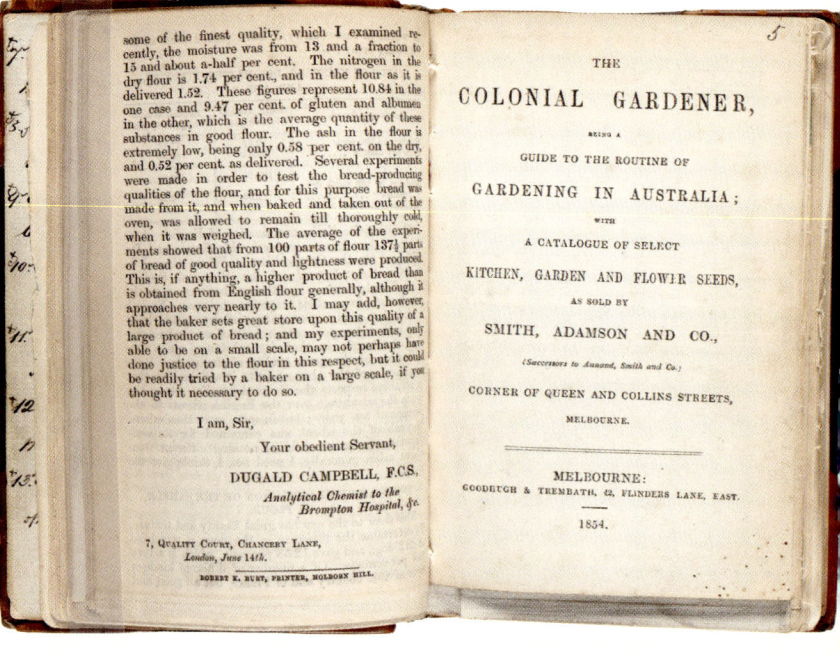

Australia's earliest gardening magazine | 1855

The *Rural Magazine*, 'A Monthly Journal of Farming, Gardening, Botany and Domestic Economy', was arguably Australia's earliest gardening magazine. Although short-lived, this Melbourne publication pioneered a genre that now provides such a vital record of our garden history. Take seed packets, for instance. The *Rural Magazine* reported that Melbourne seedsman Thomas McMillan was selling seeds 'in a fancy envelope the design of which is a shield containing the address of the firm surrounded by flowering plants'. The editor commented: 'The idea is novel, the design good, and the general effect pleasing . . . By the Bye, what an elegant present to make to a lady is one of these packets containing choice and rare flower seeds!'

RUSTIC

ADORNMENTS

FOR

HOMES OF TASTE

BY

SHIRLEY HIBBERD

Rustic Adornments
for Homes of Taste | 1856

English horticultural writer Shirley Hibberd captured the spirit of the mid-Victorian age with his book *Rustic Adornments for Homes of Taste, and Recreations for Town Folk, in the Study and Imitation of Nature* (London, 1856). Hibberd termed it the 'Age of Toys': 'The last twenty years have been marked by such a progress in domestic aesthetics as to be worthy of designation as a new era in social life . . . Our rooms sparkle with the products of art, and our gardens with the curiosities of nature . . . The mark of our progress is seen in our love for toys, plant-cases, bird and bee-houses, fish-tanks, and garden ornaments—they are the beads in our Rosary of homage to the Spirit of Beauty.'

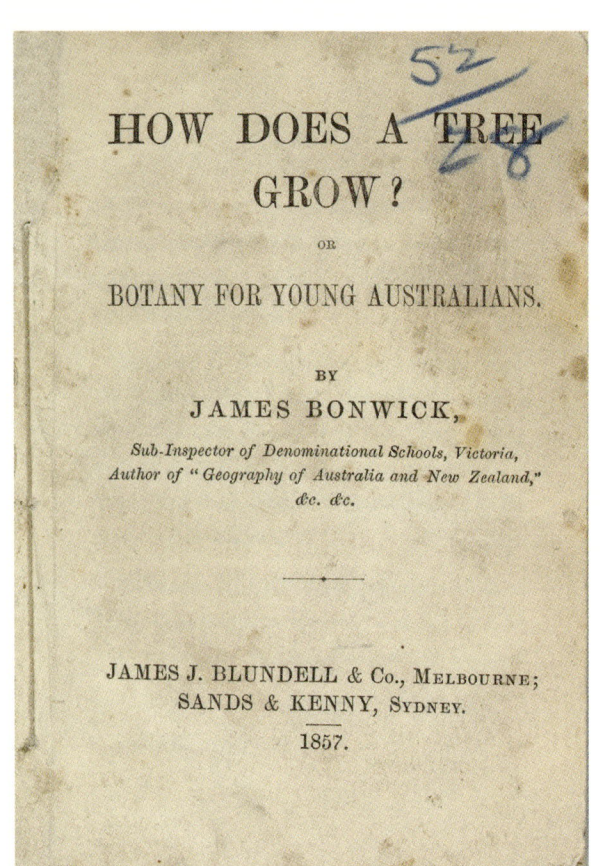

HOW DOES A TREE
GROW?

OR

BOTANY FOR YOUNG AUSTRALIANS.

BY

JAMES BONWICK,

*Sub-Inspector of Denominational Schools, Victoria,
Author of "Geography of Australia and New Zealand,"
&c. &c.*

JAMES J. BLUNDELL & Co., MELBOURNE;
SANDS & KENNY, SYDNEY.

1857.

Botany for Young Australians | 1857

James Bonwick's *How Does a Tree Grow? or Botany for Young Australians* (1857) was the earliest Australian children's book devoted to botany. A school inspector, Bonwick used dialogue between a father and son 'from a belief that the sympathies of our young friends will be excited'. His didactic tone was readily apparent: 'Will you now, dear father, explain the way in which the Monocotyledonous plants differ from the Dicotyledonous, especially in their system of growth?' Contemporary juvenile excitement seems improbable. Bonwick concluded on a non-scientific note with an exhortation: 'don't, like some philosophers, elbow God out of the field . . . Be ready to notice His thoughtfulness and goodness in the world of plants . . . [and] with heart and voice, to say, "My Father made them all."'

Breeding success | 1858

The garden of Glenara, in the folds of the Deep Creek valley on Melbourne's north-western outskirts, has been favoured by two eminent horticulturist-owners. Following completion of the homestead in 1858, Walter Clark had grounds in which to experiment and create a garden of colonial renown. Experienced in managing Macleay family properties in the Riverina, Clark planted the garden with a mix of exotic and Australian plants, ornamental and productive. The garden, depicted in von Guérard's well-known oil painting, received added horticultural lustre in the twentieth century from Walter Clark's son, Alister. His outstanding success in rose and daffodil breeding for Australian conditions made Glenara a byword for horticultural excellence.

The view from the verandah | 1859

The verandah formed a staple architectural accompaniment to the
Australian residence, favoured for cottage, villa and mansion alike.
It offered a protected transition zone between house and garden, well
suited to climbing and potted plants. For new settlers this provided the
antipodean equivalent of European window gardening. As a vantage
point overlooking gardens and the bush beyond, it was an indispensable
podium of pleasure. Sometimes partially enclosed, often elevated,
the verandah formed a virtual outdoor room, as here at Gwyllehurst
in East Melbourne in Charles Norton's vivid watercolour.

UTILITY AND ORNAMENT

(1860s–1870s)

*[Nothing can] be more beautiful that a succession of verdant lawns, broken
by graceful groups of diversified foliage and effectively arranged floral blooms.
Even the highest and most important feature in a Botanic Garden—the collection and
scientific arrangement of plants—can be advantageously carried out in this manner,
thus combining the useful with the ornamental, and gratifying the taste of lovers of the
picturesque and beautiful, while facilitating the researches of the botanical student.*

William Guilfoyle, *Annual Report of the Melbourne Botanic Gardens*, 1876

THE conjunction of utility and ornament in landscape design was exemplified by Australia's botanic gardens. There, the acclimatisation of exotic plants and trialling of economic plants demonstrated the nineteenth-century quest for the 'diffusion of useful knowledge'. The garden was a living textbook for colonial advancement. What the public rarely understood was that botanic gardens consisted of living and dead plants. The latter were the pressed and mounted herbarium specimens that supported the scientific work of the gardens. Ferdinand Mueller in Melbourne was one who lost no opportunity to showcase these two contrasting sides of botany.

When it came to ornament, though, Mueller was greatly misunderstood. His planting style, especially of trees, demonstrated a sympathy with gardenesque principles, but this was insufficient to overturn public disquiet at a perceived lack of ornament. Mueller's contemporary, George Francis at Adelaide Botanic Gardens, sniffed the wind more keenly, and introduced statues and fountains to encourage public recreation in a complementary fusion of botany and pleasure.

It was Mueller's successor at Melbourne Botanic Gardens, William Guilfoyle, who most astutely combined utility and ornament. His reworking of the gardens introduced a picturesque naturalism in place of jutting angles and fussy beds. In his design of paths and garden beds Guilfoyle's talent was especially evident. Careful vistas between and over curvilinear beds and along sinuous walks marked a new unity of utility and ornament. As J. H. Maiden, director of Sydney Botanic Gardens, later remarked: 'we thickly coat the botanical pill with the sugar of a "garden of pleasure" . . . the majority of visitors take their botany mildly'.

In the private domain, the dual attractions of utility and ornament were manifest in the rival merits of the vegetable garden and orchard compared with the flower garden and shrubbery. Many private gardens contained both—and each vied for the attention of the gardener—but most properties retained a clear line of demarcation between the two. In the suburbs especially, the vegetable garden and orchard were relegated to the side and rear, while floriculture was given centre stage. The formal decorative front garden was well on the way to its status as an Australian vernacular icon. In the country, however, a more relaxed mingling permeated garden design, with fruit trees and vines often surrounding the residence.

Ornament soon outgrew utility, especially as Australia's cities and towns developed. Public gardens, in particular, were content to leave utility to their botanic cousins, and a mode of design—which one writer christened the 'promenade style'—soon graced formerly barren wastelands. Whereas in overcrowded Britain public parks had been the 'lungs of the city', in the expanses of the colonial metropolis they were more often an 'oasis in the wilderness'. Both, though, engendered civic pride in equal measure.

Ornament also came indoors, into the parlour and onto the dining table. Architectural adjuncts in the form of bush-houses and, occasionally, glasshouses, also extended the range of horticultural environments available to the gardener. Filled with ferns and orchids, these buildings served a dual role of utility and ornament in their architecture as much as their contents. The colonial wilderness was beginning to recede.

Prize-winning plants | 1860

A competitive spirit lies close to many recreational pursuits, and horticultural societies were quick to promote the competitive possibilities of plant growing with the gloss of horticultural advancement. The number of horticultural societies increased rapidly in Australia during the 1850s and 1860s, and this brought ever greater opportunities for competitive showing. Fierce controversy arose over many aspects of garden shows and competitions, especially the question of who should receive awards—the garden owner or their gardener? Surely the first prize for 'New or Rare Plant' awarded by the Horticultural Society of Victoria to John Brown of Como, reflects the skill of his unnamed gardener, William Sangster, more truly than Brown's horticultural affluence?

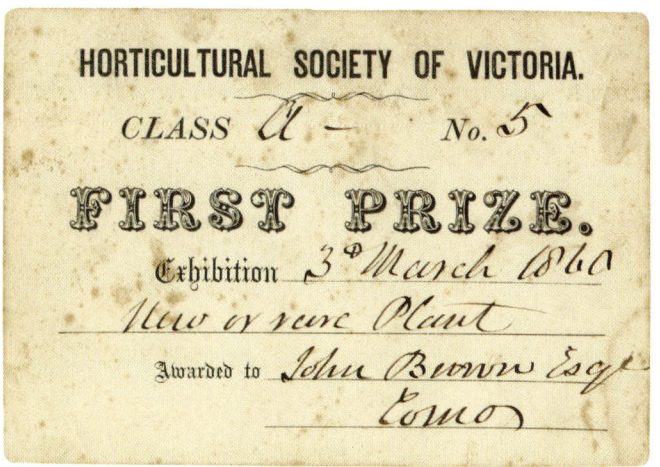

HORTICULTURAL SOCIETY OF VICTORIA.

CLASS *a* — No. 5

FIRST PRIZE.

Exhibition *3ᵈ March 1860*

New or rare Plant

Awarded to John Brown Esqᵉ
Como

Oceanian influence | 1861

The South Seas exercised a powerful fascination for botanical explorers, and the bold forms and colours of foliage and flowers found there provided a powerful stimulus to horticulture, especially in Australia.

These rarely seen photographic reproductions of paintings from a Russian expedition highlight the richness of the Pacific flora. German-born and British-trained botanist Berthold Seemann, who translated the accompanying text, praised their artistic qualities as well as their 'unrivalled truthfulness'. By means of an ingenious detachable grid (keyed to the adjoining text), F. H. von Kittlitz's paintings became a visual directory to the different floras and their ecological groupings.

The March Stand | 1862

The increasing popularity in the mid-nineteenth century of table service *à la Russe*—where guests received food plated from the sideboard instead of dishes on the table—posed a conundrum. How should the increased space on tables for floral decoration be treated? Heavy epergnes and massed displays virtually negated this new freedom. Thomas March devised a scheme of glass rods and plates that was simultaneously elegant and effective. Described in his book *Fruit and Flower Decoration* (London, 1862), the March Stand soon swept all before it. Banded colour schemes (relieved with foliage) also effectively transplanted the parterre from the flower garden to the dining table.

First Prize for Table Decoration, Royal Horticultural Society, 1861.

The gardenesque manner of planting | 1863

Horticulture received a huge boost in the wake of the gold rushes by an influx of skilled gardeners and the formation of horticultural societies to promote an earnest sharing of knowledge. In 1859 the Victorian Gardeners' Mutual Improvement Society instituted an essay book to permanently record lectures and debate. William Ferguson's 1863 essay on planting proposed the gardenesque as an appropriate style for the colony. Suited especially to the pleasure ground and near the house, he cautioned that 'the gardenesque manner of planting and managing includes the application of pruning and thinning, at all future periods of growth of trees and shrubs, so as to keep each plant perfectly distinct from those around it', advice often not heeded.

In general I would adopt the garden-esque manner of planting trees and shrubs, especially in the pleasure ground and near the house, but in more distant parts of the grounds I would adopt the picturesque mode

The all-seeing eye | 1864

The Grand United Order of Free Gardeners of Australasia was formed in 1864. Of Scottish origin, the Order drew on a mix of biblical, botanical and masonic imagery to unite working gardeners into a brotherhood of self-help and benevolence. Free Gardenery applied the art of cultivating the garden to the development of the mind in intelligence and virtue. The Order's lavish membership certificate, printed in Melbourne by Troedel, embraced these virtues. Adam and Eve jostle for space with emus and kangaroos, while overhanging palm trees proclaim loud hosannas as the deluge delivers its cleansing waters. From above, the all-seeing eye of benevolence imposes order on the disparate imagery.

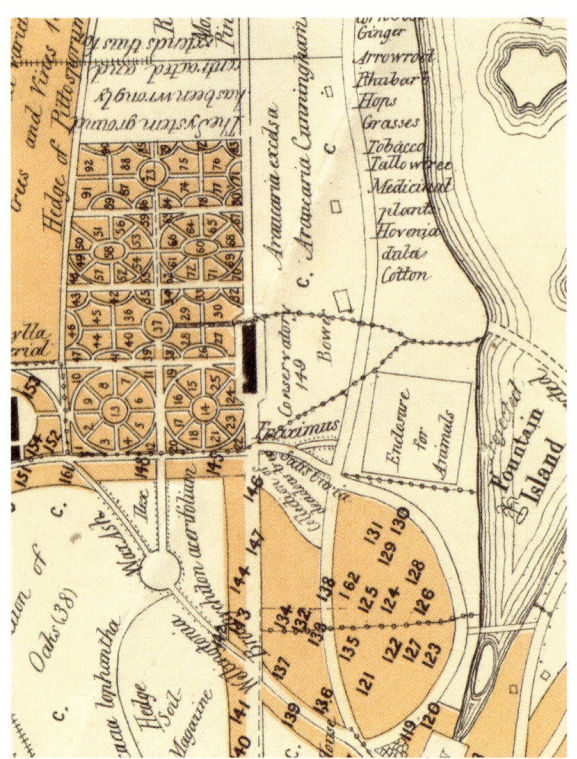

Acclimatisation in the antipodes | 1865

From the late 1850s, Melbourne Botanic Gardens consolidated under the directorship of Ferdinand Mueller as a site for experiment and education. He brought a Germanic precision and botanist's comprehensiveness to the Gardens, amply displayed in this 1865 plan. A great love was the acclimatisation of potentially useful plants, which Mueller viewed as an urgent national work. While we may now regret his enthusiasm for spreading the blackberry, acclimatisation then was akin to completing God's work. Had not the colonies been poorly endowed in their vegetal riches? Qualms were soon expressed about inappropriate introductions but successes outshone failures in the contemporary mind.

Chinese gardening | 1866

The drawings and writings of Jong Ah Sing provide an intimate glimpse into the world of Chinese gardening. A miner at Anderson's Hill, near Bealiba on Victoria's central goldfields, from 1866, Jong's expressive calligraphic images vividly convey the importance of gardening to the Chinese. Productive gardens nestle close to the tents in his plan of the encampment. The insularity of his representation was all too sadly reflected in Jong Ah Sing's personal circumstances. He was incarcerated in 1867 after a fight and ultimately admitted to Yarra Bend Lunatic Asylum. Jong's minute manuscript volume, poignantly entitled 'The Case', was tendered in 1872 in a (futile) plea for freedom.

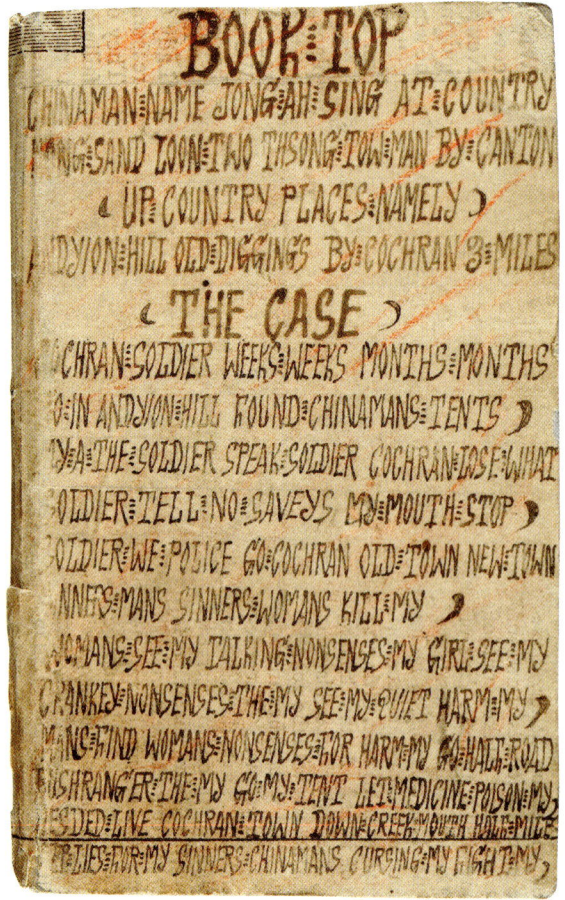

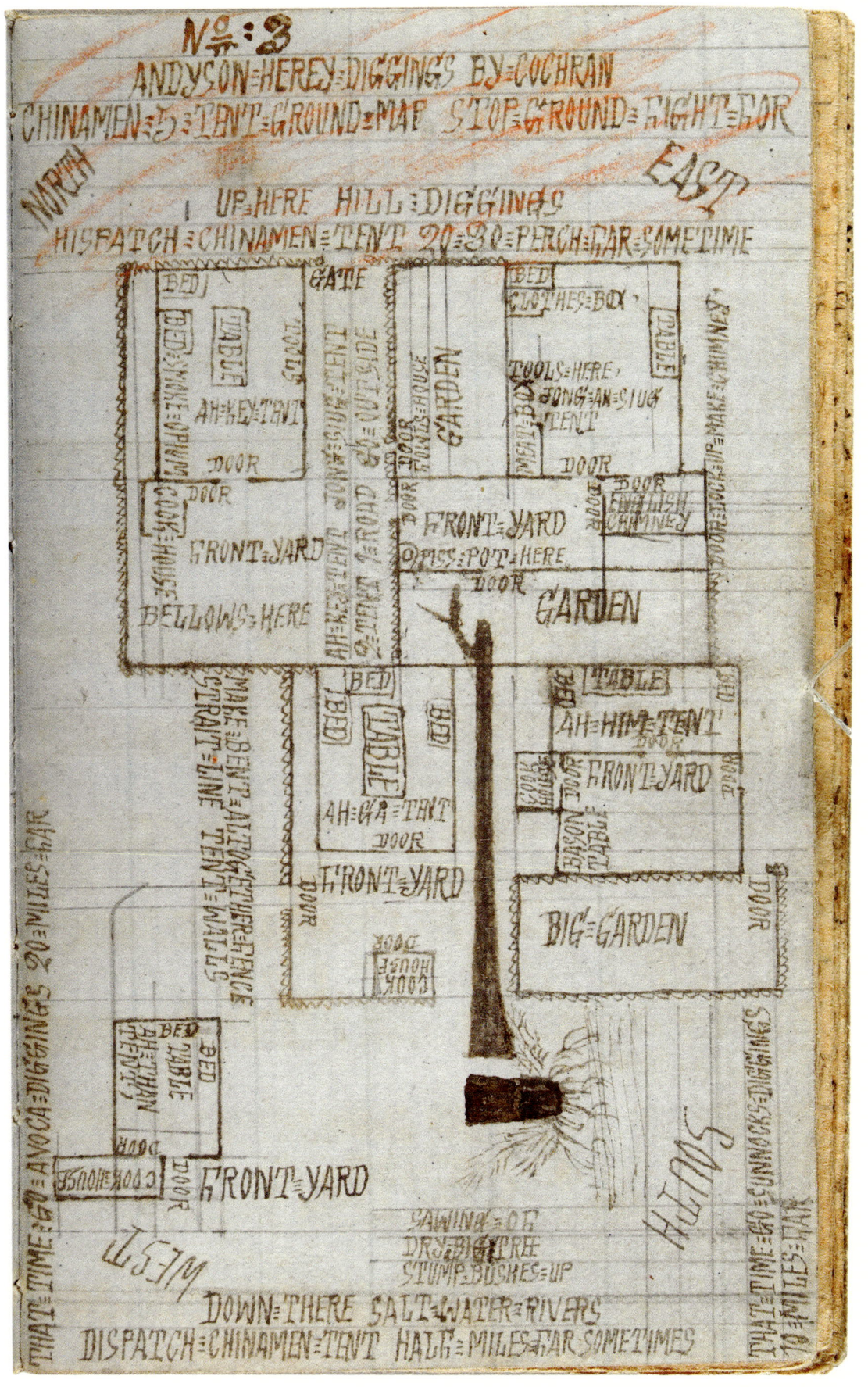

ANDY SON=HEREY=DIGGINGS BY=COCHRAN
CHINAMEN=5=TENT=GROUND=MAP STOP=GROUND=EIGHT=FAR

NORTH

EAST

UP=HERE HILL=DIGGINGS
HIS=PATCH=CHINAMEN=TENT 20=30=PERCH=FAR=SOMETIME

BED
BED=SMOKE=OPIUM

TABLE
AH=KEY=TNT

DOOR
COOK=HOUSE
FRONT=YARD
BELLOWS=HERE

DOOR

GATE

TOOLS

AH=KEY=TNT JONG=OUT=HOUSE 20=OUTSIDE
TENT 40=FENCE=UP=MAKE=CHINESE
2=TENT ½=ROAD

GARDEN

MEAT=BOX

BED
CLOTHES=BOX

TOOLS=HERE,
JONG=AN=SIUG
=TENT
DOOR

TABLE

DOOR
ENGLISH
CHIMNEY

PUNG FUNG=HOUSE
FRONT=YARD
PISS=POT=HERE
DOOR

GARDEN

MAKE=BENT=ALTOGETHER=FENCE
STRAIT=LINE TENT=WALLS

BED

TABLE

AH=GA=TNT
DOOR
FRONT=YARD

DOOR

COOK=HOUSE
DOOR

BED

BED
TABLE

AH=HIME=TENT
DOOR
FRONT=YARD

BED

DOOR

COOK=HOUSE

BASON
TABLE

DOOR

BIG=GARDEN

DOOR

BED
TABLE
AH=THAN=TENT

DOOR
COOK=HOUSE
DOOR
FRONT=YARD

WEST

SAWING=OF
DRY=BIG=TREE
STUMP=BUSHES=UP

SOUTH

THAT=TIME=GO AN OCA=DIGGINGS 20=MILES=FAR

THAT=TIME=GO CUNNACK=DIGGINGS
SHA=CHINE=GO 10=MILES=FAR

DOWN=THERE SALT=WATER=RIVERS
DISPATCH=CHINAMEN=TENT HALF=MILES=FAR SOMETIMES

Melbourne Botanic Gardens | 1867

This view of Melbourne Botanic Gardens by Henry Gritten, one of several he painted, portrays the scene with almost pastoral beauty. A self-styled 'landscape and architectural painter', Gritten had trained and exhibited in London before travelling to North America. He arrived in Victoria in 1853, and spent time in Melbourne, Sydney, Hobart and Launceston. His topographic paintings of houses and gardens exhibited a keen appreciation of garden detail. Unseen here is the turmoil that dogged the Gardens, as dissatisfaction with Ferdinand Mueller's directorship—perceived as excessively scientific and inartistic—foreshadowed the dramatic landscape transformation undertaken by William Guilfoyle in the following decade.

Plans of Flower Gardens | 1868

The role of the garden magazine as an arbiter of taste is not—as some may wish to believe—a recent development, having commenced in the early nineteenth century. Loudon's pioneering *Gardener's Magazine* (1826) had many successors, including the *Journal of Horticulture and Cottage Gardener*, established in 1848. These *Plans of Flower Gardens, Beds, Borders, Roseries, and Aquariums* (London, 1868), published by the *Journal of Horticulture*, consolidated contributors' designs into an inexpensive pattern book. The design of an elegant rosary was conveyed to readers with economical simplicity, all the more striking to modern eyes for its Dadaesque typography.

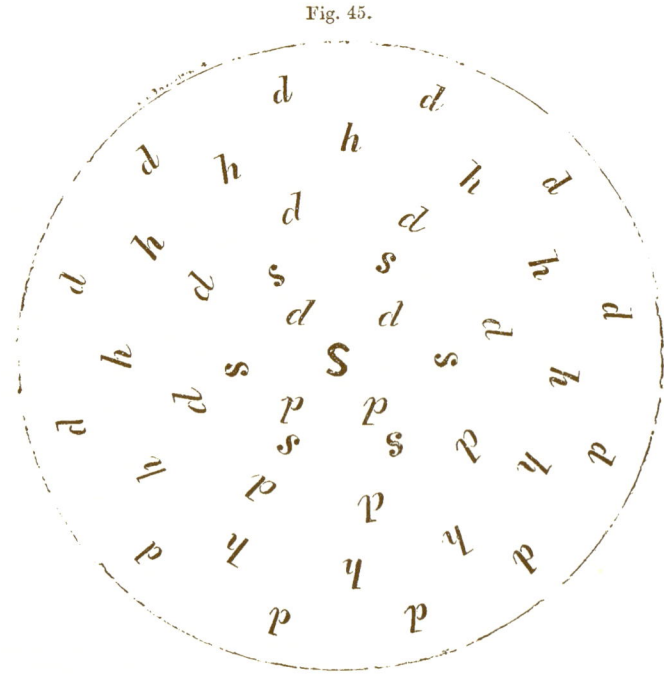

Fig. 45.

Bed 12 feet in diameter, to contain—s. Seven Standards.   H. Twelve Half-standards.   D. Twenty-four Dwarfs.

PLATE XIII.

MODE OF WATERING ROADS, DRIVES, FOOTWAYS, AND THEIR MARGINS.

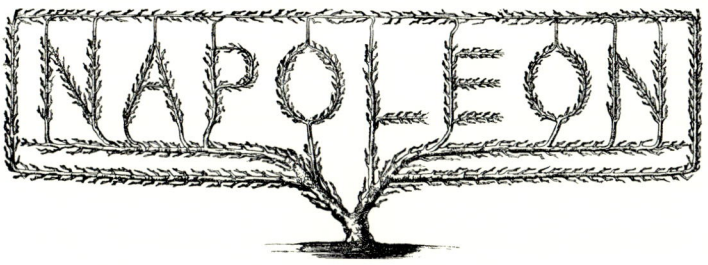

The Parks, Promenades & Gardens of Paris | 1869

William Robinson, now remembered as a proponent of horticultural naturalism, spent much of 1867 in France. Based in Paris as horticultural correspondent for the London newspaper *The Times* and the *Gardeners' Chronicle* magazine, Robinson reported extensively on advances in French gardening in the year of the Paris Exposition Universelle. His key book, *The Parks, Promenades & Gardens of Paris, described and considered in relation to the wants of our own cities and of public and private gardens* (London, 1869), provided a feast for its international audience. Although those in the colonies could hardly be expected to match the sophistication of Parisian public gardens, with their retractable metal-pipe hoses, Robinson's advocacy of the secateur, espalier pruning and bold-foliaged plantings had immediate relevance.

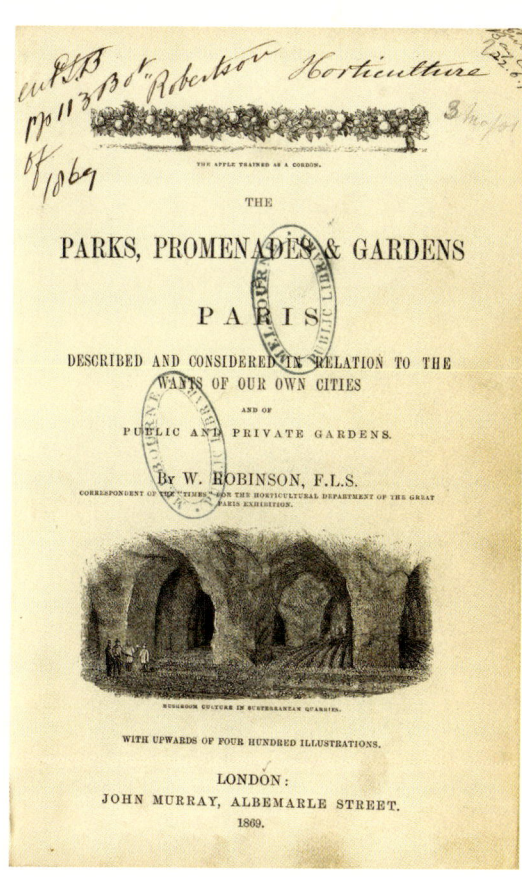

Fenceless gardening | 1870

Fences dominated nineteenth-century suburban development in Australia. A host of practical concerns underpinned this boundary making and few were willing to dispense with their symbol of possession. J. Weidenmann's book *Beautifying Country Houses: A Handbook of Landscape Gardening* (New York, 1870) illustrated an alternative where front gardens were transformed by the abolition of fences into a contiguous sward of neighbourly pride. Such horticultural nationalism was not seen in Australia until the advent of a national capital, although leasehold tenure and legislative force were critical generators of Canberra's fenceless front gardens rather than a neighbourly love of civic beauty.

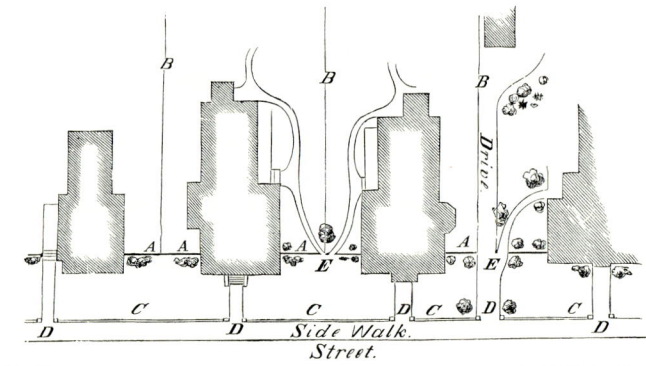

Fig.77.—PLAN FOR FRONT YARDS WITHOUT DIVISION FENCES UPON THE STREET.
AA, Fences between Front and Rear Yards ; BB, Rear Division Fences ; CC, Small Lawns ; DD, Entrances.

DISTANCE APART.	NUMBER OF PLANTS.	DISTANCE APART.	NUMBER OF PLANTS.
30 feet.	48	12 feet.	302
28	55	11	360
26	64	10	435
24	75	9	537
22	90	8	680
20	100	7	889
19	120	6	1,201
18	134	5	1,742
17	150	4	2,722
16	169	3	4,840
15	193	2	10,890
14	222	1 foot.	43,560
13	257		

12 x 13 = 156 trees with walk in centre.

209 FEET.

WALK SIX FEET.

WALK SIX FEET.   WALK SIX FEET.   WALK SIX FEET.

209 FEET.   209 FEET.

WALK SIX FEET.

209 FEET.
(A Square Acre.)

The trees require to be 16 feet apart when the walk is in the centre, and the
trees in the centre will be 21 feet apart.

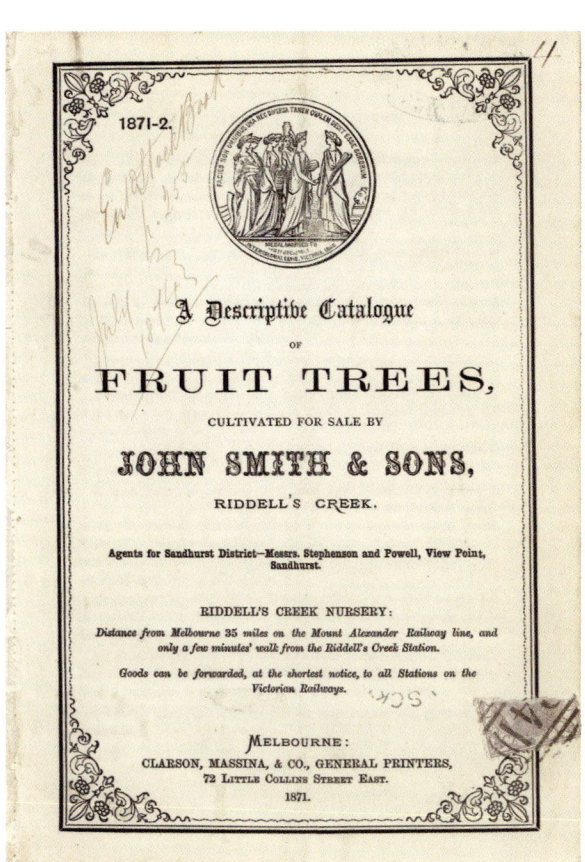

King of the Pippins | 1871

John Smith was amongst Australia's leading fruit growers. The 1871 catalogue of his Riddell's Creek
nursery listed an astonishing 131 varieties of apples, 110 pears, 48 plums, 31 strawberries, 27 cherries, 13
apricots, 5 nectarines, 17 peaches, 19 table grapes, 10 currants, 9 figs and 44 gooseberries. The catalogue
also doubled as a guide to growers, including a plan for a typical orchard, and a table of trees per acre.
The energy and care displayed by Smith and his sons led the *Australasian* to observe that 'this private
firm has done more towards the cultivation and reliable nomenclature of hardy fruits suited to this
climate than all the horticultural societies in Victoria put together'.

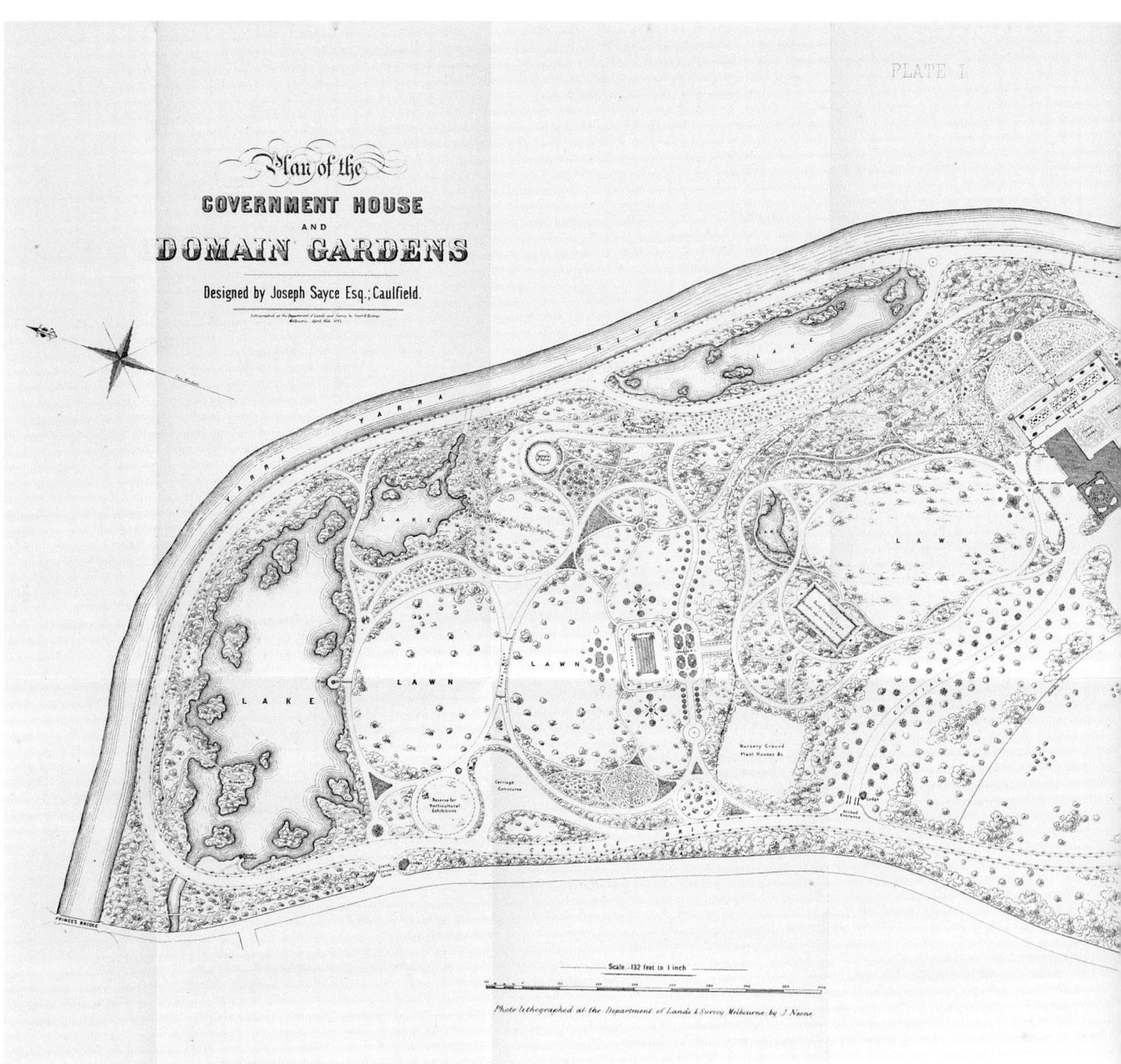

Plan of the
GOVERNMENT HOUSE
AND
DOMAIN GARDENS

Designed by Joseph Sayce Esq.; Caulfield.

Scale – 132 feet to 1 inch

Photo lithographed at the Department of Lands & Survey Melbourne by J. Noone.

PLATE I

Melbourne's Domain | 1872

Domains are a feature of all Australian capitals—the term had a distinctly local usage in describing the land around a government house. This evolved more generally into a specialised form of public land often including a botanic garden. Melbourne's Domain was formalised in the early 1870s with the erection of Government House. When no acceptable designs were produced from a competition in 1872, Joseph Sayce, a banker and amateur landscape designer, submitted a design—reminiscent of Liverpool's Sefton Park—of greater elaboration than previously considered. The scheme was adopted but the Lands Department's anxiety and spiralling costs cut short its implementation.

Summer retreats | 1873

By the 1870s, Mount Macedon had become a favoured summer retreat for Melbourne's scientific gentlemen. Their estates emulated Indian hill stations, so much so that the area was later described as the 'Simla of the South'. Charles Ryan—father of the artist Ellis Rowan—purchased land for his property Derriweit Heights in 1873. Between huge eucalypts, Ryan sculpted and smoothed the bush, interplanting between ancient eucalypt trunks with conifers and shrubberies of cool temperate plants. Nicholas Caire's photograph highlights this rich interplay between European sensibilities and the uncompromising Australian bush.

The singular pleasure
of orchids | 1874

In the realm of the vegetable
kingdom, orchids have perhaps
enjoyed the most sustained passion
of any plant. The splendour of
their blossom, the grace of their
habit and the exoticism of their
habitats have all contributed
to the pleasure of their lovers.
Mostly male and often guarded
in their passion, orchid lovers
have also produced some of the
most sumptuous of plant books.
James Bateman's *Monograph
of Odontoglossum* (London,
1874) took ten years to publish
and its plates expansively depict
the chromatic brilliance of this
orchid genus. Bateman's earlier
*Orchidacae of Mexico and
Guatemala* (1843) had adopted
an even larger format—double
elephant to the bibliophile—wryly
observed in a self-deprecatory
vignette of midgets lifting the
book with a block and tackle.

Yuccas, New Zealand Flax, Palms, India-rubber, and Ivy grouped around Sofa Arbour in the Drawing-Room.

Domestic Floriculture | 1875

Flower arranging had long enlivened domestic interiors by the time F. W. Burbidge wrote *Domestic Floriculture* (London, 1875) but the idea of decorating with live plants had only been recently revived. The new realm of indoor gardening embraced glazed plant cases, pots and tubs, aquariums and hanging baskets, as well as bouquets, wreaths, vases, floral decorations and arrangements of fruit. Burbidge's recommendations for a 'Sofa Arbour' displayed a sculptural quality more often seen in the institutional setting of a hall or ballroom. Indeed, many of his recommendations were ill-suited to Australian conditions and here it was often the shaded verandah rather than the stifling parlour that received the most concerted horticultural affection.

Select Extra-tropical Plants | 1876

Ferdinand von Mueller produced one of Australia's most successful nineteenth-century works on planting, yet it has been curiously ignored by most garden historians. The text of *Select Plants Readily Eligible for Industrial Culture or Naturalisation in Victoria, with indications of their native countries and some of their uses* (Melbourne, 1876) was first published in the proceedings of the Acclimatisation Society of Victoria. Under its more widely known title, *Select Extra-tropical Plants*, it rapidly became a horticultural manifesto for the Australian acclimatisation movement. The book was eventually published in eleven editions and translated into four languages, including German.

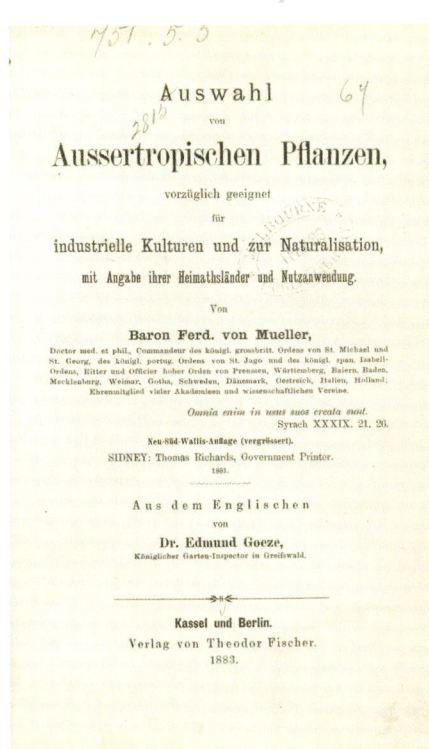

Gardening under glass | 1877

In most parts of Australia, the glazed and heated protection required in European gardens was exchanged for misted shade. One striking exception was in botanic gardens, where both forms of horticultural care were necessary to enhance the range of cultivated plants. Richard Schomburgk, German-born director of Adelaide Botanic Gardens, was responsible for Australia's most exquisite conservatory. Prefabricated in Germany and opened in 1877, Schomburgk's jewel-like Palm House consolidated Adelaide's reputation for gardening under glass. Originally designed for tropical plants, as pictured here, the building now houses rare Madagascan plants from the arid zone, highlighting changed priorities within contemporary botanic gardens.

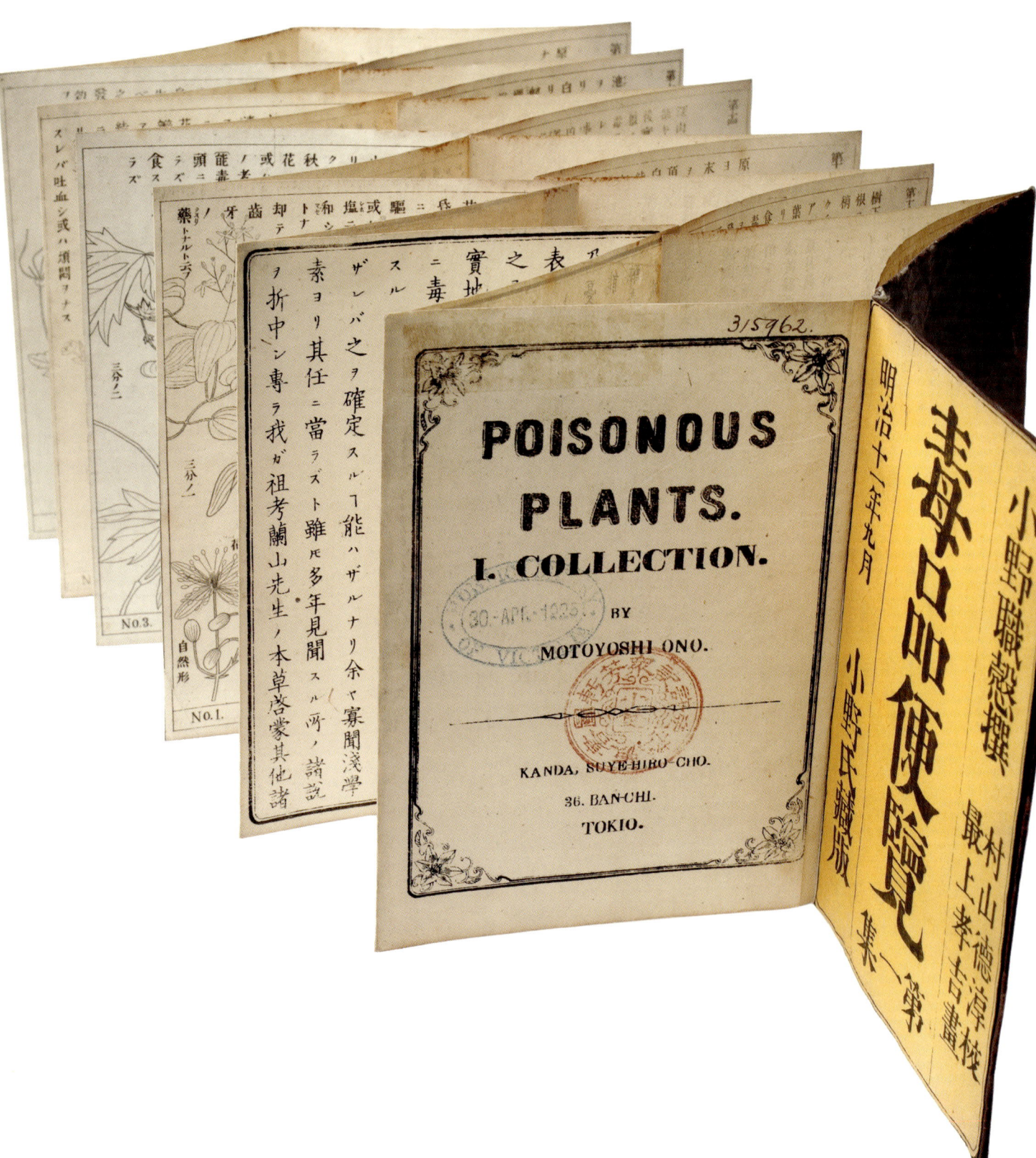

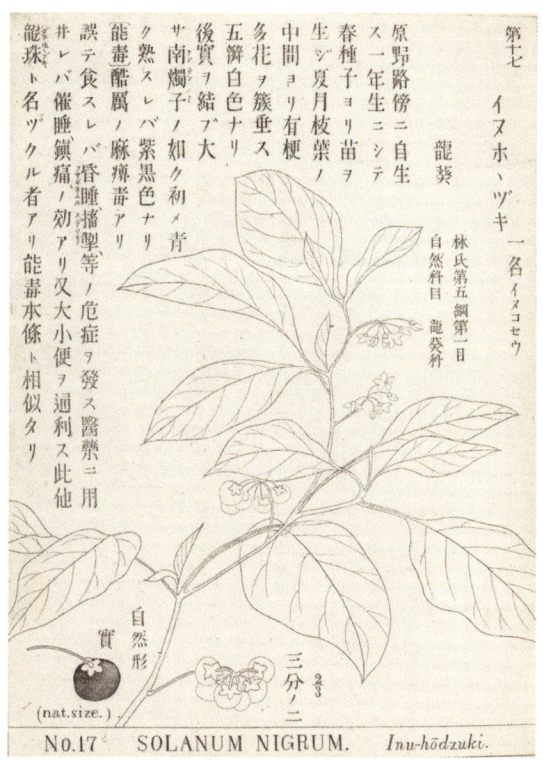

Poisonous plants from Tokio | 1878

The publication of this book in 1878 came a decade after the fall of the Tokugawa Shogunate, in a period when Japan was slowly opening to the outside world and the artistry of Japan was being revealed through many sources, including books and prints. These were combined in this beguiling publication on poisonous plants. Precisely why it found its way to Australia is not known. With its simple English translation the publication may have formed part of a chemist or pharmacist's library. Its folding pages contain elegant Japanese prints, economical of line yet rich in botanical content.

The ruins of Pompeii | 1879

Fortuna Villa, the Bendigo residence of mining magnates Christopher and Theodore Ballerstedt, was significantly extended and embellished in the late nineteenth century by mining entrepreneur George Lansell. The splendour of the estate celebrated the manner in which the goddess of fortune had favoured their risky gold-mining ventures. The Pompeii fountain, modelled on the original viewed by Lansell in 1879, lent a touch of classical grandeur to the garden, wholly in keeping with the aspirations of its gold-rich owner. Once urn-bedecked and statue-encrusted, the fountain and pool remain as a reminder of the rich cultural links transplanted to the colony's gardens.

RUS IN URBE

(1880s–1890s)

*The art which reproduces the wildness of rude nature,
and that which softens the rudeness and creates polished beauty in its place,
are equally the arts of gardening.*

Frank J. Scott, *The Art of Beautifying Suburban Home Grounds of Small Extent*, 1886

THE quest for rural contentment within Australia's burgeoning urban sprawl—that timeless quality of *rus in urbe*—reached its apogee in the late nineteenth century.

By this date, the Australian suburbanite was sufficiently dislocated from the bush and its pioneering rusticity to appreciatively re-create its distinctive qualities within the safety of pickets and palings. The primitive qualities of Australian bush architecture were now transposed into rustic arbours and arches, seats and stands. If the real stuff could not be had, then cast iron was more than acceptable, often preferred. Primal forests were tamed through their pruned and potted offspring, now gracing the verandah and transplanted to countless bush-houses and ferneries.

To its occupants, the villa once again became the Italian country house or farmstead of its seventeenth-century origins. The idea of a rural estate in the city appealed enormously to a rising generation of middle-class aspirants. Sufficiently wealthy to own their suburban estate but beyond the reach of a country retreat, their city acreage could conveniently embody the qualities of both. Scenic seclusion and urban convenience could coexist.

Contemporary depictions of the suburbs often emphasised this imaginary rural seclusion. Selectively painted or photographed through a retained clump of trees, the garden was made to appear seamless with its surrounds. Vantage points with treed foregrounds or backdrops—or better still, water and mountains—provided a graduated *mise-en-scène* for the onlooker. From within the garden, the invitee was directed to vistas of preference, generally contrived and often embellished with the aid of art. The elevated lookout was the ultimate suburban conceit, allowing one's real estate to be surveyed in the manner of a feudal lord.

In the public realm there was garden-making aplenty. Although formal avenues suited public promenading, naturalistic designs were more generally promoted. The ease with which picturesque effects could be created and the informal naturalism inherent in such plans were greatly esteemed. Was Nature not the great model?

Urbe dominated *rus* in regard to neatness though, especially in the domestic front garden and the public parterre. The suburban garden rarely achieved the quality of untamed nature—even if some advanced minds did seek to introduce a newly fashionable wild garden to their acreage. The stately trunk of the oak or elm, the floral perfection of the rose or chrysanthemum, and the rounded silhouette of the shrubbery were much desired. The roughly shod limbs of the eucalypt, the untamed habits of the forest floor and the spare qualities of the grassland were still beyond the aesthetic and horticultural sensibilities of all but the most sophisticated suburban gardener.

The harbinger of a new naturalism came in the late nineteenth century with a burgeoning appreciation of native wildflowers. Increasingly the Australian flora was eulogised by the field naturalist, paraded on the horticultural-show stage, utilised by the floral decorator and depicted in the popular press. The nursery trade helped translate this aesthetic appreciation into a horticultural nationalism through an enhanced availability of seeds and plants, yet the all-Australian garden was still many years away.

Tying Le Nôtre
down under | 1880

As suburban gardens spread, an appreciation for the past became
a hallmark of antipodean refinement. Loudon's gardenesque
had long ceased to be a style of planting and now more generally
evoked 'the art of the gardener'. Formal or 'architectural'
gardening was the rage, and even the most modest villa boasted
a flight of stairs and a terraced walk. Suitable models could be
found in popular compendiums, such as *The Famous Parks
and Gardens of the World Described and Illustrated* (London,
1880). Here the immense formal French gardens of Le Nôtre
were reduced to stock views, capable of emulation at a reduced
suburban scale. Versailles and Marly married with Malvern and
Marrickville, Chatsworth conjured with smoke and mirrors.

AVENUE AT MARLY.

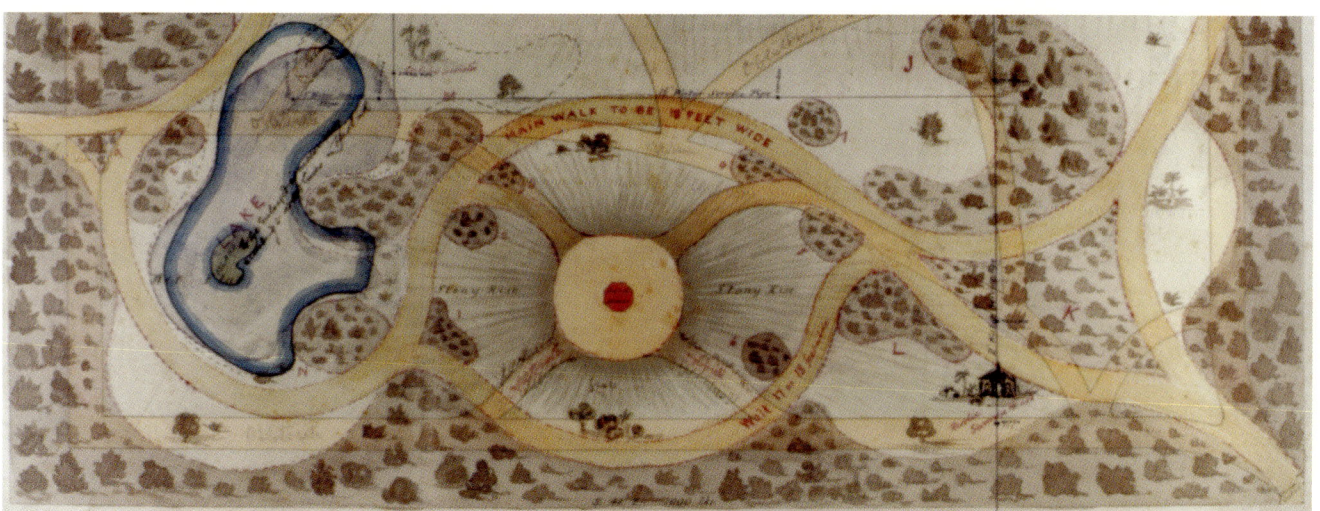

Guilfoyle's plan for Hamilton Botanic Gardens | 1881

The provision of public gardens has been accepted since the mid-nineteenth century as a
normal part of town planning, and Australia is richly endowed with fine examples. The idea
of public access, however, achieved widespread acceptance in Britain only in the 1840s, so
colonial landscape designers and bureaucrats were able to experiment with this new form of
garden. The model that evolved in Victoria distinguished *botanic* gardens from public parks
and gardens by an emphasis in the former on acclimatisation of economically useful plants
within a garden setting. In the hands of William Guilfoyle, director of Melbourne Botanic
Gardens from 1873, this was achieved with a blend of horticultural skill and elegance of design.

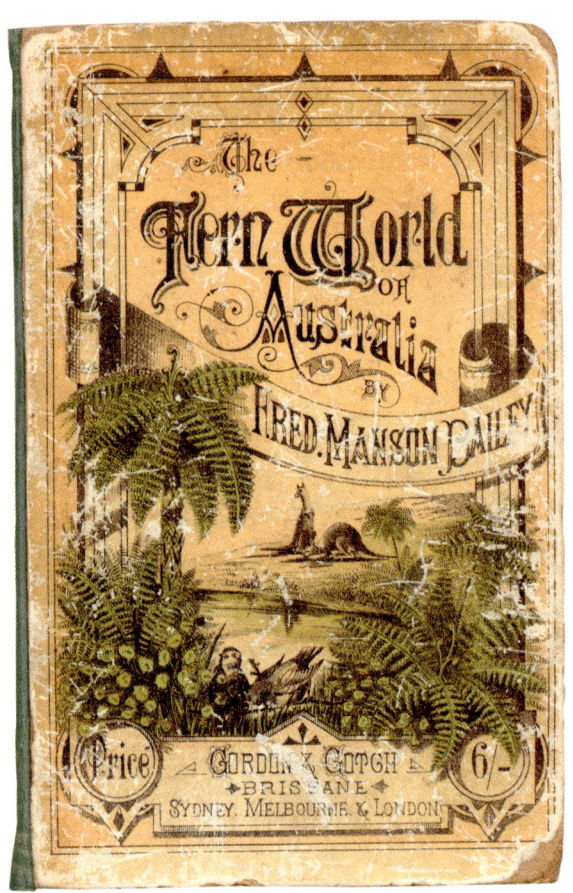

Fern mania | 1882

By 1882, when landscape designer William Sangster was appointed to re-landscape the garden at Rippon Lea, ferns were an established feature of colonial horticulture. F. Manson Bailey's book *The Fern World of Australia*, published in the previous year, had made the leap from botany text to popular handbook, and the fernery was now an indispensable component of the suburban garden. Sangster oversaw the development of a much-enlarged fernery at Rippon Lea, which remains today as a peerless reminder of the fern mania that held sway in the late nineteenth century, transporting the delights of the hills to the city.

The sustainable estate | 1883

Rippon Lea remains Australia's grandest nineteenth-century suburban garden. Established in the late 1860s by Melbourne merchant and politician Frederick Sargood, the estate achieved its pre-eminence through skilful management of water. A never-failing supply from a spring some miles away was brought to the garden via a network of pipes and reservoirs (independent of the Yan Yean reticulated supply). Rippon Lea's lake was enlarged in 1883, and the spoil used to create a mound: the mound aerated the water as it cascaded in a waterfall, while the lake provided storage and a major ornamental focus for the garden. Sargood commissioned a detailed plan of his garden to document this sophisticated system, perhaps anticipating his new role as Victoria's Commissioner of Water Supply.

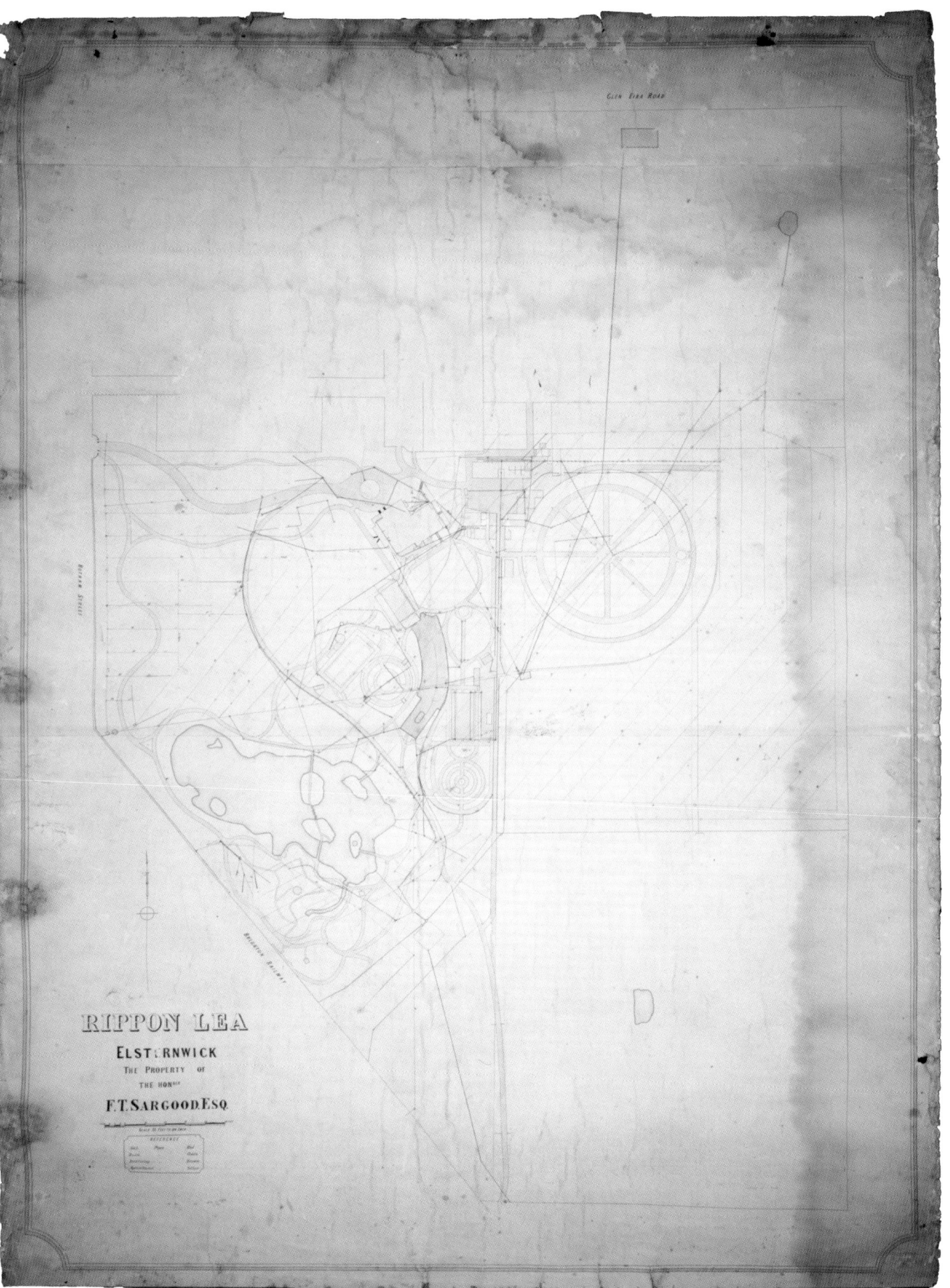

RIPPON LEA

ELSTERNWICK

THE PROPERTY OF

THE HON^{BLE}

F.T. SARGOOD ESQ.

'No connection with photography' | 1884

The pride with which owners regarded their houses and gardens was well reflected in the paintings of William Tibbits. Painting had an important advantage over photography as the artist could emphasise certain details in the creative process. Indeed, Tibbits often advertised his work with the catchphrase 'No connection with photography'. In this view of The Rest, the Abbotsford residence of Melbourne wool broker Richard Goldsborough, the vantage point has neatly exploited the tree-lined banks of the Yarra River, simultaneously giving a generous scale to the property while disguising the wool stores and drying yards adjoining the river.

'In the Realm of the Lithuanian Bison' | 1885

Forests form an indelible part of our cultural memory. Even the utilitarian literature of forestry comes under their spell. John Crombie Brown's *Forests and Forestry in Poland, Lithuania, The Ukraine and the Baltic Provinces of Russia* (Edinburgh, 1885) stands as a characteristic example. Brown came from a forestry dynasty: his brother James was an eminent Scottish authority and his nephew, John Ednie Brown, was a pioneer of Australian forestry. Within his subject, Brown frequently touched upon the social and cultural history of this landscape. Simon Schama covers the same territory with haunting effect in the opening chapter of *Landscape and Memory* (London, 1995), entitled 'In the Realm of the Lithuanian Bison'. Inspired by family memory, Schama weaves tales of the forest within a wide historical setting.

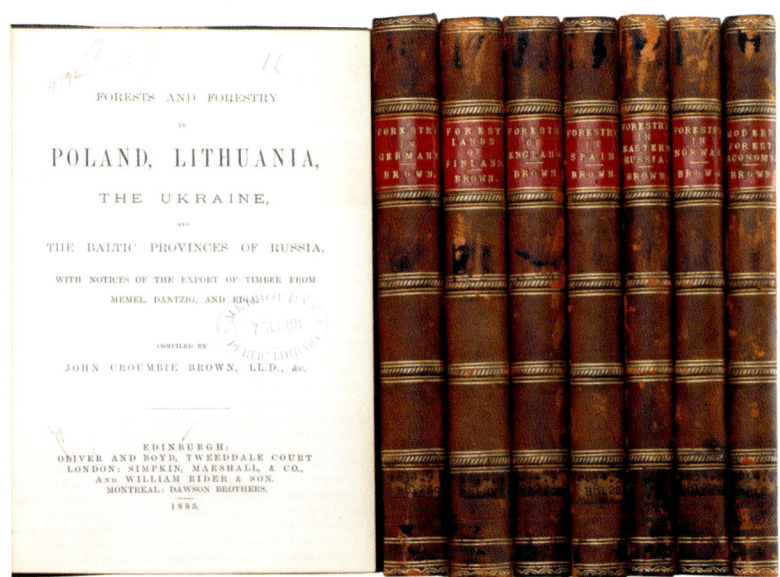

98

The Art of Beautifying
Suburban Home Grounds | 1886

It would be wrong to think that the villa garden was transferred to Australia solely from England. North America's material progress was also closely monitored, and suburban villas of the Atlantic seaboard were as keenly observed as those of Surrey. A. J. Downing was the American Loudon, and by the late nineteenth century his horticultural writings and garden designs had been reaffirmed in the books of Weidenmann and Scott. Frank J. Scott's *The Art of Beautifying Suburban Home Grounds* (New York, 1886) was first published in 1870, the year of J. Weidenmann's *Beautifying Country Houses*. The suburban idyll Scott portrays is one of polished beauty achieved through decorative planting.

Wildflower hunter | 1887

The work of Ellis Rowan, Australia's best-known painter of wildflowers, did much to popularise a love of the Australian flora. The 1870s had seen her career blossom, and during the 1880s and 1890s she travelled extensively, her adventures partially recounted in *A Flower Hunter in Queensland and New Zealand* (1898). Following a commission to execute drawings for the monumental *Picturesque Atlas of Australasia* (1886–88), she was invited by the proprietors of the *Australian Town and Country Journal* to prepare several large floral illustrations as Christmas supplements. Rowan's skill in delineating Australia's wildflowers overcame any infelicities as her paintings were reworked for the lithographer's press.

The villa garden | 1888

As Australia's towns and cities grew during the nineteenth century, a villa residence in the suburbs became an object of admiration and aspiration. The Australian prototype had been developed from the 1820s along the ridges of Sydney's Woolloomooloo Hill and on the slopes leading to Hobart's Derwent River. The villa was distinguished from the more humble cottage by the presence of a generous garden setting, yet lacked the self-sustaining qualities of the mansion estate with its expansive paddocks and orchards. By the late 1880s, sea views and distant vistas were at a premium and the villa garden had turned inward to become an oasis of contained contentment, well demonstrated in Charles Walker's photograph of an unidentified Melbourne villa.

California, due to its Pacific location, similar geography and the comparative rawness of its history, exerted considerable influence on attitudes to the Australian environment. Gold mining, national parks and the nursery trade—to name just a few areas—all felt its impact. Californian experience was also decisive in the early development of Australia's 'irrigation colonies'. When Alfred Deakin, future Australian prime minister, visited the Californian irrigation settlements of the Chaffey Brothers, he saw many parallels between the American west coast and arid areas along Australia's inland rivers. The vision of these early promoters created an expansive horticultural mood. Edward Wickson's book *The California Fruits and How to Grow Them* (San Francisco, 1889) soon became a standard reference for Australian irrigators seeking to bolster the country's navel reserves.

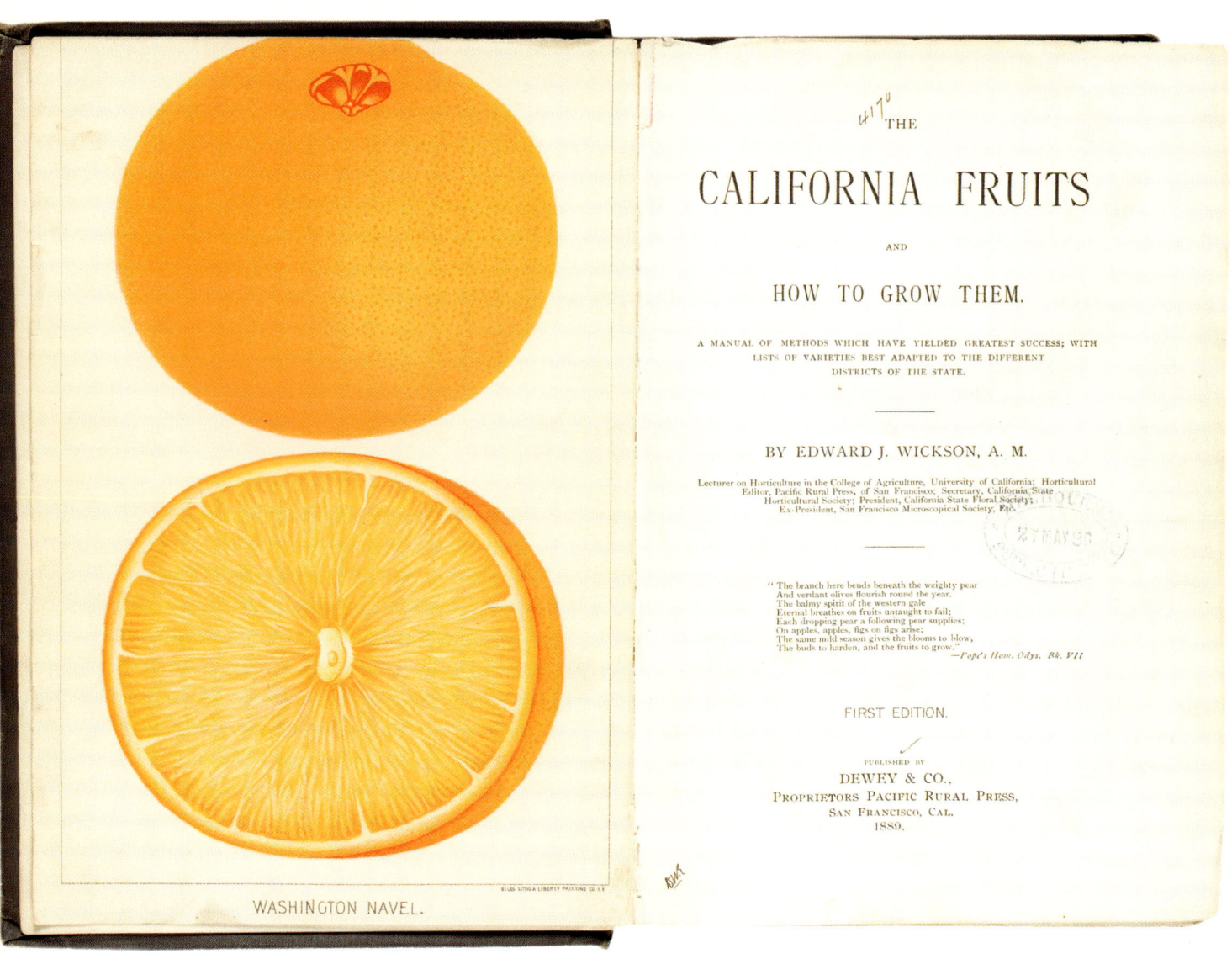

WASHINGTON NAVEL.

THE

CALIFORNIA FRUITS

AND

HOW TO GROW THEM.

A MANUAL OF METHODS WHICH HAVE YIELDED GREATEST SUCCESS; WITH
LISTS OF VARIETIES BEST ADAPTED TO THE DIFFERENT
DISTRICTS OF THE STATE.

BY EDWARD J. WICKSON, A. M.

Lecturer on Horticulture in the College of Agriculture, University of California; Horticultural
Editor, Pacific Rural Press, of San Francisco; Secretary, California State
Horticultural Society; President, California State Floral Society;
Ex-President, San Francisco Microscopical Society, Etc.

" The branch here bends beneath the weighty pear
And verdant olives flourish round the year.
The balmy spirit of the western gale
Eternal breathes on fruits untaught to fail;
Each dropping pear a following pear supplies;
On apples, apples, figs on figs arise;
The same mild season gives the blooms to blow,
The buds to harden, and the fruits to grow."
—*Pope's Hom. Odys. Bk. VII*

FIRST EDITION.

PUBLISHED BY
DEWEY & CO.,
PROPRIETORS PACIFIC RURAL PRESS,
SAN FRANCISCO, CAL.
1889.

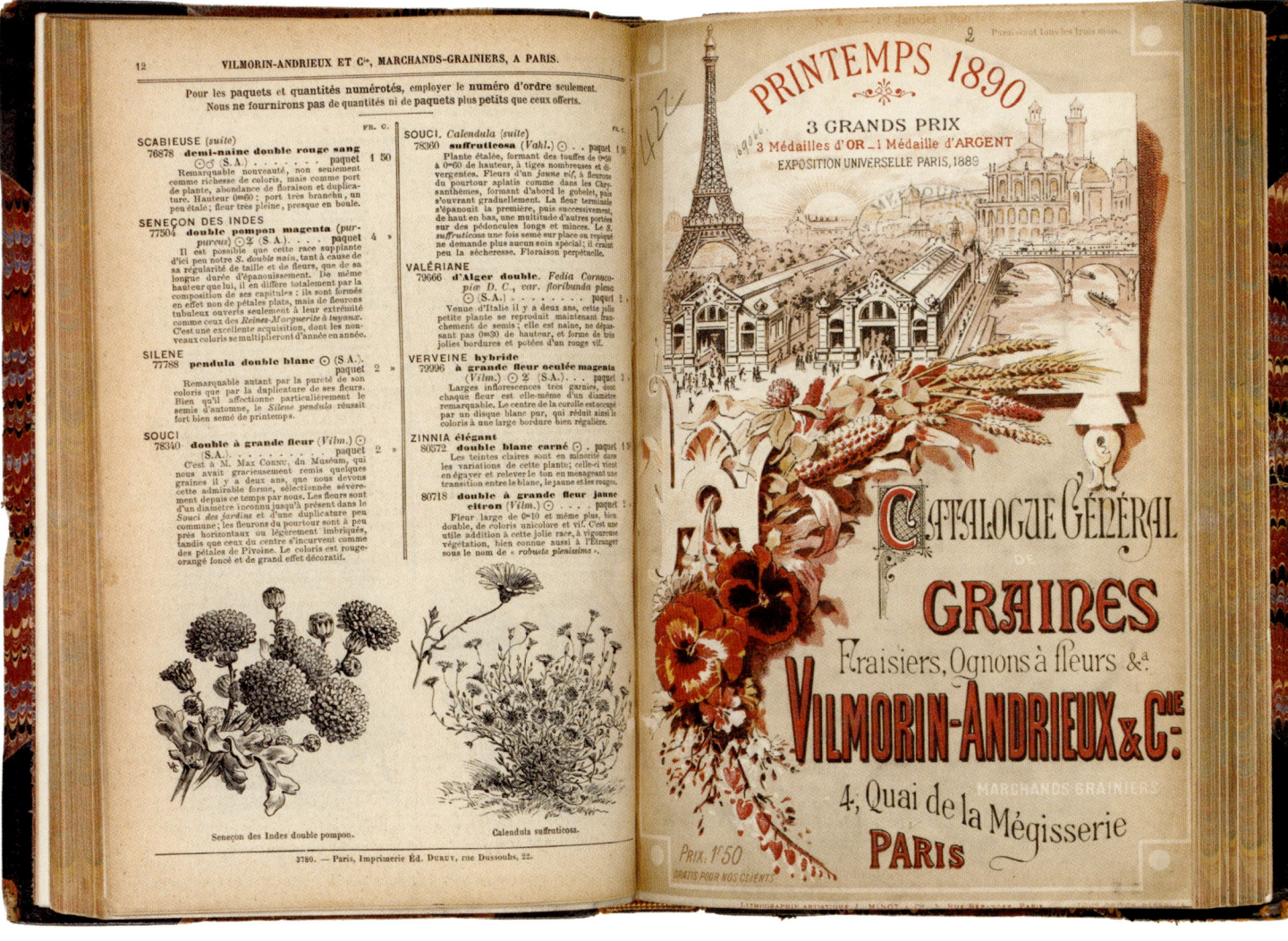

The eyes of the world were on Paris in 1889 as it hosted the Exposition Universelle. The genius of French technology was elegantly symbolised by the Eiffel Tower, but the exhibition halls below also bustled with industry. Just as the tower took the image of Paris to the world, seed merchants Vilmorin-Andrieux provided a focus for international attention in the horticultural department. The company's catalogue for the forthcoming spring contained an unmatched range of vegetable and flower seeds, much sought for their purity and reliability. Vilmorin's publications on vegetable gardening were also highly regarded and enjoyed worldwide distribution, especially through English translations edited by William Robinson.

The art of flower arrangement is a quintessentially Japanese accomplishment. It captures the essence and symbolism of that nation's intense appreciation for the transience of the seasons, its sense of occasion, and the contemplation of its spirituality. Josiah Conder, a British architect working in Japan, published the earliest English-language work on the subject, *The Flowers of Japan and the Art of Floral Arrangement* (Tokio, 1891). Its exquisite plates depict with calligraphic beauty the seasonal joys of the Japanese garden as well as practical instructions on all aspects of floral art. In 'Cherry blossoms at dusk', a mother supports her child aloft to collect blossom from a fenced garden. The cloak of dusk and the child's loss of shoes bring a furtive urgency to the scene.

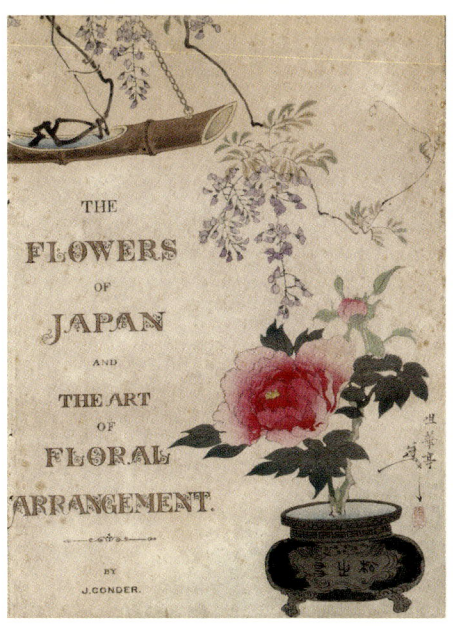

Flora for a federated Australia | 1892

H. A. James's *Handbook of Australian Horticulture* (Sydney, 1892) was the earliest Australian gardening book to include coloured illustrations. The imposing bulk of the volume and its national network of distributors combined to make the *Handbook* a publication ahead of its time. Much of the advice was also in the horticultural vanguard, particularly the inclusion of a separate chapter on Australian native plants. Horticultural interest in the Australian flora had grown during the nineteenth century, but its appearance in mainstream gardening books, and the showcasing of Australian plants by garden directors—such as J. H. Maiden at Sydney Botanic Gardens—ushered in a new phase of popular appreciation.

NATIVE FLOWERS.

The Fruit Salad Plant | 1893

Whilst migration since World War II has immeasurably enriched our diets, the nineteenth century witnessed the uncertain beginnings of Australia's exotic fruit industry. David Crichton's book *Australasian Fruit Culture* (Melbourne, 1893) was the product of long horticultural experience. His list of recommendations seems strikingly modern: guava, jackfruit, litchi, rambutan and even the native geebung. Although now regarded more for the boldness of its foliage, Crichton recommended *Monstera deliciosa* (Fruit Salad Plant) as a suitable subject for the semi-tropical fruit garden. Lightly brushing off a 'slight tickling sensation in the throat' caused by eating its fruit, he extolled the rich luscious flavour, highly appreciated in its native Mexico and Guatemala.

Towards a national estate | 1894

The formation of the Melbourne Amateur Walking and Touring Club in 1894 was one small step in the creation of a unified national park system. Colonial governments, and their Lands Departments in particular, had long viewed national parks with suspicion, wary of any challenge to the credo of exploitation. However, the concerned voices of botanists, ornithologists, recreational walkers and lovers of unspoiled scenery—often unified under the field naturalists' banner—combined to pressure governments from the 1870s to reserve successively greater tracts of land. The use of the term 'national parks' signified a wish to transcend parochial concerns and to let nature dictate boundaries that formed a national estate.

The horticultural expert | 1895

By the 1890s the state apparatus of agriculture in Australia had widened from its early focus on broad-acre cropping and pastoralism to embrace intensive horticulture. The newly created departments and bureaux of agriculture and horticulture responded to advances in entomology, chemistry and plant pathology, bringing scientific productiveness to the land. A new public servant—the horticultural expert—was also born. Dispensing advice through lectures, field days, periodicals and books, the expert soon became a fixture. French-born Adrian Despeissis fulfilled this role for the Western Australian Bureau of Agriculture and his popular *Handbook of Horticulture & Viticulture of Western Australia* (Perth, 1895) typified a new genre of handbooks.

The Wombat | 1896

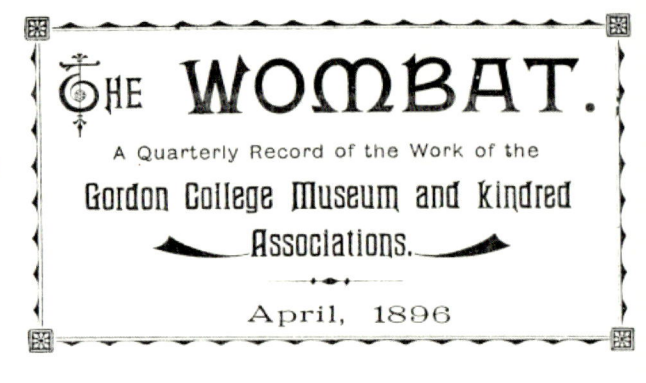

London has *The Times*, Melbourne has the *Age*, and Geelong had the *Wombat*. It is difficult to imagine a more distinctive name for an Australian natural history journal. Published by the Gordon College Museum and kindred associations during 1895–96, the *Wombat* was an organ for the new age of field naturalists. Whereas royal societies had previously covered a wide field of scientific endeavour, the various field naturalists' societies established from the 1880s emphasised first-hand observations of nature. Such groups made vital contributions to botany, nature study in schools, and the promotion of Australian flora in our gardens.

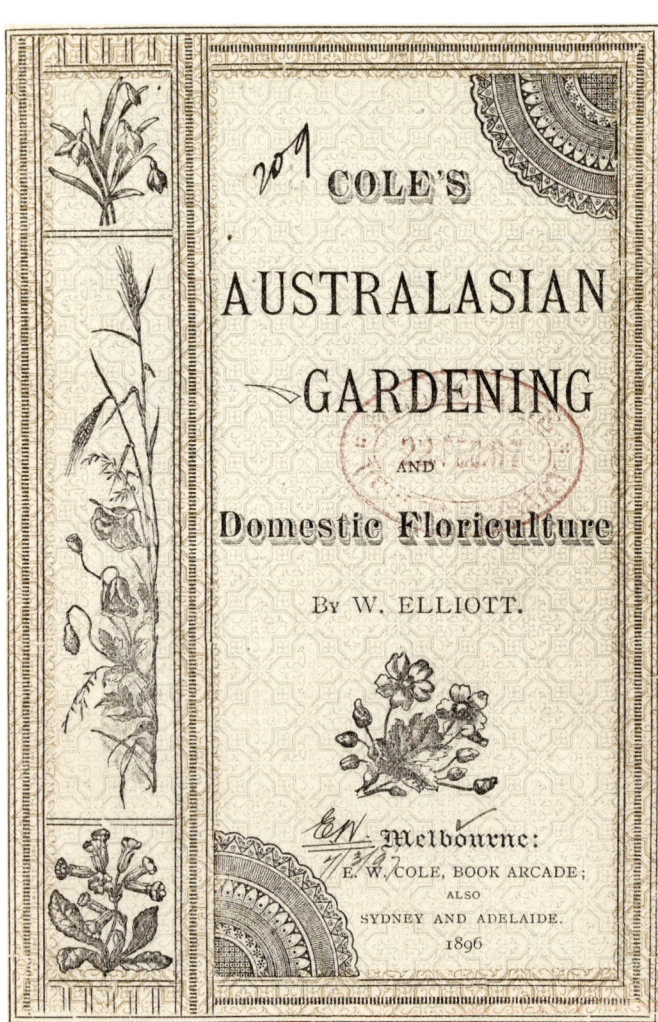

Australasian Gardening and Domestic Floriculture | 1897

The quest to publish a popular national gardening handbook intensified in Australia during the 1890s. The works of H. A. James (*Handbook of Australian Horticulture*), F. Hamilton Brunning (*The Australian Gardener*) and Arthur Yates (*Yates' Garden Guide*) all sought this mantle. It was William Elliott's *Australasian Gardening and Domestic Floriculture* (Melbourne, 1897) that arguably achieved the greatest contemporary popularity. Sadly, Elliott—one of Victoria's most experienced horticulturists and for many years horticultural editor of the weekly *Leader* newspaper—did not live to see his book published. He modelled his design advice on Edward Kemp's *How to Lay Out a Garden* (London, 1864), bringing the gardenesque to a new generation.

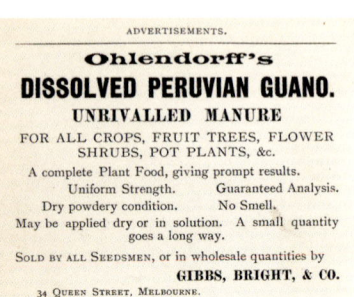

Aspects of Nature | 1898

The aspects of nature prescribed for students in late-nineteenth century Victoria were those of Milton, Cowper, Wordsworth, Shelley and Ruskin. For good reason: the subject being taught was entitled 'English'. Although youthful readers of Thomas and Mabel Harlin's matriculation text *Aspects of Nature* (Melbourne, 1898) may have struggled to reconcile its predominantly British literary extracts with the local environment, the universal message of Romanticism was unmistakable. In its horticultural guise, Romanticism was perhaps best represented by William Robinson's book *The Wild Garden* (London, 1870). The wild garden, though, was at the cutting edge of suburban values, its ability to survive with little maintenance often at odds with confined suburban neatness.

'Marvellous Smelbourne' | 1899

Sewage flows downhill. A truism to be sure, but one that led to an unparalleled documentary record of the nation's suburban gardens. Responding to insanitary conditions and alarming mortality rates, colonial and local governments joined forces from the late nineteenth century to implement metropolitan sewerage systems. Colonial engineers and surveyors met the challenge with characteristic Victorian thoroughness. The need for accurate levels and pipe placement ensured a detailed survey of each suburb at large scale, recording not only major built features but, in many cases, garden paths, fences and horticultural buildings. When compared with paintings and photographs the worth of these plans to the garden historian is magnified.

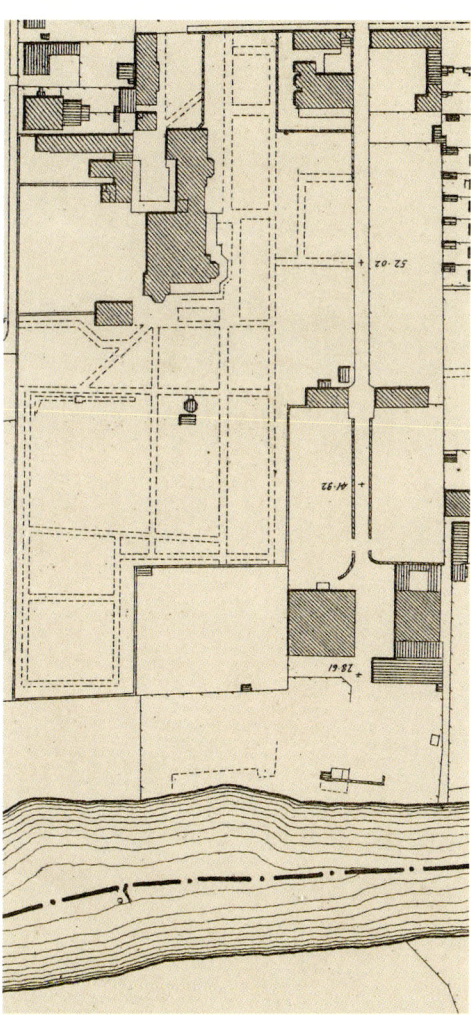

NATIONALISM
AND NATURALISM
(1900s–1910s)

Any emblem worth notice at all should be a real and living expression
of something precious to its people, and a source of inspiration as well . . .
If we are to be worthy of our Wattle we must make it true that it stands
both for us and our country, a symbol of Australia's golden prosperity,
and the hospitality of its citizens.

Tullie C. Wollaston, *Our Wattles*, 1916

THE distinctive Australian flora, already appreciated for the isolated horticultural potential of its flowers, foliage and habit— and to a lesser extent, its bark and scent—was increasingly linked to national sentiment. For those who had supported Federation, this nationalism was further proof of the potential of 'Young Australia'. It was manifest in the debate over a national floral emblem and in the establishment of Wattle Day. More generally it was invoked in the teaching of nature study in schools, where Arbor Day provided a civic focal point for tree planting and an opportunity for enlightened voices to champion the Australian flora.

Increasingly, these enlightened voices emanated from the city, as the harsh realities of bush life slipped further into the memory.

After decades of colonial landscape painting depicting a pioneering and often heroic rural Australia, the velvet-suited painters of the Heidelberg School looked no further than outer suburbs for their inspiration: a day's work in the country was but a short train ride away. These 'city bushmen', as art historian Leigh Astbury christened the Australian Impressionists, joined with the '*Bulletin* school' of writers to create a rural mythology for Australian suburbanites in which the Australian flora was accorded a central role. In the decorative arts, this was seen in the vogue for 'gumnut nouveau', where the sinuous forms of buds, nuts and leaves soon adorned myriad objects. Garden beds outlined as maps of Australia were an unmistakable manifestation of popular nationalism.

The link between appreciation of Australian plants in the wild and their planting in domestic gardens was a significant advance. Many proponents of the Australian flora were also keen members of horticultural societies or influential in institutions such as botanic gardens and museums, where the message was spread to a receptive but cautious audience. Landscape designers and educators too played an important role. Walter and Marion Griffin, for example, as designers of the new federal capital, Canberra, were well placed to speak with a voice of authority. They were especially captivated by the potential for a new ecological sensibility in Australian landscape design. The facility with which the Australian native flora complemented informal garden designs was periodically advanced by such enlightened voices, yet formality—both in garden design and maintenance regimes—dominating the suburban garden.

Within two decades of the federation of Australia's colonies (1901) one of the earliest Australian-plant gardens had been created in suburban Melbourne, at Maranoa Gardens in Balwyn. Yet this was in advance of contemporary popular taste, and it would not be until the 1960s that nationalism and naturalism achieved a lasting fusion.

The nineteenth century witnessed dramatic and irrevocable changes for many of Australia's Indigenous peoples. In almost every facet of life, traditions attuned to the cycles of the land were overturned by transplanted cultures. Coranderrk, an Aboriginal settlement reserved by Victoria's colonial government in 1863, was intended to house and educate those people whose lands had been invaded. Yet benevolent paternalism governed life at Coranderrk—regulations prescribed nominated times for hunting and fishing, for instance. The growing of hops was introduced as a means of generating work and income, and by the turn of the century was well established. But even this was imbued with great irony: Coranderrk hops were greatly sought by colonial brewers whose grog wrought such havoc.

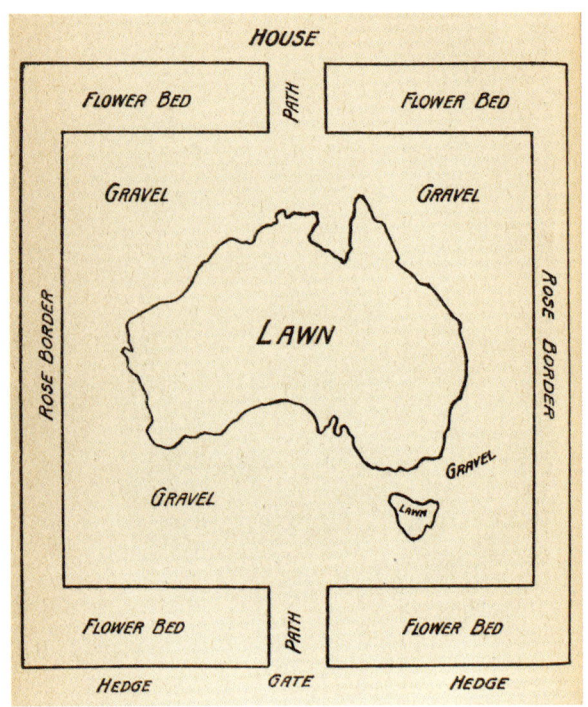

Carpet bedding for a new Commonwealth | 1901

During the Commonwealth inauguration celebrations in January 1901, visitors to Sydney Botanic Gardens could inspect a novel horticultural tribute—a garden bed representing a map of Australia. A later published illustration of such a bed was accompanied by instructions for the home gardener: 'as an alternative to turf, the coast could be delineated in coloured-foliage plants, pot plants half sunk to represent cities, and different states worked out in carpet-bedding plants of contrasting colours'. One advertiser in *Home and Garden Beautiful* delineated the Australian coast with rubber hose, placing the sprinkler rather ironically over arid central Australia: perhaps this was a subtle reference to the confident mood engendered by irrigation and other projects of national interest.

'Gardencraft' for women | 1902

When Frances (later Viscountess) Wolseley founded her School for Lady Gardeners at Glynde, Sussex, in 1902, there were few professional opportunities in horticulture for women. Wolseley had a vision of women making a socially acceptable livelihood from gardening and, in the process, reviving the welfare of rural communities. 'Gardencraft'—a term Wolseley was fond of using—extended far beyond horticulture, and embraced the full range of garden design and management. Wolseley's books *Gardening for Women* (1908), *In a College Garden* and *Women and the Land* (1916), and *Gardens: Their Form and Design* (1919) greatly extended her educational influence, and her ideas for close-knit communities found a practical expression in Australia at Edna Walling's Bickleigh Vale estate.

THE RIGHT KIND OF WOMEN-GARDENERS.

The Principles of Gardening for Australia | 1903

In a work that stands apart from the overwhelmingly practical canon of Australian gardening books, C. Bogue-Luffmann produced a theoretical manifesto for his preferred picturesque naturalism. His inspiration for garden beds, derived from watching clouds on a lazy day, gives a potent demonstration of his unconventional and even transcendental approach to garden design. An enigmatic figure who had trained in Spain, Luffmann was responsible for admitting the first women students to Melbourne's Burnley School of Horticulture. In his *Principles of Gardening for Australia*, Luffmann spoke from the heart in a manner not seen until the emergence a generation later of Edna Walling, one of the beneficiaries of his liberal views on education.

The Forest Flora of New South Wales | 1904

Australia's busiest and most influential botanic gardens directors often lacked the time or inclination to publish gardening books. Instead, many used other avenues to indirectly disseminate their thoughts on horticulture and landscape design. Just as Ferdinand Mueller addressed suitable economic plants for acclimatisation in his book *Select Extra-tropical Plants*, so Joseph Maiden used his monumental work *The Forest Flora of New South Wales* (Sydney, 1904–24) to convey the horticultural potential of his subject. Maiden was a great champion of the Australian flora, and this was his most detailed and sustained advocacy of indigenous trees. The *Forest Flora*—depicted here by the first plate, *Grevillea robusta* (Silky Oak)—was illustrated with outstanding delicacy by Margaret Flockton.

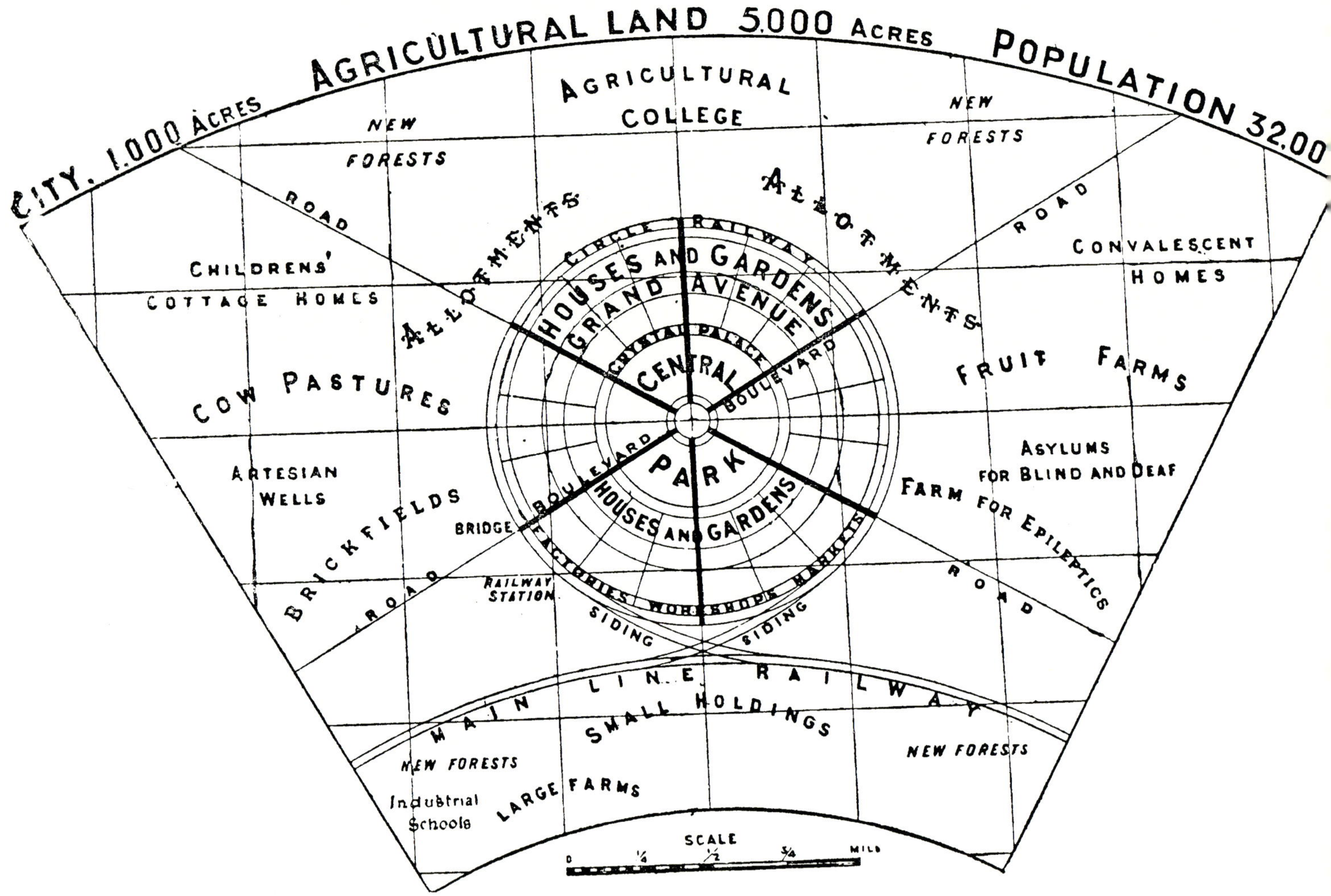
CITY, 1,000 ACRES
AGRICULTURAL LAND 5,000 ACRES
POPULATION 32,00
AGRICULTURAL COLLEGE
NEW FORESTS
NEW FORESTS
ALLOTMENTS
ALLOTMENTS
ALLOTMENTS
ROAD
ROAD
CHILDRENS' COTTAGE HOMES
CONVALESCENT HOMES
CIRCLE RAILWAY
HOUSES AND GARDENS
GRAND AVENUE
CRYSTAL PALACE
CENTRAL
BOULEVARD
COW PASTURES
FRUIT FARMS
PARK
ARTESIAN WELLS
ASYLUMS FOR BLIND AND DEAF
BOULEVARD
FARM FOR EPILEPTICS
BRICKFIELDS
BRIDGE
HOUSES AND GARDENS
ROAD
ROAD
RAILWAY STATION
FACTORIES WORKSHOPS MARKETS
SIDING
SIDING
MAIN LINE RAILWAY
SMALL HOLDINGS
NEW FORESTS
NEW FORESTS
Industrial Schools
LARGE FARMS
SCALE
0 ¼ ½ ¾ MILE

The Garden City movement | 1905

The town planning ideal of basing the city on a garden gained credence with the publication of Ebenezer Howard's book *Garden Cities of To-morrow* (London, 1902). Howard's ideas and conceptual designs were publicised through lectures, conferences, journal articles and republication in the works of others, such as A. R. Sennett's *Garden Cities in Theory and Practice* (London, 1905). Howard represented the ideas underlying garden cities in the form of three magnets: Town, Country and Town–Country. Sennett chose to republish Howard's diagram of a circular garden city that reconciled the competing forces of the three magnets.

'A National Rose Idea' | 1906

Amongst the first acts of newly federated Australia was a national flag competition, in which the judges sought inclusion of a six-pointed star 'representing the six federated States'. This federation star formed the basis of a model rosary in Melbourne's Domain, planted under the aegis of the National Rose Society of Victoria. (The Society's naming displayed ambitious nationalism, as had Mueller's National Herbarium of Victoria half a century earlier.) The states were worked out in different colours, the main star was graduated in height, and chains on poles supported climbing roses. An extra point, officially added to the flag's star in 1908 to represent the various Australian territories, rendered this worthy rosary problematic.

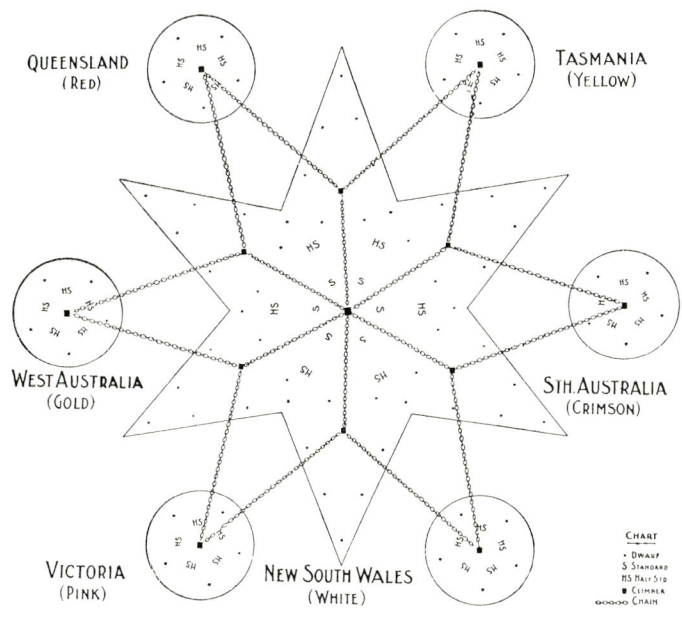

QUEENSLAND
(RED)

TASMANIA
(YELLOW)

WEST AUSTRALIA
(GOLD)

STH. AUSTRALIA
(CRIMSON)

VICTORIA
(PINK)

NEW SOUTH WALES
(WHITE)

CHART
• DWARF
S STANDARD
HS HALF STD
■ CLIMBER
ᴑᴑᴑᴑ CHAIN

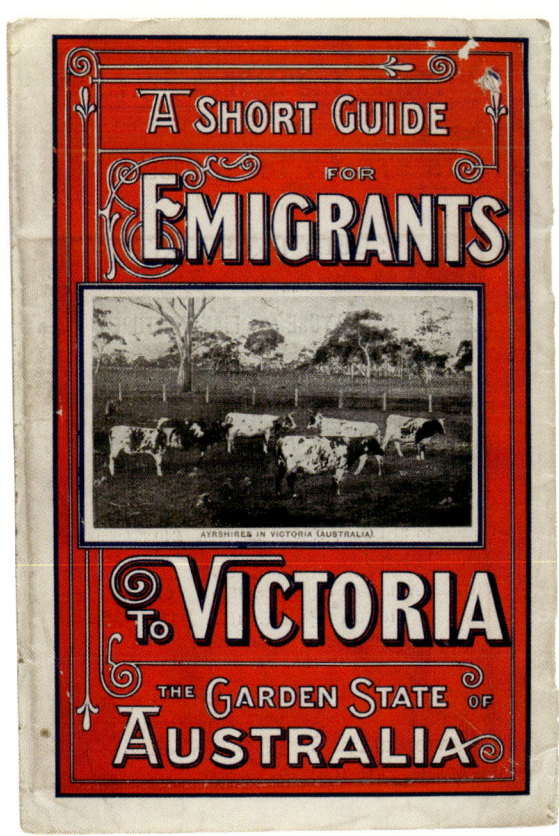

A SHORT GUIDE FOR EMIGRANTS TO VICTORIA THE GARDEN STATE OF AUSTRALIA

AYRSHIRES IN VICTORIA (AUSTRALIA).

Cultivating the Garden State | 1907

The Garden City was, by 1907, a town planning initiative that enjoyed international currency, signifying wide boulevards, generous parks and tree-lined residential areas. The Garden State slogan was, by extension, used as a catchphrase for agricultural and horticultural productivity. One of the earliest known uses was in *A Short Guide for Intending Emigrants to Victoria, the Garden State of Australia* (Melbourne, 1907). Boasting rich agricultural land and a population density of 14 persons per square mile, Victoria was touted as 'The Garden State . . . The Granary of the Continent'. The appeal was made to attract hardworking, sober immigrants 'of white race' to farm estates, newly subdivided by the state's Closer Settlement Board.

Pussies in the garden | 1908

Whether providing habitat for native birds or a suburban savanna for pet cats—to take two extremes—the garden has long been a source of enjoyment for animal lovers. Gertrude Jekyll introduced the subject in her book *Children and Gardens* (London, 1908) with an entertaining chapter entitled 'Pussies in the garden'. Musing on the pleasures of her 'perfect garden companions', Jekyll captured her delight in photographs and sketches. Blackie leaps in ecstasy in the catmint, Tabby sleeps in her photographic bag and three kittens drink from a saucer of milk, forming an 'equicateral triangle' for Jekyll's observant pen.

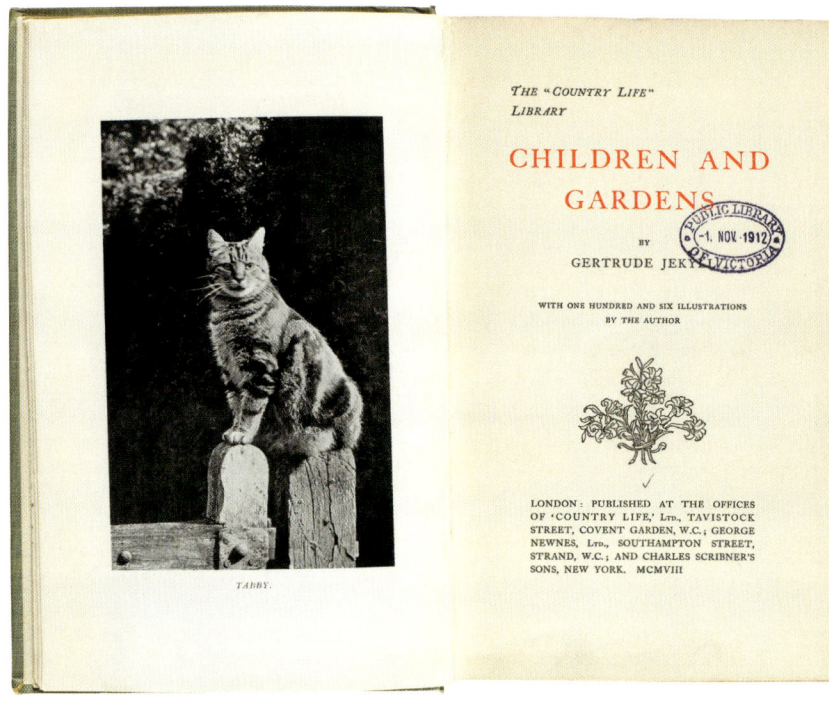

Naturalism and scenic effect | 1909

William Guilfoyle's landscape designs were derived from close observation of scenery throughout Australasia and the Pacific. Guilfoyle had sailed throughout the Pacific immediately prior to his appointment in 1873 as director of Melbourne Botanic Gardens. He also retained vivid memories of the Tweed River in northern New South Wales, where his family farmed. Guilfoyle's liking for scenic effect was expressed in his outstanding skill in recapturing this in a garden setting by sculpting land and massing plants. This plan, published in the Melbourne Botanic Gardens' *Descriptive Guide* at the close of his directorship, recorded his finest achievement—if further proof was necessary, Guilfoyle also included a retrospective plan to remind visitors of the layout he had inherited from his predecessor.

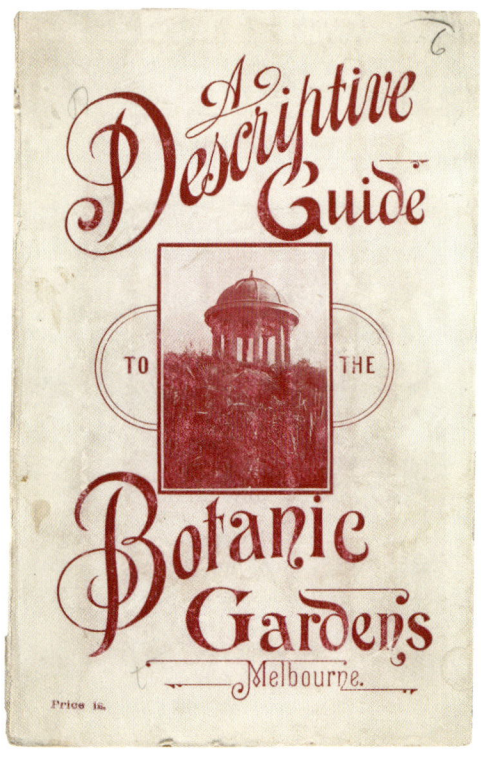

BOTANIC GARDENS, 1909,
SHOWING ALTERATIONS AND ADDITIONS EFFECTED SINCE 1873.
BY W.R. GUILFOYLE. DIRECTOR. Ⓐ TO Ⓗ SHOW ENTRANCE GATES.

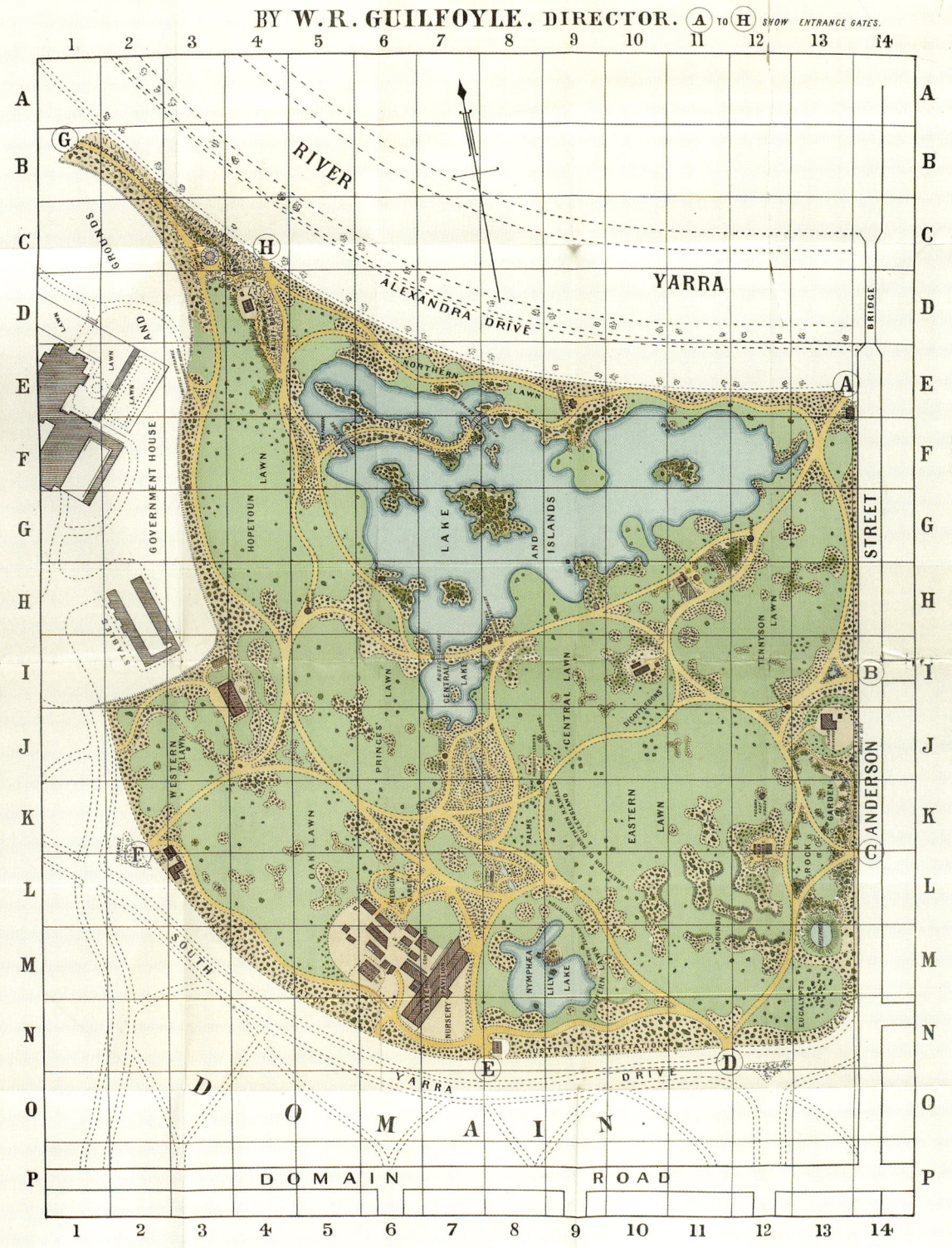

By means of this Plan, which has been divided into blocks indicated perpendicularly by letters and horizontally by numbers in the margins, the exact position of certain plants, special groups, conservatories, plant and rest houses, favorite views and other spots of interest to Visitors can be readily located on consulting the General Index, and there ascertaining in which block the object desired is situated.

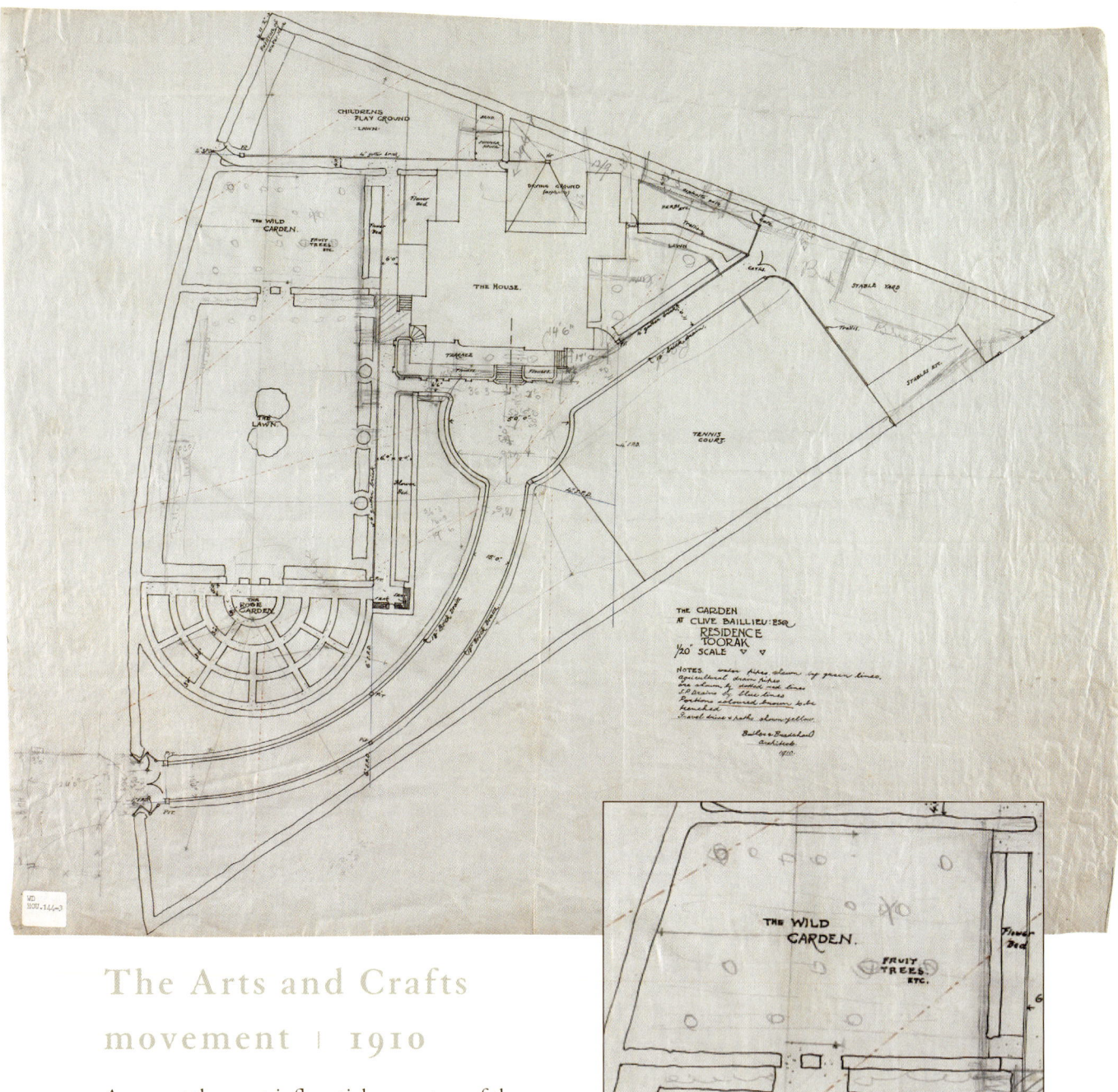

The Arts and Crafts

movement | 1910

Amongst the most influential promoters of the
Arts and Crafts movement in Australia was architect
Walter Butler. Prior to his emigration in 1888, Butler had trained in England under architect
J. D. Sedding, and moved in the circle of William Morris. The Arts and Crafts movement stressed
a respect for local materials and building traditions, and an appreciation of Romantic and medieval
literature. The garden was seen as an extension of the house, and it seemed logical that the architect
would design both. In this 1910 plan for the garden of Clive Baillieu's house, Kamillaroi, in Toorak,
Butler envisaged a series of outdoor rooms, planned with a simple and appropriate formality.

Carving out a capital | 1911

The most integrated linking of garden and state occurred in Australia at Canberra. Following the 1911 competition for a national capital—to be sited with political exactitude between Melbourne and Sydney—the winning entry by Walter and Marion Griffin brought a bold new landscape architecture to Australia. Their vision was inspired by the undulating topography, with natural features determining the broad formal setting for a garden city in the bush. Hotel Canberra's landscaping provides an intriguing example of this transfer of ideas into practice. But politics bit hard as Australia carved out its capital and development proceeded at such a pace that for many years the respected French encyclopaedia *Petit Larousse* advised 'La capital est Bombala'.

'Young Australia and his flower' | 1912

The first Wattle Day was celebrated on 1 September 1910, two years earlier than this portrait. National sentiment symbolised by the wattle had been formalised in 1889–90 when a Wattle Blossom League was formed in Adelaide under the aegis of the Australian Natives Association. So great was the public response that the symbolism of Wattle Day was almost overshadowed by indiscriminate and over-enthusiastic ravaging of blossom from metropolitan hinterlands. There could, however, be no mistake amongst readers of the *Australasian* that this lad would have a brighter future through his love of the wattle. The message of national pride was reinforced through school nature study lessons, tree-planting ceremonies and quickening interest in the Australian environment generally.

Fantasy garden | 1913

The garden as a place of imagination and fantasy is beautifully captured in Hugh O'Rorke's photograph of a girl dressed as an elderly lady, engrossed in her knitting. In the convincing simplicity of her generational transformation, she seems to stand as a symbol of pre-war innocence in an ageless garden setting. Yet the Edwardian fantasy is almost over.

The backyard was commonly associated during wartime with vegetable gardening, where individual or communal productivity aided a greater national cause. Rarely is it associated with aircraft manufacture, yet during the Great War this Brighton back garden in suburban Melbourne became an industrial garden. The outbreak of war in 1914 coincided with advances in aviation, sufficient to unleash a potent new weapon. Fresh from British experience as a test pilot, Basil Watson used the backyard of his parents' house to construct this biplane, modelled on the Sopwith Scout. Still in his early twenties, Watson was feted as a pioneering Australian aviator. Sadly the wings of Watson's biplane buckled over Laverton on one fateful flight in 1917, ending a career of rare ingenuity.

The Australian Flora in Applied Art | 1915

Richard Thomas Baker, curator of Sydney Technological Museum, was a passionate advocate for the Australian flora. Succeeding J. H. Maiden in the position, Baker did much to advance the cause of economic botany through innovative museum displays and publications. Although only one volume of his projected series *The Australian Flora in Applied Art* was published, in *Part 1: The Waratah* (1915) Baker included the designs of artist Lucien Henry to produce a work of originality and great vitality. Baker's text and Henry's inventive waratah-derived designs formed a virtual manifesto for a national style of decorative art.

School gardening | 1916

The school gardening movement commenced in the early 1900s as progressive educators sought to instil values of cooperation, self-reliance and civic pride in their students. The Young Gardeners League was a specifically wartime manifestation of the movement, aimed at raising funds for war relief through the sale of flowers and vegetables. Managed by the Victorian State Schools Horticultural Society, the work of the League was supplemented by nature study lessons and the annual observation of Arbor Day.

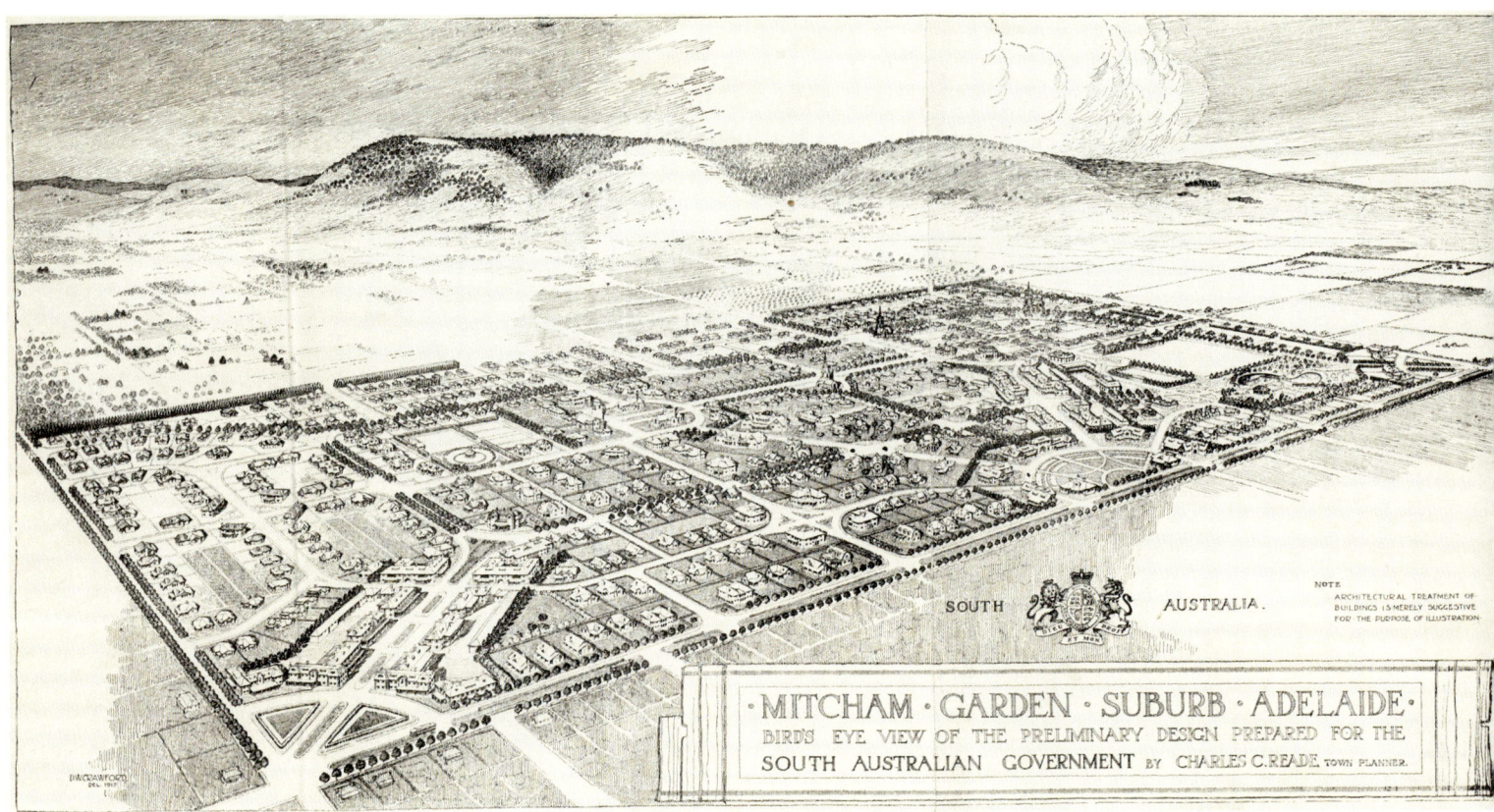

SOUTH AUSTRALIA.

NOTE
ARCHITECTURAL TREATMENT OF
BUILDINGS IS MERELY SUGGESTIVE
FOR THE PURPOSE OF ILLUSTRATION

· MITCHAM · GARDEN · SUBURB · ADELAIDE ·
BIRD'S EYE VIEW OF THE PRELIMINARY DESIGN PREPARED FOR THE
SOUTH AUSTRALIAN GOVERNMENT BY CHARLES C. READE TOWN PLANNER.

Colonel Light Gardens:
model garden suburb | 1917

Adelaide's well-ordered grid plan formed a perfect town-planning
laboratory. With each rectangle a potential test tube, the city now
contains some of the best examples nationally of key international
design influences. Charles Reade, the first Government Town Planner
to be appointed in Australia, undertook his major experiment at
Mitcham with a model garden suburb. Now known as Colonel Light
Gardens, Reade's 1917 scheme provided the country with its most fully
worked example of the Garden City movement. Drawing on strong
socialist convictions, Reade promoted the social, economic, aesthetic
and cultural benefits of town planning to a wide audience.

The Carnation, Dahlia and Sweet Pea Society of Victoria | 1918

The quickening pace of urbanisation in the late-nineteenth and early-twentieth centuries created rings of new suburbs around Australia's major cities and towns. On newly subdivided blocks, an ever-increasing wave of new-home owners fuelled the ranks of hobby gardeners. This egalitarian style of home gardening saw a rise in plant specialisation, enthusiastically embraced by plant nurseries and horticultural societies. The Carnation, Dahlia and Sweet Pea Society of Victoria (established 1901) had achieved sufficient longevity by 1918 for Thomas Patterson to present his 'Reminiscences of an Amateur Carnation Enthusiast', and a year later to write a history of the Society.

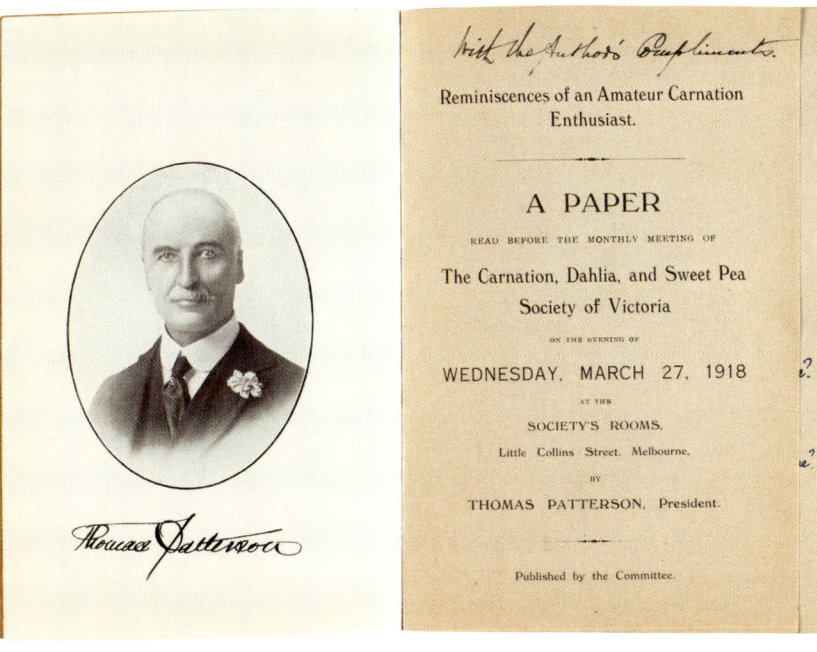

Maranoa Gardens, Australian showpiece | 1919

When Maranoa Gardens was first opened to the public in 1919, the Melbourne public was able to inspect, for the first time, a garden composed entirely of Australasian plants. Created in semi-rural Balwyn as a private garden in 1901–26 by mercantile broker John Watson, the site was comfortably distant from his residence and the quizzical gaze of his neighbours in suburban Canterbury. After Watson's death the garden was transferred to public ownership and members of the Field Naturalists' Club of Victoria were instrumental in its upkeep. Although Watson's exact motives are not known, in public ownership the garden has become a showpiece for the Australian flora and a fine example of the bush-garden ethos.

GAY ABANDON

(1920s–1930s)

Our land abounds in nature strips/of beauty rich and rare.

Advance Australia Fair, unintentional rendition

ALTHOUGH a shadow was cast over the inter-war period by the Great Depression of the late 1920s and early 1930s, this followed an expansive era of metropolitan development. New rings of suburbs had developed around Australia's capital cities—some were served by electrified suburban train services and many lay within commuting distance of workplaces by the motor car, an increasingly popular mode of personal transport. The period saw the rise of the quarter-acre block and a consolidation of suburban plots as the gardens of the masses.

Gaiety was a much-sought attribute of inter-war gardens, private and public alike. With floriculture in the ascendant, flower shows and specialist horticultural societies catered for enthusiastic local audiences.

Even after the advent of wireless—or radio, to use the American term—in the late 1920s, gardening remained a localised pursuit. Many nurseries operated on pocket-handkerchief sites in the suburbs, close to their clients, while larger firms maintained city retail outlets and outer suburban plant farms. Parochialism was kept at bay by gardening magazines such as *Australian Home Beautiful* and *Australian Garden Lover*, although even these market leaders struggled to achieve comprehensive national circulation and coverage.

Gay abandon came to the flower garden with ever brighter and larger varieties of popular flowers. Dahlias, gladioli, irises and (as ever) roses all achieved great popularity, with new annual novelty selections bringing colour to the garden and valuable profit to the seed merchant and nursery proprietor. However, not all was fleeting effect: in his rose and narcissus hybridisation, Alister Clark—one of several enthusiasts dedicated to advancing Australian horticulture in this manner—placed a new emphasis on plant breeding suited for Australian climatic conditions.

The popularity of the motor car necessitated concessions in the suburban garden. Although the carriageway, turning loop and stables had always been a feature of the mansion, homestead and villa, space for a drive and garage was now needed on far smaller plots. The drive and front path now rivalled one another in prominence, and paired gates at the nature strip—that ironically titled ribbon of concrete-edged lawn—set the family home apart from its earlier inner suburban prototypes.

Car travel also revolutionised sightseeing and holidays. Oil companies were quick to promote the virtues of motor travel to view wildflowers in their native habitats. Seaside cottages and shacks in the nearer hills were also now a realistic goal for many—these seasonal or weekend homes inspired a new casual approach to gardening. Motoring and modernism were comfortable bedfellows, but gardening took longer to respond to the new modern aesthetic.

Modernism, from its advent in the wake of the Great War, influenced art, architecture, gardens, typography and many other forms of design. Whereas Edna Walling's gardens of this period echoed the earlier Arts and Crafts movement, modernist architects were experimenting with a new landscape aesthetic to match their severe built forms. The seemingly random forms of Australian trees used sparingly as a sculptural interplay between organic vegetation and inanimate architecture, was an early response. But it was not until the social and cultural cataclysm of World War II that modernism truly remade Australian society.

The essence of eucalypts | 1920

Horticultural experimentation has long been associated with the public interest of botanic gardens
and the commercial gain of the nursery industry, yet in every generation there are also individuals
who make significant private contributions. Russell Grimwade combined business and philanthropy
in the service of horticulture. Eucalypts were a passion, uniting his love of the Australian flora, his
professional pharmaceutical interests and a keen aesthetic appreciation. His city garden, Miegunyah
in Toorak, and rural acreage, Westerfield near Frankston, formed his experimental grounds.
Grimwade's photographs in *An Anthography of the Eucalypts* (Sydney, 1920) distilled his interests
into abstract images of haunting beauty.

Playtime | 1921

John Sulman, a pioneer of town planning in Australia, included a chapter entitled 'Sports Reserves, Playgrounds, Gardens, and Trees' in his *Introduction to the Study of Town Planning in Australia* (Sydney, 1921). Amongst the subscribers to the book was Miss M. Josephine Bedford, Honorary Secretary of the Playground Association of Queensland. Bedford—known as the 'little Admiral'—was a formidable advocate for the playground movement in Australia, stressing the moral, physical and social benefits of supervised play. She had attended lectures on the playground movement in Berkeley, California, in 1911, and influenced many playground designs, including this widely admired example in the Brisbane suburb of Ithaca.

Half-hours in the Bush-house | 1922

A. E. Cole came to prominence with his book *The Bouquet: Australian Flower Gardening* (*c*. 1914). Cole's last publication was devoted to that most Australian of garden buildings, the bush-house. *Half-hours in the Bush-house* (Sydney, 1922) advocated differential lath spacing to provide multiple environments as well as specialised houses to suit different horticultural requirements. Such sophistication was, however, beyond the reach of many Australian gardeners, for whom shade was a rudimentary necessity rather than a designer accessory.

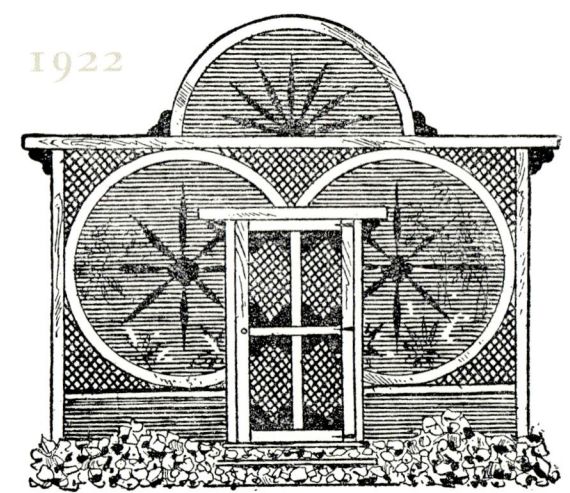

Gardens of industry | 1923

Match making, like many nineteenth-century industries, exposed its workers to appalling conditions. 'Phossy-jaw', a necrosis of the jawbone, eventually caused a worldwide ban on phosphorus match heads, with Victoria being late to legislate (1916). By that date the impressive factory of Bryant & May had been erected in Richmond, and its working conditions were considered amongst the country's best. Tennis courts were installed in 1923 as part of a suite of recreational facilities for workers. This garden of industry recalled the benevolence and humanity of the Quaker founders of the company, a religious link shared by many Garden City proponents in industrial England.

Backyard icon | 1924

Gilbert Toyne remains the unsung hero of the Australian rotary clothes hoist, a backyard icon. Although now marketed with such success by others, Geelong-born Toyne advertised his innovative design in *Australian Home Beautiful* as early as 1924. Primitive timber versions of a rotary clothes line were known in the nineteenth century, but the defining features of Toyne's hoist were two meta cross arms supporting wires and a central post with winding mechanism (facilitating raising and lowering to suit the user). The suburban backyard revolved around the hoist until the invention of the tumble dryer.

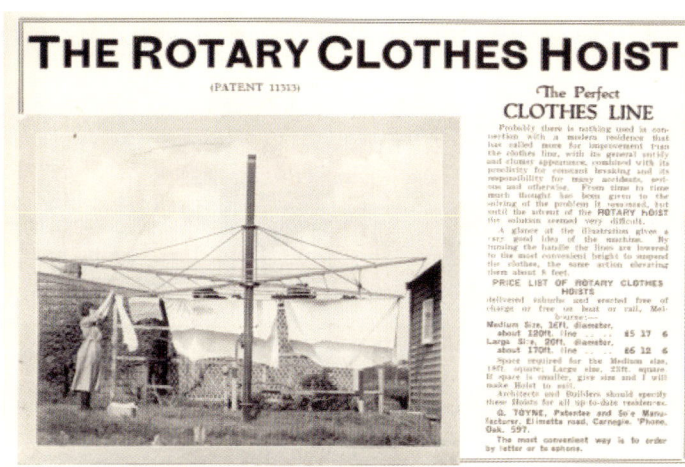

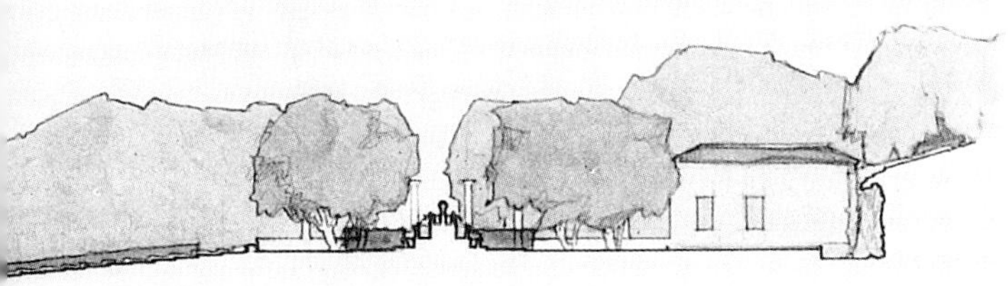

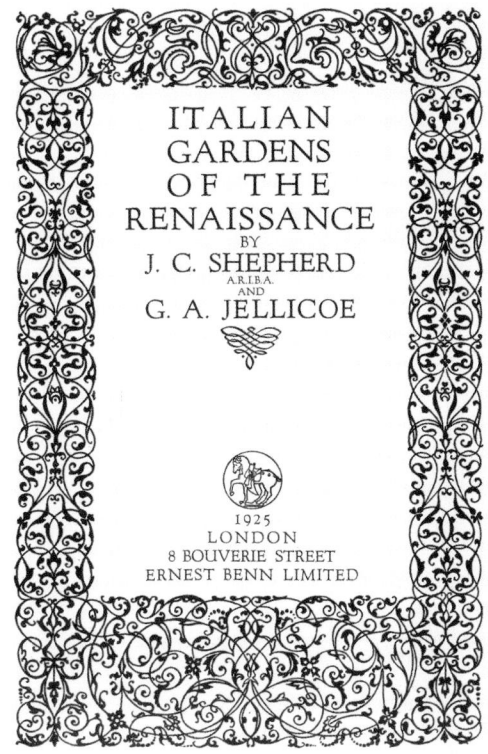

ITALIAN
GARDENS
OF THE
RENAISSANCE
BY
J. C. SHEPHERD
A.R.I.B.A.
AND
G. A. JELLICOE

1925
LONDON
8 BOUVERIE STREET
ERNEST BENN LIMITED

There could be no greater inspiration for a twentieth-century revival of formal landscapes than the gardens of Italy. The names now roll off garden-lovers' tongues like the rosary: Villa d'Este, Villa Lante, Villa Gamberaia. Say them often enough and the glories of the Renaissance can be yours. Created around sixteenth- and seventeenth-century palazzi, these gardens—including Villa Lante at Bagnaia, pictured here—were assiduously documented by two young architects, J. C. Shepherd and G. A. Jellicoe, in the lavish folio *Italian Gardens of the Renaissance* (London, 1925). Edna Walling was amongst the disciples. She owned the book, and the authors' remarks on formality and design read like a manifesto for her early gardens.

Front gardening | 1926

For horticultural writer E. E. Pescott and his publishers, gardening in Australia in 1926 was above all a matter of floriculture. Cover images are revealing, and Pescott's book *Gardening in Australia* was firmly pitched at home gardeners in the new metropolitan arteries developing along suburban railways. On generous blocks, lawns and wide paths were enlivened by flower beds and pergolas. Trees were noticeably absent from these new cottage gardens, and a widespread interest in shrubs was still some years away. The front garden was low and neat, a setting for the house—more public park than botanic garden.

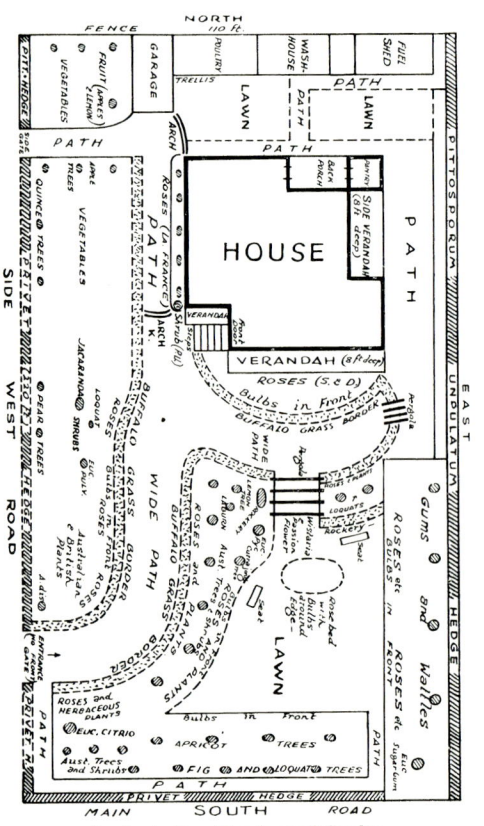

An Australian "Landscape" Garden.

WHITCOMBES AUSTRALIAN GARDENING HANDBOOKS

Gardening
in AUSTRALIA

1/6

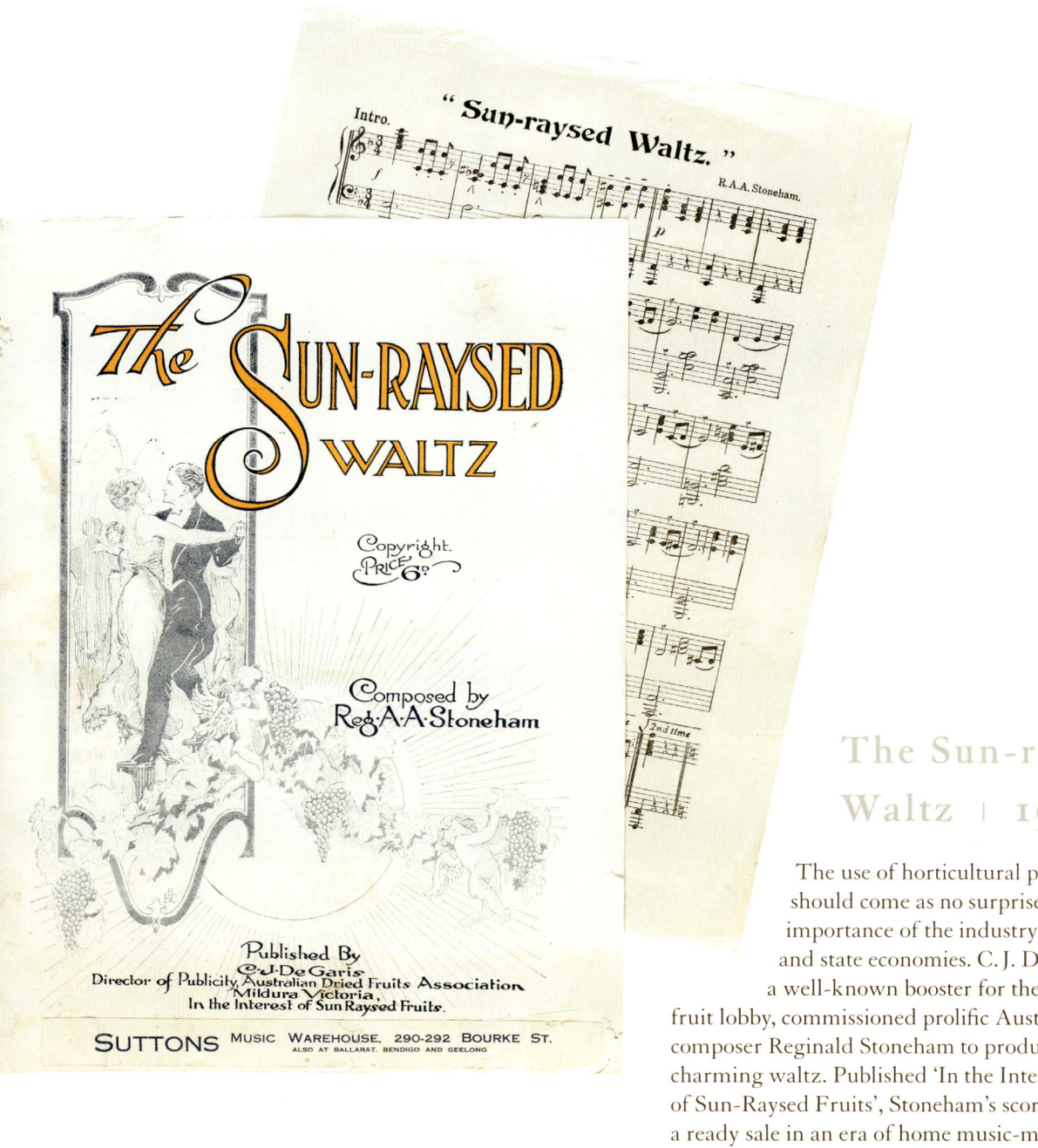

The Sun-raysed Waltz | 1927

The use of horticultural propaganda should come as no surprise given the importance of the industry to local and state economies. C. J. De Garis, a well-known booster for the dried fruit lobby, commissioned prolific Australian composer Reginald Stoneham to produce this charming waltz. Published 'In the Interest of Sun-Raysed Fruits', Stoneham's score found a ready sale in an era of home music-making poised on the cusp of the wireless revolution. Victorian Railways Chairman Harold Clapp was another who promoted the Mildura fruit industry, optimistically selling sultanas at railway refreshment rooms as a means of boosting traffic to Victoria's most remote railway destination.

During the early twentieth century, designers searched for a distinctive Australian style. In architecture, the Mediterranean countries came under close scrutiny, not only for climatic similarities but also for the colourfulness of the vernacular architecture and its materials. In gardening, the same sources were tapped. Mrs Philip Martineau's book, *Gardening in Sunny Lands* (London, 1924), drew together similarities between The Riviera, California and Australia. The gardens of Spain were also much admired. Mildred and Arthur Byne's *Spanish Gardens and Patios* (Philadelphia, 1928) promoted their virtues, and it was the Spanish influence on North America as much as direct European models that was an inspiration for Australian garden designers and architects.

The Metropolis of Tomorrow | 1929

Architects are accustomed to drawing on the natural world for inspiration. Think of the analogies between buildings and trees: foundations rooted in the earth, stout log columns, rusticated balustrading, roofs sheathed leaf-like. By contrast, architectural delineator Hugh Ferriss proposed geo-morphological analogies in his prophetic work *The Metropolis of Tomorrow* (New York, 1929). Ferriss foreshadowed the 'lofty terraces' of high-rise living, with roof gardens as 'sun porches', planted with trees in two feet of soil. His frontispiece, 'Buildings like Mountains', showed the skyscraper growing organically from the earth. This was his inspiration—in his imaginary metropolis he visualised 'Buildings like crystals . . . No Gothic branch, no Acanthus leaf; no recollection of the plant world'.

The dahlia in Australia | 1930

By 1930 the dahlia had made great strides in Australia. In that year, a second impression of Edward E. Pescott's lyrical title *The Dahlia in Australia* was issued and nursery catalogues were bursting with newer and larger cultivars. A century earlier, dahlias had also enjoyed considerable popularity in colonial gardens, adding colour and vibrancy to bed and border. 'The majestic mien of the plant, the size and symmetry of the flowers, the brilliant and infinite variety of its splendid colours, combined with easy management, growing and flowering in every soil and in every climate . . . finds a hearty welcome', wrote Sydney horticulturist Luke Wooff in 1864.

Wildflower show | 1931

The 1931 Melbourne wildflower show was apparently well attended, but no visitor was more enthusiastic than the owner of this booklet *Wild Flowers of Australia*. Floral emblem plebiscite results and nursery catalogue extracts sat alongside eagerly scribbled notes in this de facto notebook and scrapbook. A larger wildflower show was, of course, on display in the Australian bush and with motoring now commonplace, oil companies were quick to promote travel by field naturalists and tourists. 'It behoves us then to make sure of seeing [wildflowers] . . . to their best advantage in their natural setting' exhorted The Shell Company of Australia, publishers of this booklet.

Flower farming | 1932

The seeds and seedlings that provided a splash of colour in countless Australian front gardens during the 1920s and 1930s originated in farms such as this. Wartime restrictions of trade with Germany had cut off a major seed supply and had encouraged Australian companies to expand and develop local facilities. The Yates company, founded in Manchester in 1826, had entered the Australasian market in the 1880s. In 1916, as the Great War raged in Europe, the company's Tasmanian flower farm on the Derwent River was established where fertile alluvial soils provided perfect ground for farming the seeds that were the company's lifeblood.

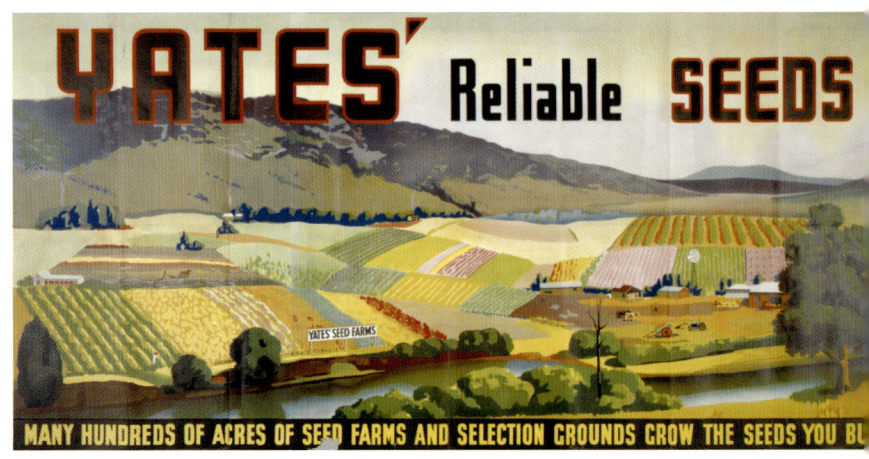

New Way Gardening | 1933

The cactus revolution gathered momentum during the 1930s. Spikes and spines began to protrude from gardens in a manner unexpected, yet wholly appropriate given the hot, dry climate across many parts of the continent. Above all, the 'New Way Gardening' embraced specialised garden features such as the bush-house, rockery and window gardens, suited not only for cacti, but also native shrubs, wildflowers, ferns and succulents.

CLAREMONT
BULBS · SEEDS
KOOKABURRA
"For a Sure Return"
Registered Trade Mark

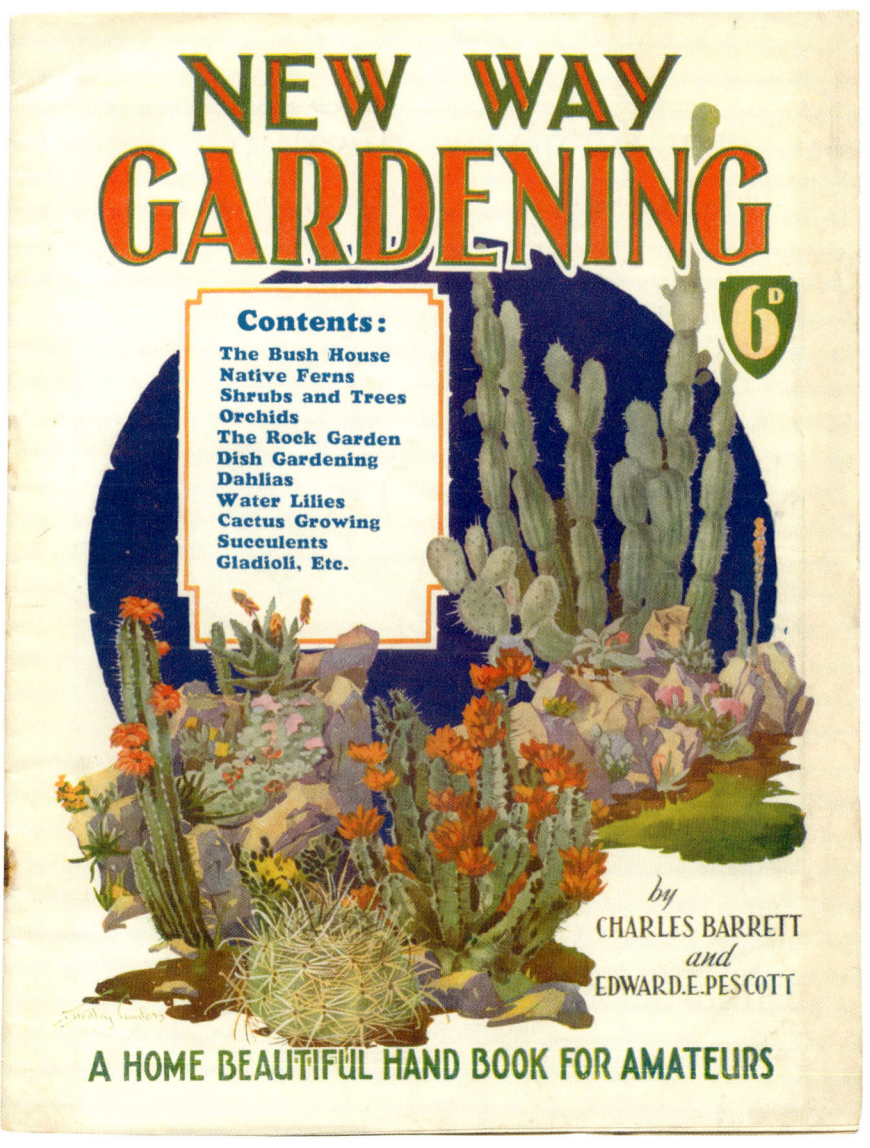

NEW WAY
GARDENING
6D

Contents:
The Bush House
Native Ferns
Shrubs and Trees
Orchids
The Rock Garden
Dish Gardening
Dahlias
Water Lilies
Cactus Growing
Succulents
Gladioli, Etc.

by
CHARLES BARRETT
and
EDWARD. E. PESCOTT

A HOME BEAUTIFUL HAND BOOK FOR AMATEURS

Tarnagulla Presbyterian Church

FLOWER SHOW

AND

Centenary Fair

VICTORIA THEATRE

THURSDAY, 4TH OCTOBER, '34

Open 3 to 10 p.m.   ::   No Entries Received on Show Day

PRIZE SCHEDULE

Class A.—CUT FLOWERS.
(Distinct varieties and colors wherever possible.)
1. Best collection, 3 Cut Flowers.
2. Best collection 6 Bulbs and Tuberous Blooms.
3. Three hardy annuals.
4. Three hardy Perennials.
5. Three Penstemons.
6. Three Delphiniums.
7. Collection Fuchsias.
8. Three Single Stocks.
9. Three Double Stocks.
10. Three Verbenas.
11. Three Petunias.
12. Three Carnations.
13. Three Pelargoniums.
14. Three Phlox.
15. Six Geraniums.
16. Six Iceland Poppies.
17. Six Poppies.
18. Six Snapdragons.
19. Three Pæonies.
20. Three Larkspur.
21. Three Gaillardias.
22. Six Pansies.
23. Three Dianthus.
24. Three Canterbury Bells.
25. Three Watsonias.
26. Three Columbines.
27. Three Sweet Williams.
28. Six Sweet Peas.
29. Three Ranunculus.
30. Three Schizanthus.
31. Three Cactus.
32. Three Calliopsis.
33. Three Scabious.
34. Cornflowers (3 stems of each).
35. Three Clarkias.
36. Three Sprays Climbing or Rambler Rose.
37. Three Sprays Polyanthus Roses
38. Six Roses.
39. Three Dark Roses.
40. Three Light Roses.
41. Champion Rose, selected from any exhibit. Special prize, 5/- (gift of Mr. J. H. Allen).
42. Arranged Bowl of Flowers.
43. Arranged Bowl of Roses.
44. Four Gent's Buttonholes.
45. Three arranged Vases of Flowers.
46. Bridal Bouquet.
47. Arranged Basket of Flowers.
48. Hand Bouquet.

Class B.—POT PLANTS.
Entries to be the property of the Exhibitor.
1. Three Ferns.
2. Asparagus Fern.
3. Maiden Hair Fern.
4. One Fern.
5. Three Pot Plants (any kind).
6. One Pot Plant in Bloom (any kind).
7. Foliage Plant.
8. One Begonia.
9. One Hanging Basket.
10. Any Special Exhibit

Class C.—FLOWERS.
(Children under 15).
1. Three Gent's Buttonholes.
2. Posy.
3. Arranged Basket of Flowers.
4. Arranged Bowl of Sweet Peas.

Class D.—VEGETABLES.
Entries to become the property of the Committee.
1. One Cabbage.
2. One Cauliflower.
3. Two Lettuce.
4. Three Carrots.
5. Three Parsnips.
6. Bunch Radishes.
7. Three Turnips.
8. Three Onions.
9. Bunch Tree Onions.
10. Six Shallots.
11. Three Rhubarb.
12. Dish of Green Peas.
13. Dish of Beans.
14. Bunch of Spring Onions
15. Six Potatoes.
16. Collection Vegetables.
17. Three Red Beet.
18. Six Lemons.

Class E.—PRODUCE.
Entries to become the property of the Committee.
1. One Dozen Hen Eggs.
2. One Dozen Duck Eggs.
3. Half Dozen Turkey Eggs.
4. Three Geese Eggs.
5. Dressed Fowl.
6. Pair Dressed Rabbits.
7. 1 Pot Honey.
8. 1 lb. Butter.
9. Half Bushel Wheat.
10. Half Bushel Oats.

Class F.—JAMS, JELLIES, and PRESERVES.
1. Marmalade.
2. Fig Jam.
3. Quince Jam.
4. Apricot Jam.
5. Dark Plum Jam.
6. Light Plum Jam.
7. Melon Jam.
8. Raspberry Jam.
9. Apple Jelly.
10. Quince Jelly.
11. Melon Jelly.
12. Collection of Jellies.
13. Strawberry Jam.
14. Tomato Sauce.
15. Plum Sauce.
16. Six Bottles Preserved Fruit.
17. Collection Pickles.
18. Collection Chutney.

Class G.—CAKES.
Entries to become the property of the Committee.
1. One loaf home-made Bread.
2. One loaf Fancy Bread.
3. Victoria Sandwich.
4. Sponge Cake.
5. Pound Cake.
6. Six Cream Puffs.
7. Plate Scones.
8. Plate Sweet Scones.
9. Collection Six Plain Biscuits.
10. Rainbow Cake.
11. Ginger Bread.
12. Plate of Laminatons.
13. Plate Short Bread.
14. Plate Pastry.
15. Jam Roll.
16. Collection home-made Lollies.
17. Sponge Sandwich.
18. Best Decorated Cake.

Class H.—NEEDLEWORK.
1. Prettiest Tea Cosy, mounted white.
2. Prettiest Tea Cosy, mounted colored.
3. Collection three D'Oyleys, crochet.
4. Collection three D'Oyleys, not crochet.
5. One Tray Cloth, crochet.
6. One Tray Cloth, not crochet.
7. Three Pieces of Crochet.
8. Prettiest Cushion, mounted.
9. Table Centre, crochet.
10. Table Centre, not crochet.
11. Duchesse Set.
12. Pillow Shams.
13. Ladies' Night Dress.
14. Best Pair Knitted Sox.
15. Infant's Singlet.
16. Infant's Modesllos.
17. Infant's Bootees.
18. Infant's Jacket.
19. Infant's Bonnet.
20. Worked Apron.
21. Three Handkerchiefs.

Class I.—CHILDREN'S WORK.
1. Child's Frock, under 16.
2. Embroidered D'Oyleys, under 16.
3. Best Dressed Doll, under 14.
4.
5. Hemmed Handkerchief, under 10.
6. Pair Socks, under 11.
7. Kettle Holder, under 9.
8. One Darned Sock.
9. Knitted Jumper, under 16.

Class J.—NOVELTIES.
1. Most Useful Article, made from material costing less than 1/6.
2. Most Useful Article made from Waste Material.
3. Open Novelty.
4. Best Hobby Exhibit.

Class K—PHOTOGRAPHY
Negatives not necessarily to be printed and developed by the exhibitor.
1. Six Local Views.
2. Twelve Snapshots.
3. Three Comics.
4. Three Animal Studies.
5. Novelty Snap.
6. Three Child Studies.

Class L.—SCHOOL WORK.
All entries to be certified by Head Teacher to be the work of the exhibitor.
Show Age on Entry Form.
(Under 15).
1. Handwriting, Verses 1 to 3. "Arbor Day," April School Paper, Grade 7.
2. Essay, 300 Words. "Victoria, it's Development and Progress." First prize, 2/6 (gift of Mr. D. Ross).
3. Pastel Work. A Colored Bowl or Vase.
4. Best School Workbook.
5. Best Sample of Hobby Work.
(Under 12).
6. Handwriting, Verses 1-2, "Anzac Day Thoughts," April school paper, Grade 5.
7. Essay, 100 Words. "A Bush Ramble." First prize, 2/6 (gift of Mrs. D. Ross)
8. Pastel Work. An Orange.
9. Best School Workbook.
10. Best Sample of Hobby Work.
(Under 8).
11. Handwriting, 1st Verse "From a Railway Carriage," P. 76, 2rd Grade school paper.
12. Hobbies.

REGULATIONS.
All entries must be in the hands of the Secretary by 8 p.m. on October 3rd, and exhibits to be in the Hall by 10 a.m. Show Day.
Entry for Classes C, D, E, G, is free, all other Classes 3d for each exhibit.
Exhibits in Classes D, E, and G become the property of the Committee.
The First Prize in each Section will be 1/-. The Second prize, Certificate. Where there are less than three entries the Prize will be Certificate only. Entries in Classes G, H, I, J, K, must be the work of the exhibitor.
Special Exhibits cordially invited. Contributions of Produce or other articles will be gratefully received.
The decision of the Judges is final.

Admission 6d; Children under 14 Free   ::   Novelty Attractions

Refreshment and Usual Stalls

MISS H. PATTERSON, } Hon. Secs.
MRS. B. ALLEN,

T. Page & Son, Printers, Quambatook, Ultima and Manangatang.

The flower show prize schedule, distributed some weeks ahead of time, always heralded a day of horticultural festivity in the country. In 1934, the Tarnagulla Presbyterian Church Flower Show took the form of a Centenary Fair, one of countless celebrations of European settlement in Victoria. Well supported by local sponsors, the schedule provides a snapshot of inter-war floral favourites—Canterbury bells, clarkias, columbines, delphiniums, dianthus, fuchsias, gaillardias, geraniums and pelargoniums, Iceland poppies, pansies, penstemons, pæonies, petunias, phlox, ranunculus, roses, schizanthus, snapdragons, stocks, sweet peas, verbenas and watsonias.

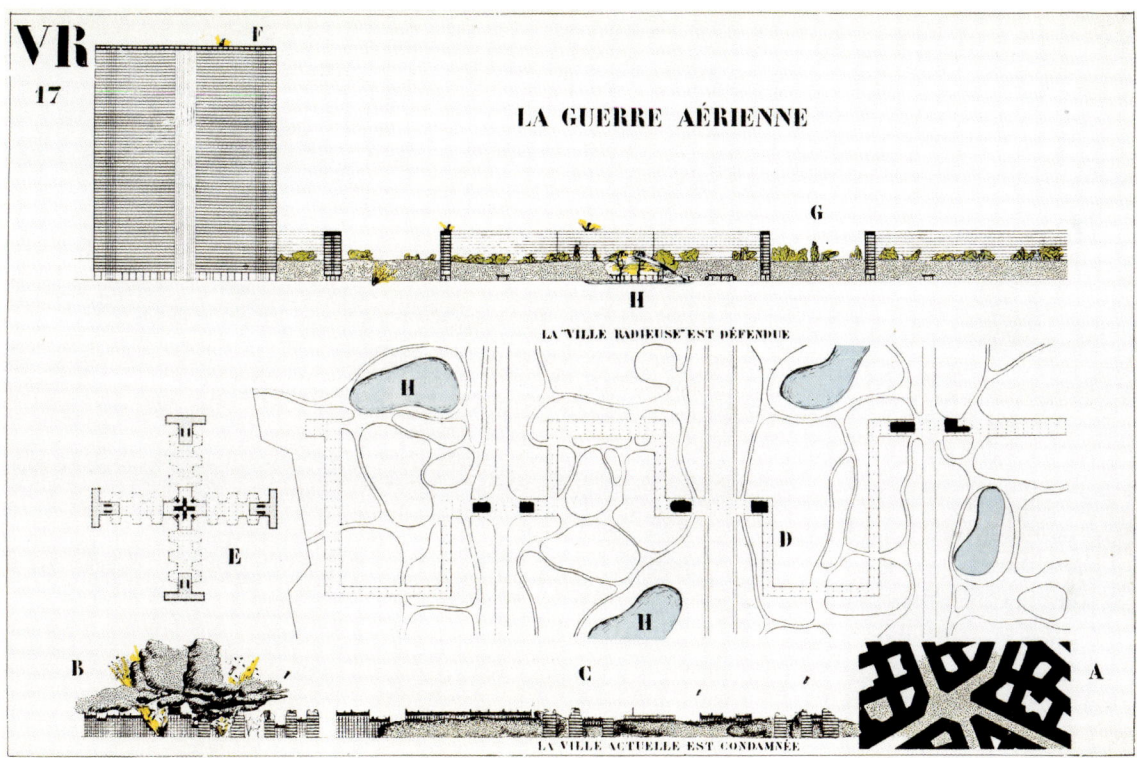

The Radiant City | 1935

French architect Le Corbusier published his modernist manifesto *La Ville Radieuse*—or *The Radiant City: Elements of a Doctrine of Urbanism to be used as the basis of our Machine-age Civilization*—in 1935. He believed that suburbs must be eliminated and nature brought into the cities themselves—a Green City. 'All those suburbanites rescued from their miserable mock existence', he exalted, 'To live! To breathe!' Corbusier's plans even catered for aerial warfare, with a stepped line of thin high-rise buildings providing a minimal target compared with the old low-rise town planning. Swimming pools in large communal parks provided reserves of water to drive off poison gas from attacks. Truly this was urbanism at the pointy end.

Identity crisis | 1936

Poor Melbourne. No harbour, no surf beaches, no mountains, not even much of a river. How then could tourist organisations promote the Victorian capital? In 1936, Melbourne's intact Victorian-era qualities were not yet highly regarded, except perhaps that most residents and visitors greatly appreciated the nineteenth-century gardens which so richly imbued the metropolis. Just as the promoters of closer settlement had coined the 'Garden State' tag, now the railway department promoted the 'Garden Capital'. Poster artist James Northfield presented a dramatic oblique aerial view, with the grid of the metropolis backed by the Domain's informal greenery and just a hint of order in the distance provided by Government House and the Shrine.

MELBOURNE
The Garden Capital of Victoria. Australia.
TAKE A 'KODAK'

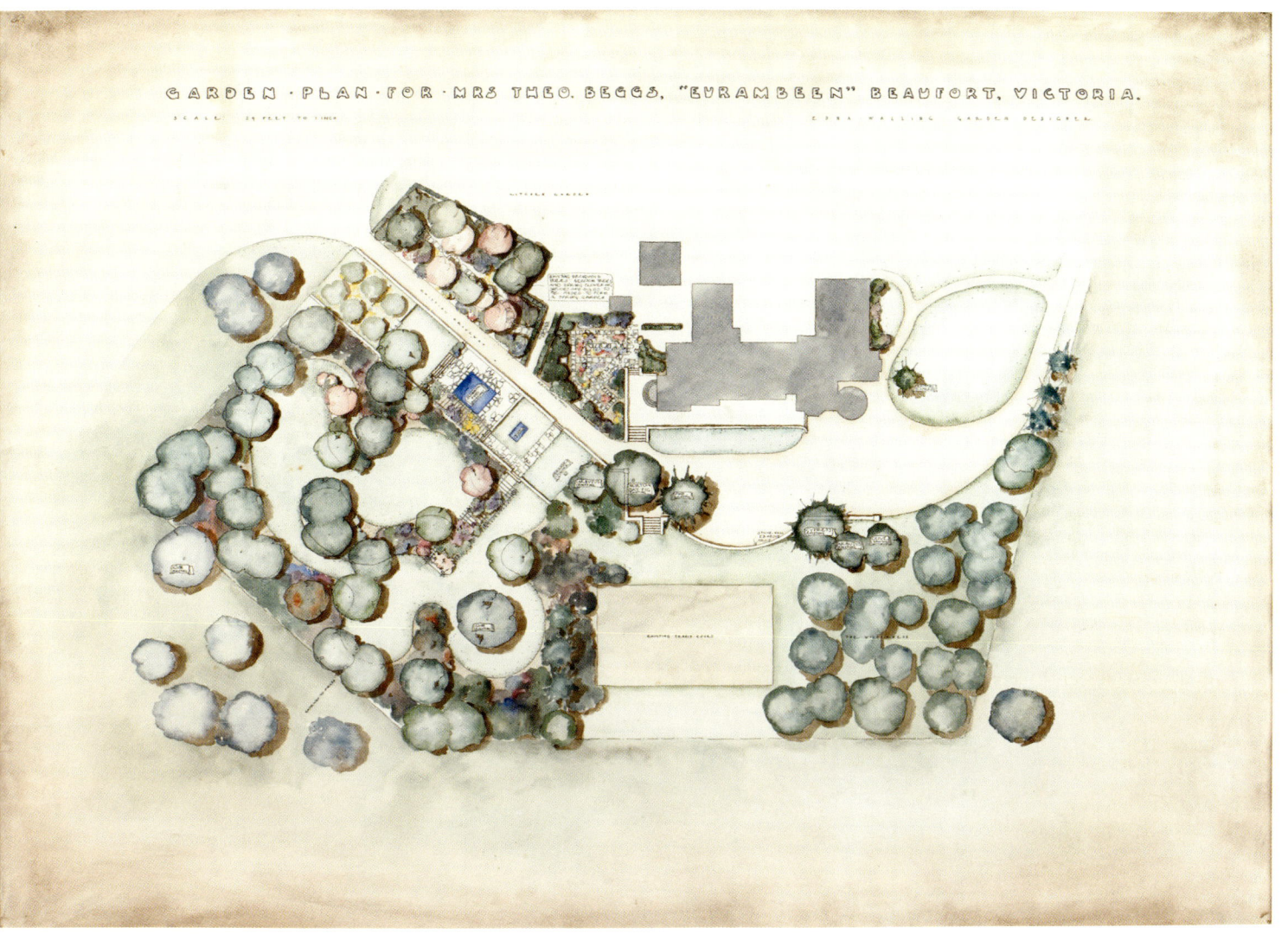

Walling in perpetuity | 1937

Edna Walling had a sharp sense of self. Her writings in *Australian Home Beautiful* addressed readers in a most personal manner, with quick and memorable turns of phrase. But it is in Walling's drawings that we best see a legacy in the making. Using heavy-grade Whatman's paper and watercolour over pencil and ink, she created works of great beauty and lasting appeal. Some bear the casual jottings of construction, but generally the extraordinarily high survival rate of her drawings testifies to her careful attention to client expectations and needs. In the footsteps of Repton, her writings and drawings were the Red Books of their age and now speak for her generation.

143

6D
The Garden Year
WITH
MR. BEAR

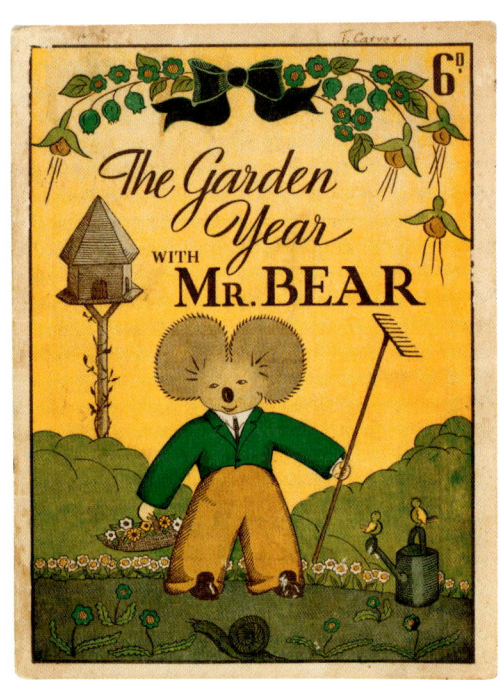

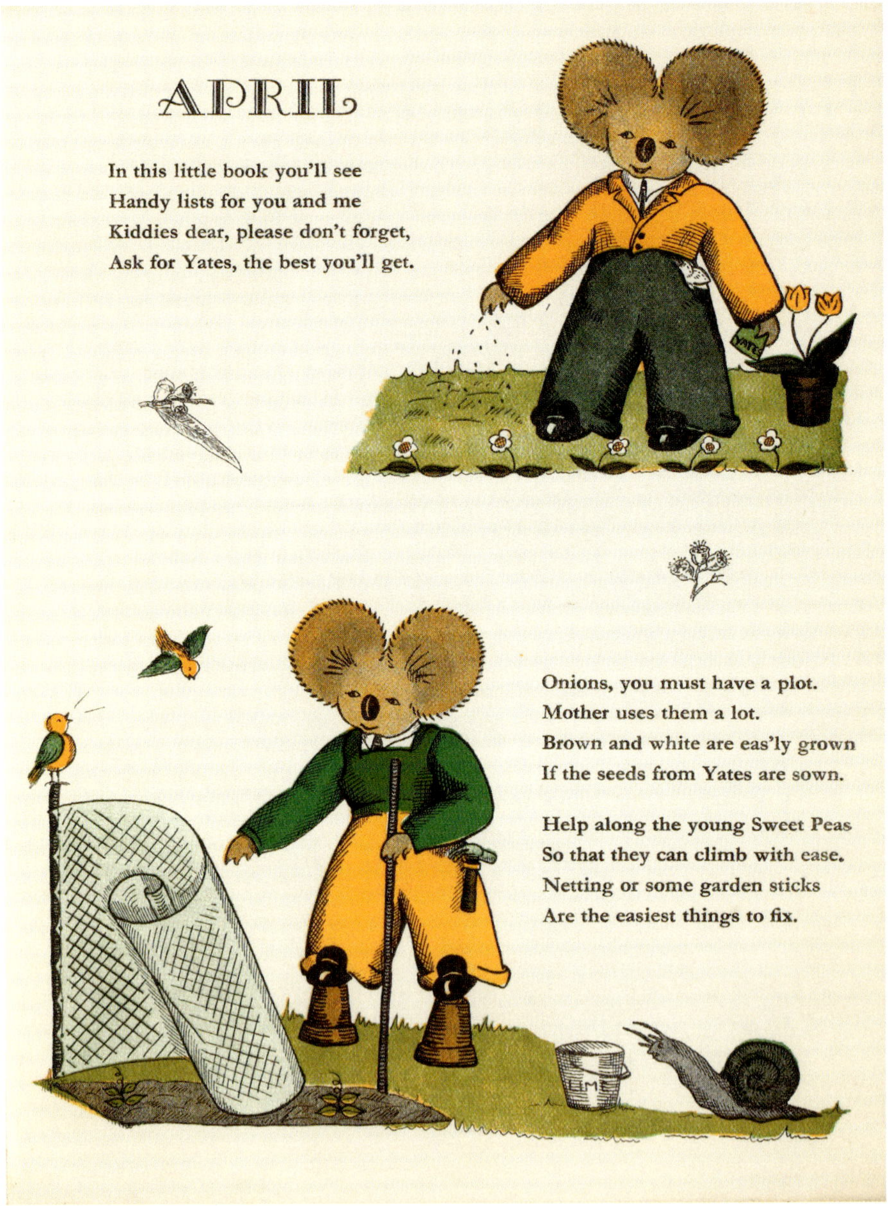

APRIL
In this little book you'll see
Handy lists for you and me
Kiddies dear, please don't forget,
Ask for Yates, the best you'll get.
Onions, you must have a plot.
Mother uses them a lot.
Brown and white are eas'ly grown
If the seeds from Yates are sown.
Help along the young Sweet Peas
So that they can climb with ease.
Netting or some garden sticks
Are the easiest things to fix.

'In this little book you'll see
Handy lists for you and me
Kiddies dear, please don't forget,
Ask for Yates, the best you'll get.'
So begins *The Garden Year with Mr Bear* (Sydney, 1938), a charming children's book published by the Yates seed company. Aided by beguiling vignettes of Mr Bear, we sow flower seeds, plant onions and erect netting for sweet peas—all subtly identified with the publisher's product.

Garden in a Valley | 1939

Dunedin, the garden created by Jean Galbraith in a valley near Tyers, in the Gippsland hinterland, retains a special place in the memory of Australian gardeners. Galbraith, an accomplished botanist, lovingly described the making of her garden in the *Australian Garden Lover* during the 1930s. Published in book form in 1939 the story was immediately popular with those who had known Galbraith from her columns written under the pen-name 'Correa'. Such sensitive and intuitive words came naturally to this gifted writer, yet when her first columns were published, Galbraith's gender was mistaken by some readers, surprised by the polished observations of a twenty-year-old girl.

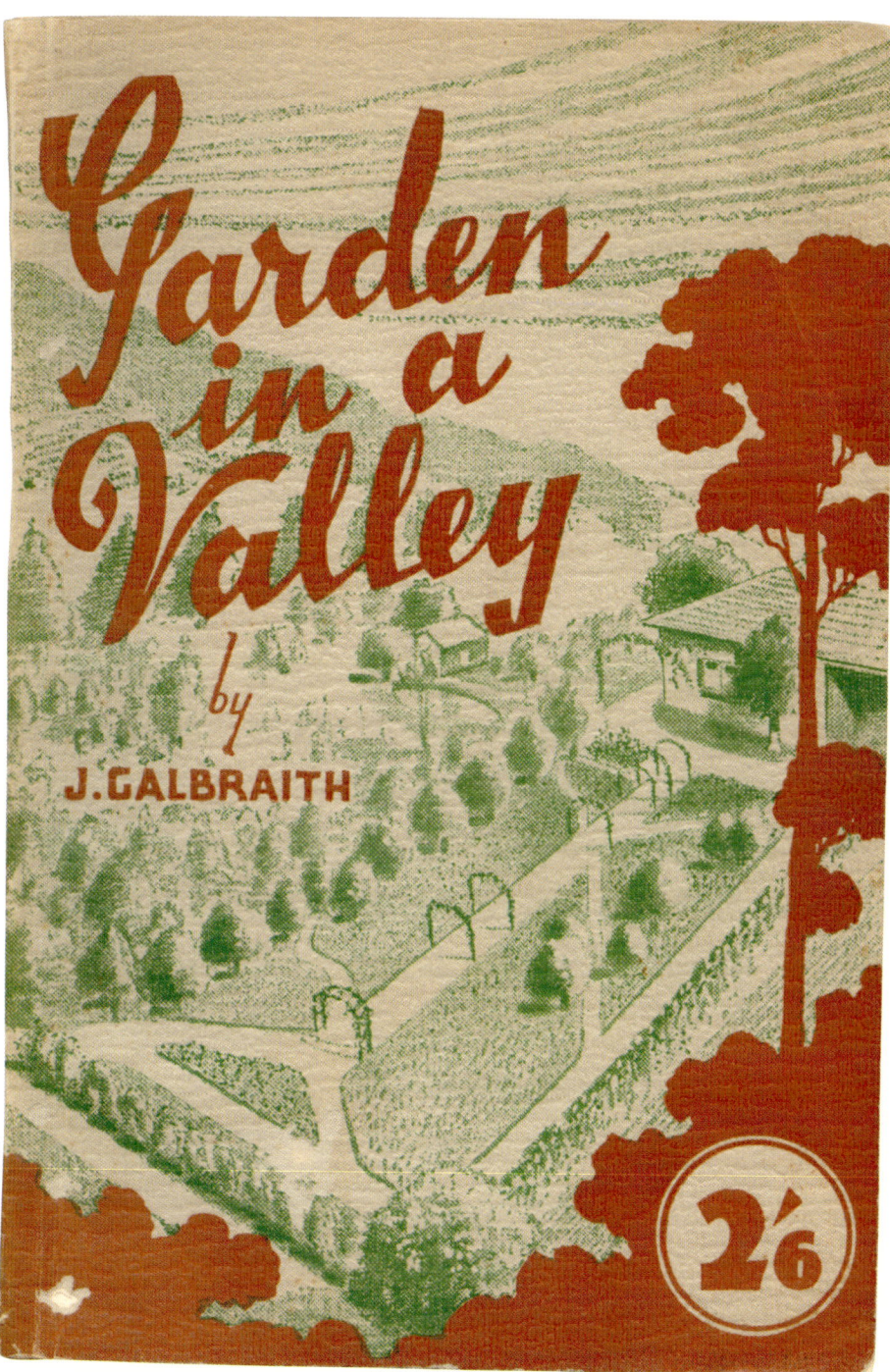

VELVET LAWN

(1940s–1950s)

*Yes, we just met on the cover—Velvet Lawn is my name and I work
for Ogden Industries. My job is to tell you why Ogden Industries do a better job
of caring for your lawn with so little personal effort on your part.*

Catalogue of Ogden Garden Products, c.1959

GARDENING, although performed under hardship and in restricted circumstances, brought practical and pleasurable benefits to Australians during the long dark years of World War II. Wartime restrictions swept aside normal commercial considerations as seed companies worked cooperatively with governments to assist the war effort. In an era marked by strict rationing, emphasis was placed on vegetable seed production as home gardeners were exhorted to 'dig for victory'. (Even on the front line in New Guinea, Australian defence personnel were provided with pocket-sized booklets to identify 'Friendly Fruits and Vegetables' in the fecund but oppressive tropics.) As backyard supplies of fruit and vegetables were bolstered, attention was also being placed on the flower garden, to bring cheer in uncertain times. Wartime gardening was promoted and widely perceived as a morale-boosting and socially acceptable pursuit.

As the immediate threat to Australia receded, architects, engineers and town planners turned to the task of post-war reconstruction. The exigencies of wartime production and a consequent hiatus in non-essential development encouraged visionary thinking. This was especially evident in town planning, where gardening and landscape design were treated as part of the continuum of urban design. Walter Bunning, an influential voice, prefaced his book *Homes in the Sun* (1945) with an historical overview. 'This is what we were promised', he thundered, and 'This is what we got'.

While decrying the planning of suburban Australia, Bunning and his colleagues realised that this was where great opportunity existed for improved design to enhance the living standards of ordinary Australians. Yet radical visions filtered slowly to the populace as rationing of materials checked building approvals. While a cooperative community approach to post-war reconstruction was widely advocated, individual action—especially through owner-built and owner-occupied houses—triumphed. The do-it-yourself ethic—so much an Australian way of life—came to the fore as home owners dressed their blocks with new lawns and terraced garden beds, set off by splendid letterboxes that proudly addressed their newly landscaped envelope. Much of this was a response to recently commercialised aspects of DIY purveyed through magazines and catalogues—modernism in subtle guise.

Uncurbed demands on horticulture meant that some gardens were now a garish parody of nature, as dinner-plate begonias, clipped shrubs and even oversize concrete crowns and baskets arose unchecked. Lawns and their maintenance reached a state of enthusiastic perfection, providing the perfect velvet backdrop for dotted features. This style reached its full flowering in the Fletcher Jones Garden, which soon became a model for the post-war generation of suburban gardeners. Floral clocks epitomised this style in the public realm.

Against this background, it is perhaps no wonder that environmentalism found an increasingly sympathetic ear, even amongst gardeners. Pragmatic concerns over soil erosion soon widened to community unease at bushland destruction. If Edna Walling's writings are taken as a barometer of the horticultural mind, her increasing interest in native plants from the late 1940s—resulting in her book *The Australian Roadside* (1952)—represented a crucial shift in opinion. The establishment of the Society for Growing Australian Plants in 1957 under the slogan 'Preservation by Cultivation' heralded a united voice for Australian flora. Soon it was not only those in leafy outer suburbs who were advocating Australian-plant gardens, but as the 1960s approached the climate was ripe for wider public acceptance of the bush garden.

Item 5.—

ARBOR DAY

Kate Louise Brown   Ernst Schmid

1. The sunbeams are twinkling, the air, soft and free, Is tell-ing a
2. Though now it is slender, no tall-er than I, It soon will be

message to you and to me. Come out! Come out! We're
growing straight up to the sky. A tree! A tree! That

planting a tree; Come out! Come out! We're planting a tree.
touches the sky; A tree! A tree! That touches the sky.

Arbor Day | 1940

Although Arbor Day had been celebrated in Australia since the late nineteenth century, World War II gave a renewed national purpose to its message. North American in origin, Arbor Day had long been an annual fixture in the Australian school calendar. Thistle Harris was at the forefront of nature education and her *Arbor Day Book* (Sydney, 1940) assembled a collection of relevant songs, poems and plays. American content was still prominent, but Harris drew on many Australian sources to present a distinctive mix of fact, folklore and ritual. Support for Arbor Day by the Australian Forest League recalled the age-old link between trees and national sentiment.

An idyll for the outskirts | 1941

Earnestly held beliefs and values underpinning planned communities were often expressed through dramatic art. Walter and Marion Griffin's Castlecrag estate in Sydney and Edna Walling's Bickleigh Vale village on Melbourne's outskirts both incorporated outdoor stages for performance. Here Walling's shutter has captured dancers as living sculptures, a leggy chiaroscuro of torsos and trunks. The ballet may be raising funds for the wartime work of the Red Cross but the image is filled with intensely private thoughts. Romanticism and Modernism seem to have collided.

Dig for victory | 1942

As the 1940s progressed, the proximity of war in the Pacific gave Australians a new sense of national urgency. Government control over production dictated rationing of goods to ensure that the war effort was accorded the highest priority. Home-grown produce not only lessened the demand on rationed goods, but gave householders a greater choice and more certain supply of food. Posters lined the billboards of railway stations giving commuters seasonal planting selections. Complementary booklets, compiled by Australia's departments of agriculture, disseminated detailed advice on weighty matters such as the staking of tomatoes and destruction of slugs.

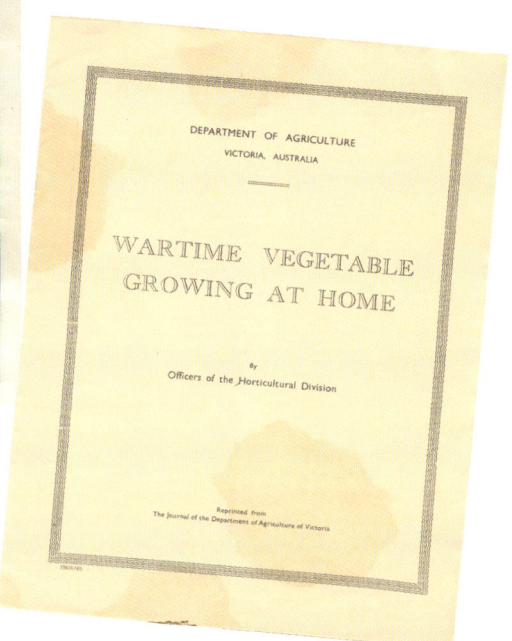

Seeds and the war | 1943

As wartime restrictions cut deeper into civilian life, rituals and routines eased hardships. Seed merchants trod a fine line, assisting government programmes as necessary, yet also stressing the value of gardening to the home front. 'Surely as the pot of beer, the "smokes", the horse and dog race, and the picture show are necessities even in war-time, how justified is the request of those who ask . . . for the flower seeds and plants with which they may produce in their own homes by their own spare time efforts, that abundance of flower and foliage, of colour and scent, which brings such joy and comfort to them and to their fellows, and especially to the sick, the lonely and the distressed.'

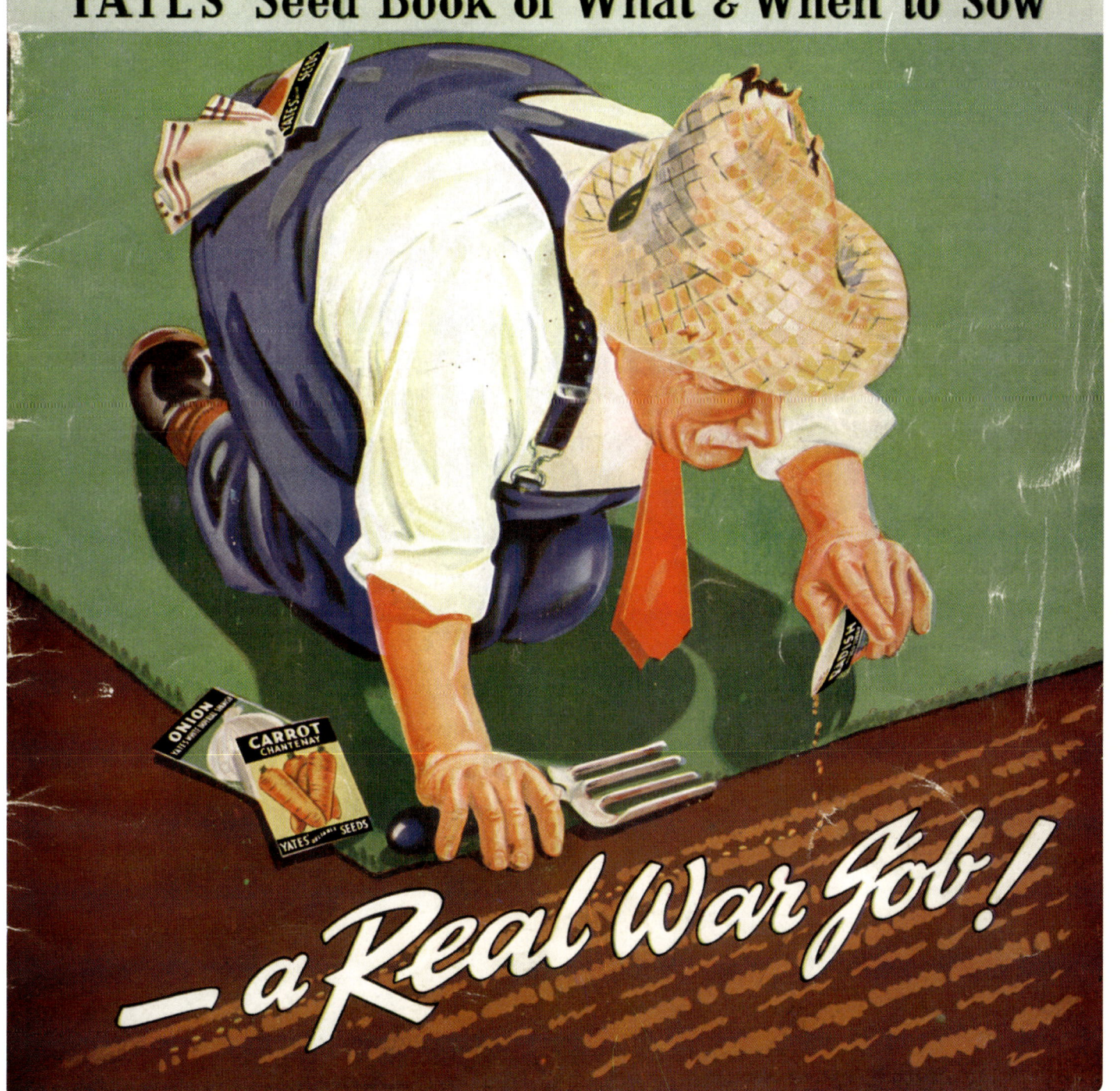

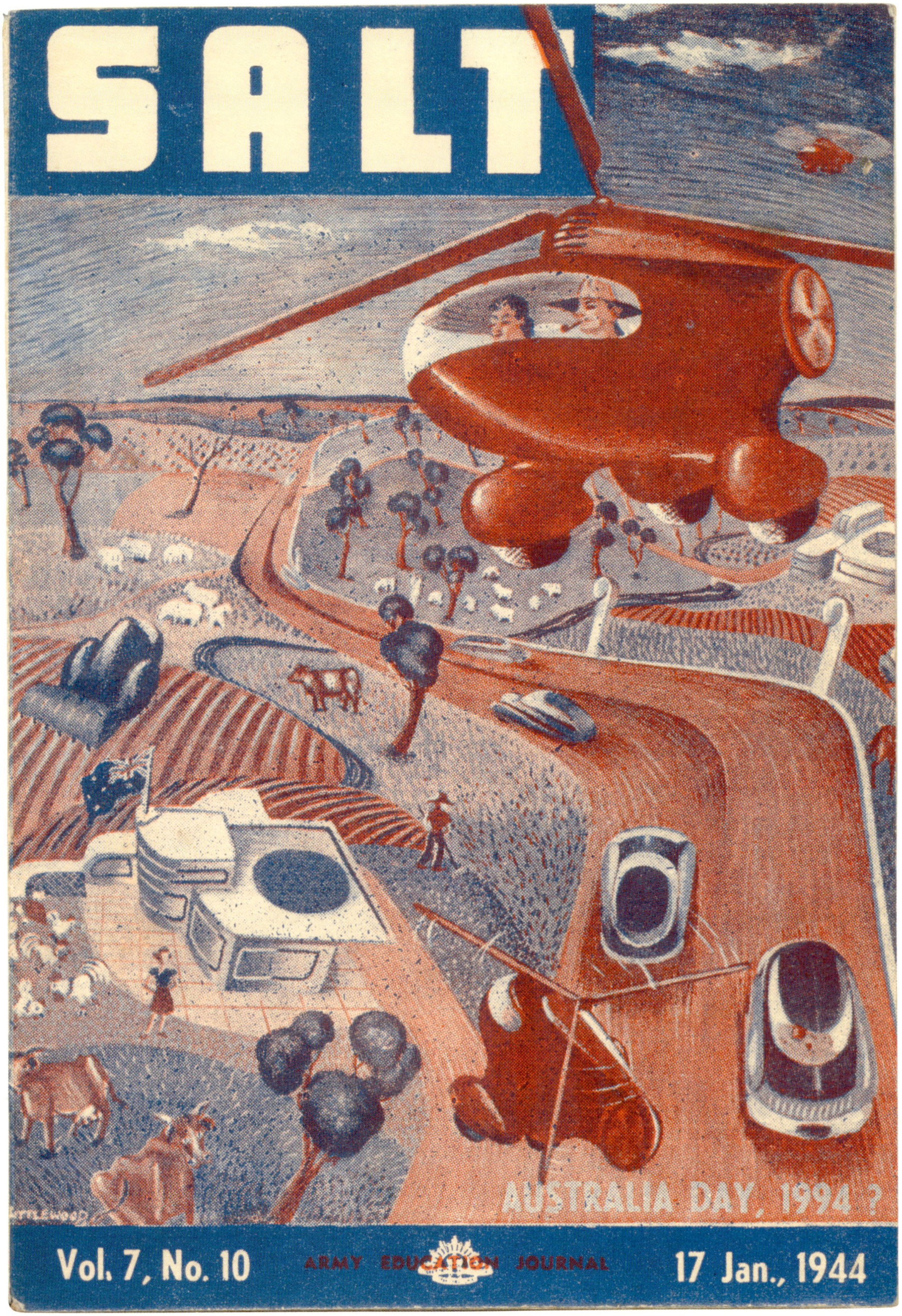
SALT
AUSTRALIA DAY, 1994 ?
Vol. 7, No. 10
ARMY EDUCATION JOURNAL
17 Jan., 1944

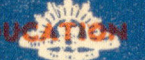

Tell him he's dreaming | 1944

When journalist Clive Turnbull wrote in January 1944 of his forecast for 'Australia—1994'
he claimed without apparent irony that the country would be '156 years old this month'. During
wartime conditions, time became magnified—'25 years of normal development have been telescoped
into the last three high-pressure years'. Warming to his task, Turnbull postulated that 'The world
of tomorrow could be found in miniature today': the wartime laboratory would be tomorrow's
factory. Turnbull's article was published in Salt, journal of the Australian Army Education Service.
Artist John Littlewood's visionary cover illustration set the tone for a world where town planners,
transport engineers and industrial designers would change the face of the Australian countryside.

Homes in the Sun | 1945

Town planning received a major boost with post-war
reconstruction. Walter Bunning was an influential
voice with his book *Homes in the Sun* (Sydney, 1945).
He lamented that the early promise of good living
conditions for Australians had not been fulfilled.
Bunning sought improved housing and landscape
design through an alliance with town planning.
He linked family needs with 'shelter answers':
thus an 'elevator apartment' might answer for an
individual or couple while a single dwelling would
suit an invalid or a couple with children. Bunning's
favoured individual dwelling was the 'Suntrap House',
which incorporated appropriate solar orientation
and penetration, links between indoor and outdoor
spaces, and adequate ventilation.

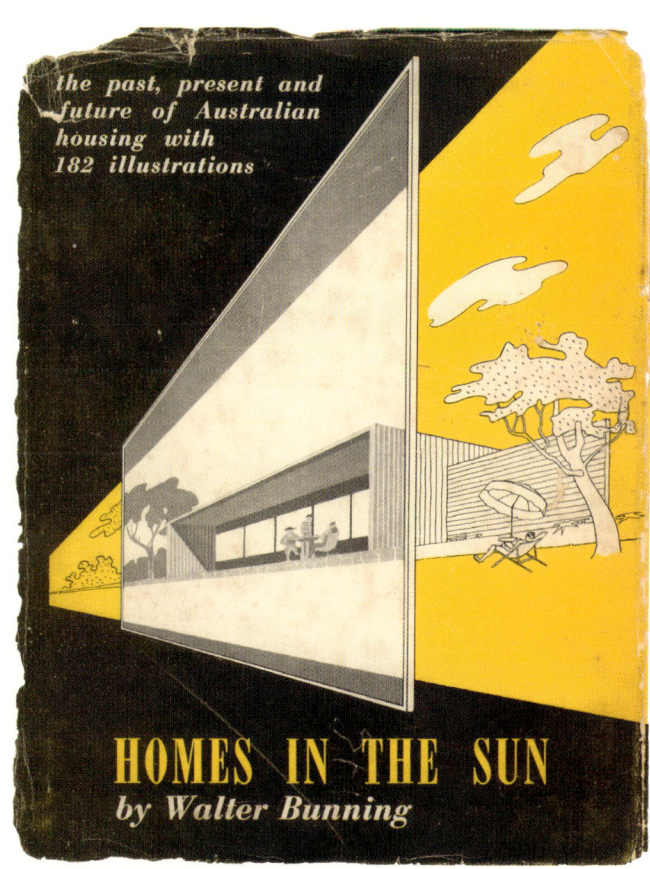

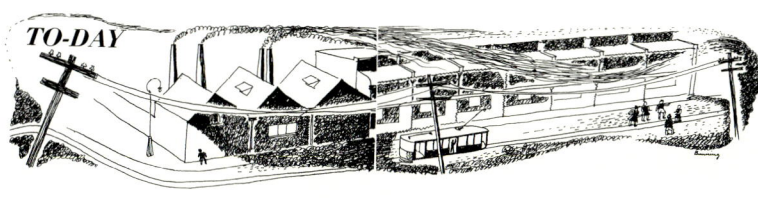

Soil and Civilization | 1946

Elyne Mitchell, free-spirited daughter of celebrated military commander Harry Chauvel ('Chauvel of the Light Horse' and an uncle of the pioneering Australian film director Charles Chauvel), used her writings to promote concern for the Australian environment. Her grazing property on the upper Murray at the foothills of the Snowy Mountains was the inspiration for *Australia's Alps* (1942) and *Speak to the Earth* (1945). Her third book, *Soil and Civilization* (Sydney, 1946), was an impassioned plea to safeguard our country's fragile soil, a rapidly eroding resource. To Mitchell, the soil was 'an integral part of the unity which is our bodies and our deeper selves, our thoughts and our inspiration'.

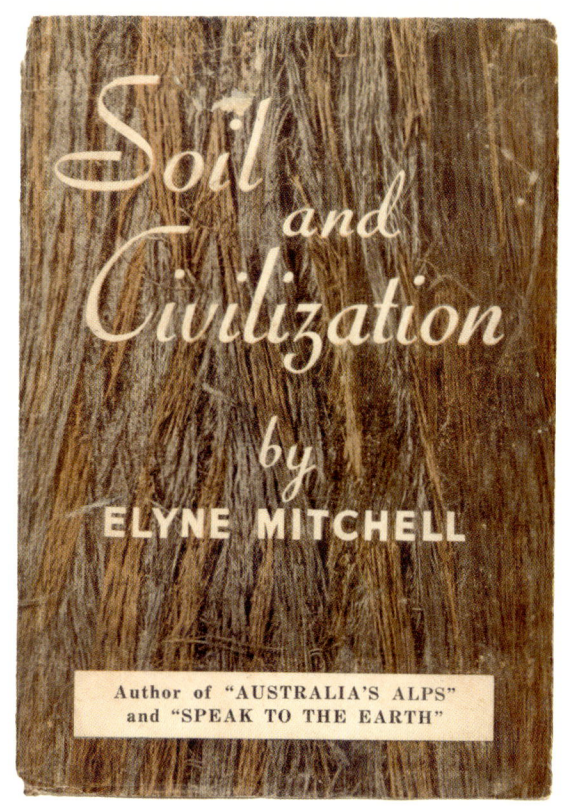

'Garden Silhouette' | 1947

Who knows what goes through the minds of photographers? Perhaps tiring of mountains, waterfalls and rivers, the official photographer for the Victorian Railways here captures a private moment, entitled 'Garden Silhouette'. The personal vision through the viewfinder becomes a shared public image, just as the horticulturist or landscape designer can share an intensely personal expression through the gardens they create. Perhaps in a transcendental moment, the photographer was carried away by the evanescence of his subject. Was this a self-portrait with friend, or a stolen moment of horticultural congratulation?

154

Fletcher Jones Gardens | 1948

This landscape of industry was developed in Warrnambool from 1948 when clothing manufacturer Fletcher Jones sought to beautify its Pleasant Hill works. Postcard views reveal that neatness ruled, and the garden became a model for the post-war generation of suburban gardeners. A quintessential FJ man—in bas-relief near the lily pond—subtly brought the image of permanent press trousers and crisply ironed shirts into the open: garden and product reinforced one another. The lawn was dotted with floral baskets, spaced like sunbathers on a crowded beach trying hard—but never quite succeeding—to achieve the least possible contact with their neighbours.

Horticultural chutzpah | 1949

The post-war years witnessed a resurgence of interest in horticultural shows and competitions. New magazines such as *Your Garden* joined established titles in the buoyant gardening marketplace, while horticultural societies reported expanding memberships and large attendances at functions, all giving oxygen to the competitive urge. The nursery trade responded to a great interest in competitive floriculture with larger and brighter blooms. The rose had never lost its devotees, but worshippers of the dahlia, gladiolus and chrysanthemum were rewarded for their faith with show-stopping cultivars that pushed the bounds of decency.

155

Gardening by male order | 1950

These erect trunks, shaved swards and pendulous forms show that the masculine garden is a thing of curious and perverse beauty. As early as the 1930s, the male gardener was under the microscope. A leading article in the *Garden and Home Maker of Australia* on 'The husband in the garden' was sub-titled 'A warning as to the perils involved in having both'. Warming to the task, the journal continued: 'Damage done to such inanimate stuff as furniture and household gear may be very easily repaired . . . but turn a man loose in a garden and the harm that ensues may take at least two planting seasons to correct.'

Backyard traditions | 1951

For readers of *Australian House and Garden* in 1951 the suburban backyard was still a working garden, yet to make the leap of sophistication into an outdoor living space. Vegetables, fruit trees, clothes drying and even the occasional chook still ruled the roost. Swimming pools, decks, patios and sundry gadgetry still only featured occasionally in popular home-making magazines, but within a decade such trappings of modernism had unleashed irrevocable changes in the Australian backyard.

herbert young

The Australian Roadside | 1952

In the post-war years, Edna Walling increasingly promoted the scenic and horticultural values of the Australian flora. Her book *The Australian Roadside* (Melbourne, 1952) used evocative photographs to reinforce an inspirational message that natural scenery should be valued not only for its intrinsic beauty but as a model for garden planting and design. Walling was fond of photographing roadside vegetation—on the rear of this print she wrote 'Red Gums (*E. camaldulensis*) seem always to convey the restful atmosphere of a park. We are fortunate when, as here, they survive along our roads, framing the landscape and arching the road with grey limbs splashed and patched red.'

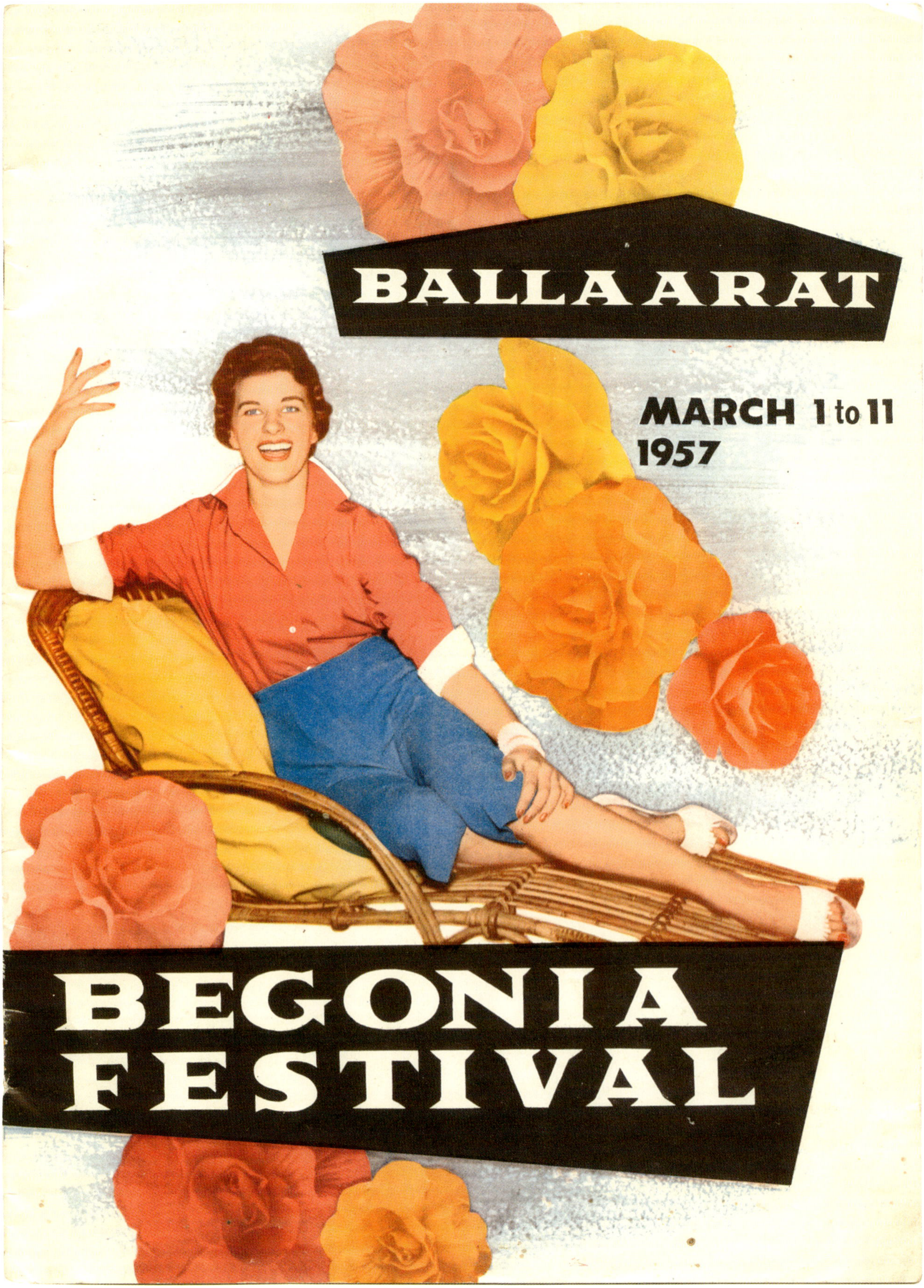
BALLAARAT
MARCH 1 to 11
1957
BEGONIA
FESTIVAL

1953 Begonia Queen, in her floral float
(Miss Beverley Coles)

Ballarat Begonia Festival | 1953

Ballarat's Begonia Festival, inaugurated in 1953, is perhaps the best known of Australia's floral festivals. Civic leaders—representing a heady mix of local government, real estate and tourist interests—drew on British precedents to give Ballarat a truly 'Australian Festival of National Interest'. With an emphasis on floral queens and princesses, royal imagery has become a distinctive feature of Australian floral festivals, seemingly at odds with nationalist ideals. Perhaps responding to the need for an irreverent local identity, the pristine qualities sought in Ballarat's Miss Begonia Queen have recently been challenged in Queensland by the Melon Queen award, a highlight of Chinchilla's week-long Melon Festival.

Who wants a republic? | 1954

Monarchists unite! All hail Arthur Pickford, King of Mosaics, Prince of Ballarat, Duke of Wendouree, late of Lindisfarne Crescent. When Queen Elizabeth II visited Ballarat in 1954, it was predicted that 'love, flowers and loyalty will greet her'. But few could have imagined the giant Imperial Crown that greeted curious visitors to Arthur Pickford's 'shell house', only a stone's throw from the royal dais at Ballarat Botanic Gardens. With splendid suburban candour, Pickford expressed his loyalty in a uniquely personal—but now ominously unfashionable—garden tribute.

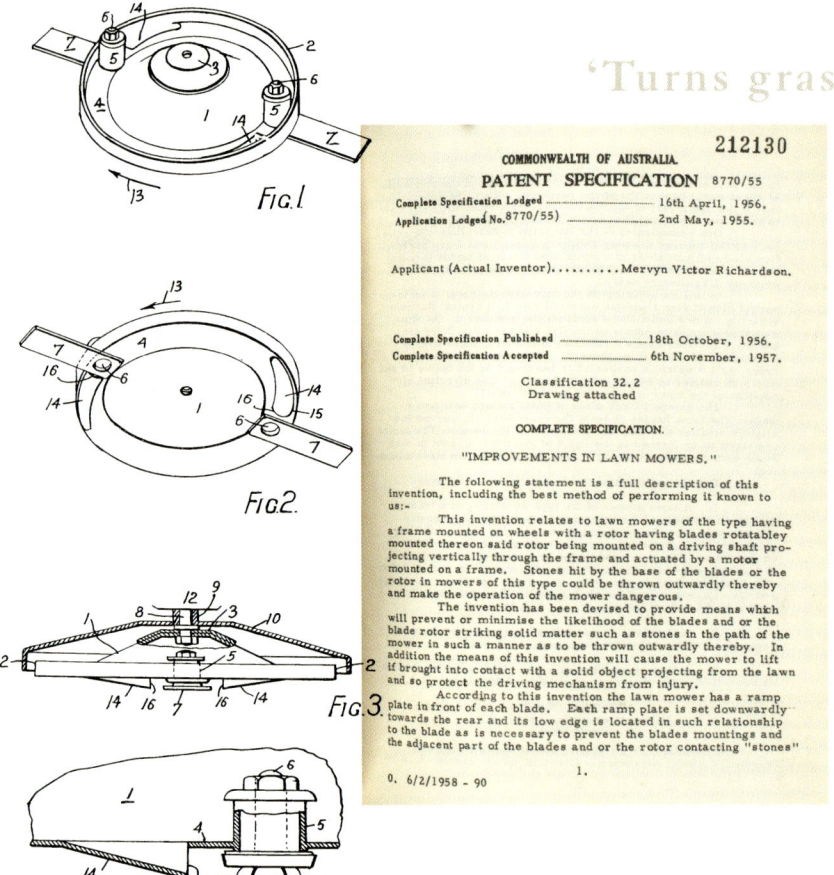

Fig.1.

Fig.2.

Fig.3.

Fig.4.

COMMONWEALTH OF AUSTRALIA.

212130

PATENT SPECIFICATION 8770/55

Complete Specification Lodged .... 16th April, 1956.
Application Lodged No.8770/55 .... 2nd May, 1955.

Applicant (Actual Inventor)......... Mervyn Victor Richardson.

Complete Specification Published .... 18th October, 1956.
Complete Specification Accepted .... 6th November, 1957.

Classification 32.2
Drawing attached

COMPLETE SPECIFICATION.

"IMPROVEMENTS IN LAWN MOWERS."

The following statement is a full description of this
invention, including the best method of performing it known to
us:—
      This invention relates to lawn mowers of the type having
a frame mounted on wheels with a rotor having blades rotatabley
mounted thereon said rotor being mounted on a driving shaft projecting vertically through the frame and actuated by a motor
mounted on a frame. Stones hit by the base of the blades or the
rotor in mowers of this type could be thrown outwardly thereby
and make the operation of the mower dangerous.
      The invention has been devised to provide means which
will prevent or minimise the likelihood of the blades and or the
blade rotor striking solid matter such as stones in the path of the
mower in such a manner as to be thrown outwardly thereby. In
addition the means of this invention will cause the mower to lift
if brought into contact with a solid object projecting from the lawn
and so protect the driving mechanism from injury.
      According to this invention the lawn mower has a ramp
plate in front of each blade. Each ramp plate is set downwardly
towards the rear and its low edge is located in such relationship
to the blade as is necessary to prevent the blades mountings and
the adjacent part of the blades and or the rotor contacting "stones"

0. 6/2/1958 - 90

1.

'Turns grass into lawn' | 1955

Mervyn Victor Richardson did not
invent the lawn mower, but his
lightweight contraption of piping,
billycart wheels and a peach-tin
petrol tank revolutionised its design.
Yet Richardson required a distinctive
feature to achieve patent protection.
His application, lodged in 1955 and
approved two years later, specified a
mode of fixing the blades to a solid disk
such that stones would not be thrown
outwards by the rotating mechanism.
Patents were one thing, but it was
effective marketing that really launched
the Victa. 'Turns grass into lawn' was
perhaps the most memorable piece
of corporate copywriting of its time.

Northern contentment | 1956

Australia has a long and rich tradition of regional
gardening guides. In part this derived from colonial
and state parochialism, born of remote distances and
political insularity. More important, from a horticultural
standpoint, were the extremes in climate across the
continent. This variation produced—and continues to
produce—distinctive planting combinations and garden
designs, nowhere more evident than in the tropical and
semi-tropical climates of northern Australia. Always keen
to promote its defining qualities, Queensland produced
some of the nation's most distinctive and charming
gardening handbooks. Despite climatic differences, the
sixteen-perch Brisbane block produced tropical contentment
equal to that of a more temperate Melbourne quarter-acre.

Nôtre Dame Abbey, Tarrawarra | 1957

Irish Cistercian monks were sent to Australia in the 1950s to set up a monastery in Victoria's Yarra Valley. Here, they followed the medieval traditions of the French Cistercian order—a largely self-sufficient community, growing fruit and vegetables, including grapes, and running a dairy and beef cattle farm. The regimented order of monastic life, and its intertwined worlds of prayer and hard physical work, is reflected in this silent, purposeful scene. In the labour-saving enthusiasm of post-war Australia the adoption of this centuries-old self-sufficient lifestyle appears anachronistic, yet it expressed the ethos of B. A. Santamaria's Catholic Rural Movement and the emerging co-operative environmental idealism of the 1960s.

Notre Dame Abbey, Tarrawarra, Vic.   On Way to Work.

Build Among Our Trees

Not Over Them

As suburbia expanded in the post-war years, so environmental issues rose to the surface. Few decried the destruction of orchards and paddocks, but threatened bushland and native trees roused a new vocal constituency of tree preservation and civic amenity groups. In leafy Eltham, on Melbourne's north-east fringe, the circle of landscapers and designers centred around Peter Glass, Alistair Knox, Gordon Ford and Ellis Stones formed a prominent voice of concern. The Glass papers contain correspondence, photographs and ephemeral items from the Eltham Tree Preservation Society that highlight suburban battles. 'To chop is to cheapen, bury your axe' was the rallying cry.

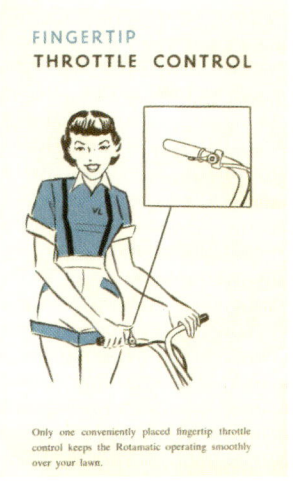

So easy a woman could do it | 1959

With advances in lawn mower design came a corresponding proliferation in advertising. Women were often featured during this period, providing a finely honed message of convenience and ease. Velvet Lawn played her part, eyeing sharp blades, demonstrating streamlined beauty (without a mower in sight), toying with the fingertip throttle control. The link between ease of use and women in advertising was even more blatant for electric lawn mowers, as manufacturers shamelessly bridged a credibility gap in this traditionally male market.

LIVING IN THE ENVIRONMENT

(1960s–1970s)

The conservation of the planet for the habitation of mankind requires
a clarification of the issues involved . . . The Universe will win in the end but,
unless we change our ground, it may only be at the cost of all civilisation
being totally destroyed in the process.

Alistair Knox, *Living in the Environment*, 1975

THE progressive ethic of modernism received a jolt in 1962 when American biologist Rachel Carson raised the spectre of a *Silent Spring* in her best-selling book of that name. Unfettered use of pesticides, particularly DDT, was endangering life on planet Earth in a manner that required urgent global action. Carson's impassioned plea was magnified by a groundswell of environmentalism, united under the slogan 'Think globally, act locally'.

In Australia, this new environmental consciousness took many forms. At a basic level it encouraged organic gardening. Chemical-free horticulture (and agriculture) was advocated by a loose coalition of devotees, who regarded organic practices as part of a continuum of natural living. Journals such as *Earth Garden* and *Grass Roots* brought this message to a dedicated audience. Their experimental lifestyle prefaced a more systematic approach to organic farming and gardening through Bill Mollison's Permaculture system.

Returning to nature also suited those promoting horticultural use of the Australian flora. The idea of gardening with Australian plants had progressed in sophistication to a stage in the 1960s where aesthetic considerations were merging in the popular mind with a nationalistic message. The best-selling publications of Betty Maloney and Jean Walker, Ellis Stones, and Glen Wilson brought bush gardens into the suburbs. Acceptance of the new landscape aesthetic also encouraged revegetation projects, including those using techniques such as the Bradley method of clearing weed species and encouraging natural regeneration. This ecological awareness became increasingly important, especially as the profession of landscape architecture had so recently emerged as a distinct discipline in Australia. Seminal works such as Ian McHarg's *Design with Nature* (1969) prefaced the rise, a decade later, of landscape ecology which united the aesthetics of landscape design with environmental factors.

Landscape architecture, gardening and architecture increasingly forged a complementary design ethos. Rough hewn beams, natural earthy colours and the rugged forms of Australian trees and shrubs produced a distinctive Australian palette. In Sydney this gave rise to the 'nuts and berries school' of architecture. In Melbourne, the Eltham group of artists, architects and landscape designers promoted the suburb's bushland amenity under the slogan 'Build among our trees, not over them'. The fusion of Australian culture—

in particular the arts—and politics reached a new high point in 1972 with the election of the Whitlam government, symbolised by the leafy expressionism of Clifton Pugh's prime ministerial portrait.

The books of Maloney and Walker invoked the motto 'naturalness with order' to describe their bush garden designs. This tag recalled the late eighteenth-century term 'sharawadgi', used by the English to describe the Chinese manner of designing gardens perceived as embodying calculated disorder. Such diluted orientalism was not confined to the asymmetry and casual artlessness of bush gardens as the fashion for bonsai and pebble gardens also expressed a version of carefully manipulated modernism in the home garden. Bush gardens were equally well adapted to modernism and the ceaseless search for an Australian garden identity, especially in the casual ease with which they transformed the garden into a place of leisure.

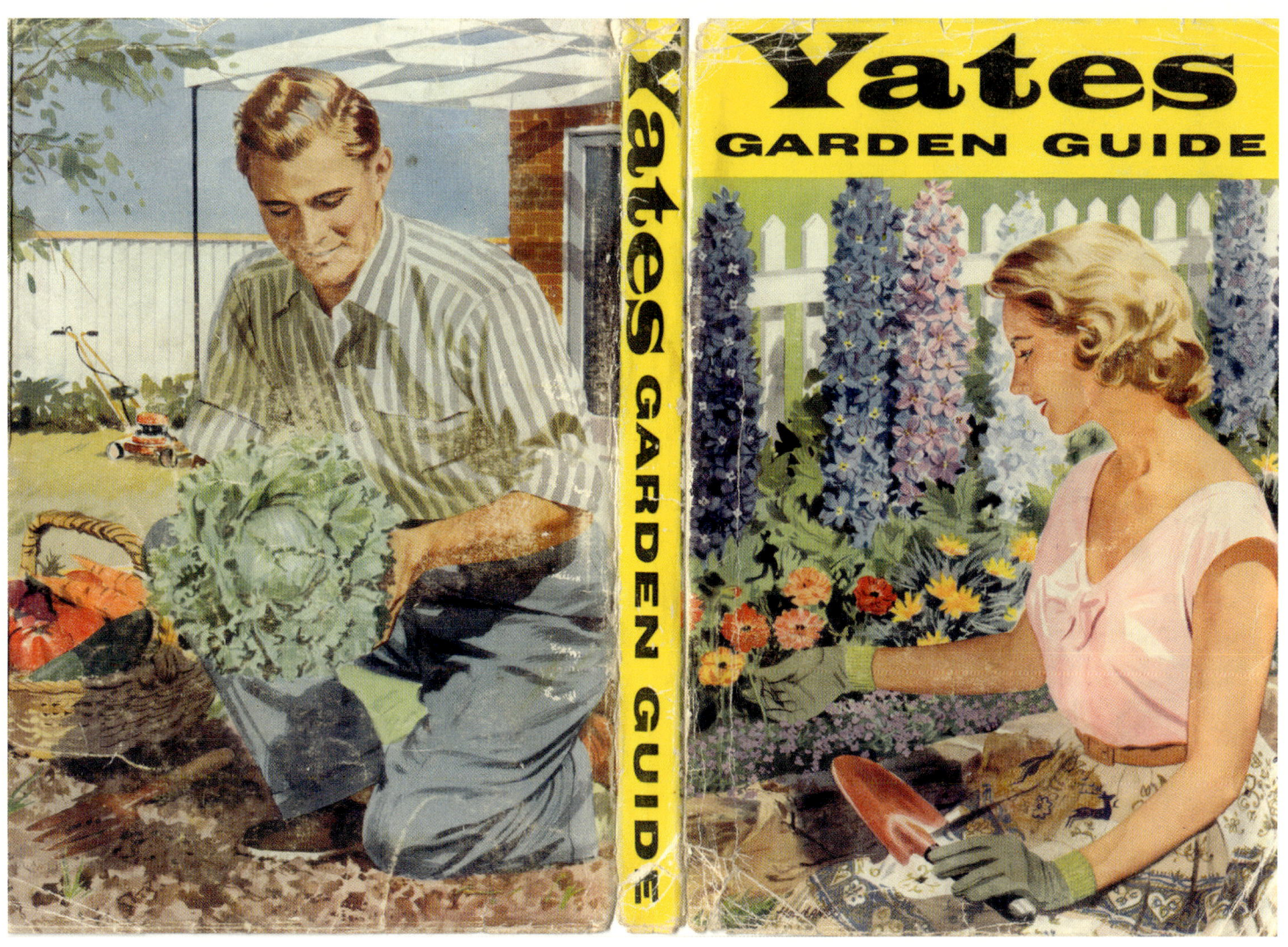

Gender in the garden | 1960

For historians, subsidiary texts can often reveal a more telling message or provide a more vivid
contemporary snapshot than the entire contents of a book or similar work. In particular, in packaging
and advertising one or two images must represent the product. For those interested in representations of
gender in the garden, book covers, seed catalogues and other forms of advertising make up a compelling
record. Within the beguiling simplicity of this dustwrapper, feminine floriculture is contrasted with
vegetable virility and mowing masculinity more sharply than a dozen written texts.

Southern comfort | 1961

Who could want for more? A backyard, a coffee table, some comfy chairs and a television. This image of the post-war migrant dream is notable for the ease with which the traditional Australian backyard has been converted into an outdoor room—the spare setting of the backyard stage has been transformed by its temporary props. Yet the moment is fleeting. The scene is ripe for the improver's hand.

Mardi Gras meets Sunny South | 1962

The singlemindedness of rosarians is captured with alarming clarity in this garden plan. Each rose has been plotted and its variety named, painting a satisfying mental picture for the devotee but an enigma for the uninitiated. The names read like a disjointed history lesson: Kleopatra, Grace de Monaco, Chrysler Imperial, President Herbert Hoover. Elsewhere, some fractured geography is snatched: Los Angeles, Mojave, Montezuma, Sunny South. Mardi Gras joins Roundelay and Garden Party. The rosarian sees ordered rows of Hybrid Teas and Floribundas, a kaleidoscope of colour. Old favourites stand discreetly between more numerous and boisterous newcomers. The rose world comes to life in the mind's eye.

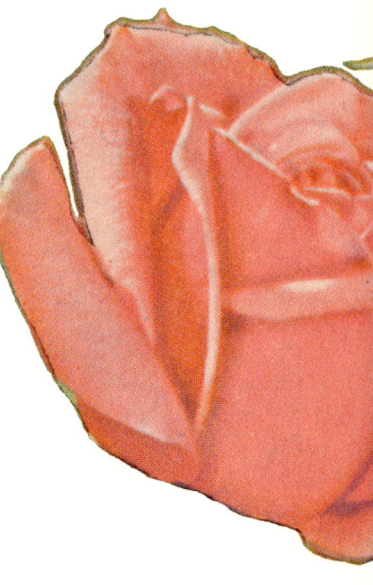

168

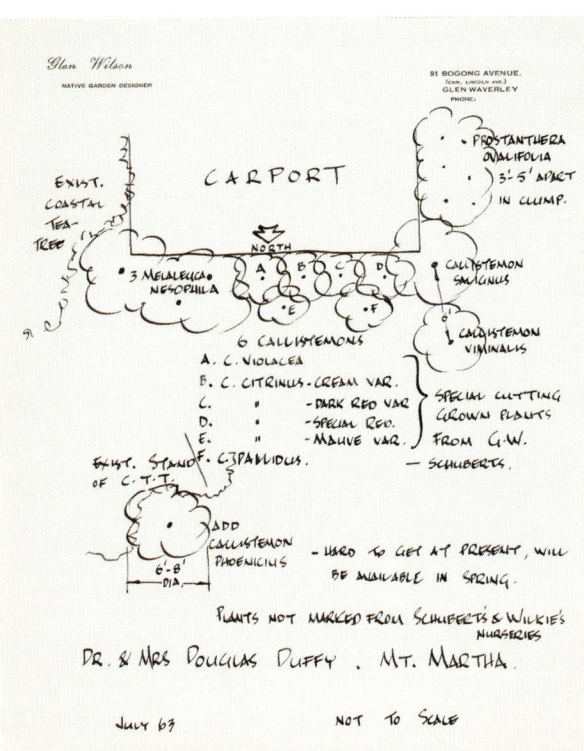

Australian-plant gardening | 1963

The 1960s were a decade of experimentation for landscape design using Australian plants. This sketch design, prepared for a client of the pioneering Australian-plant nursery of Bernhardt and Dulcie Schubert, highlights this phase. Glen Wilson, identified on his letterhead as a 'Native garden designer', has blended red-flowering Callistemon phoenicius against the existing white-flowering Coastal Tea-tree in what he termed 'picture making'—grouping plants of similar foliage and shape but with contrasting flower colouring. Reflecting increasing horticultural interest in the Australian flora, many of the plants used by Wilson and his colleagues were variations raised from seed and subsequently registered as cultivars (cultivated varieties) for commercial distribution.

Australian Outrage | 1964

The exhibition *Australian Outrage* was organised by the Royal Australian Institute of Architects in 1964 to highlight the decay of our visual environment. A book of the same name, edited by Donald Gazzard, brought the message to a wider audience, who were shocked at the damning images it contained. Power poles, proliferating signage, jerry-built amenities and vehicular wastelands all felt the icy glare. Just as Robin Boyd had parodied 'arboraphobia' in his 1961 critique of the Australian environment, *The Australian Ugliness*, so Gazzard illustrated similar visions of lopped trees and blighted landscapes, grimly quoting the Australian saying: 'If it moves, shoot it; if it doesn't, chop it down.'

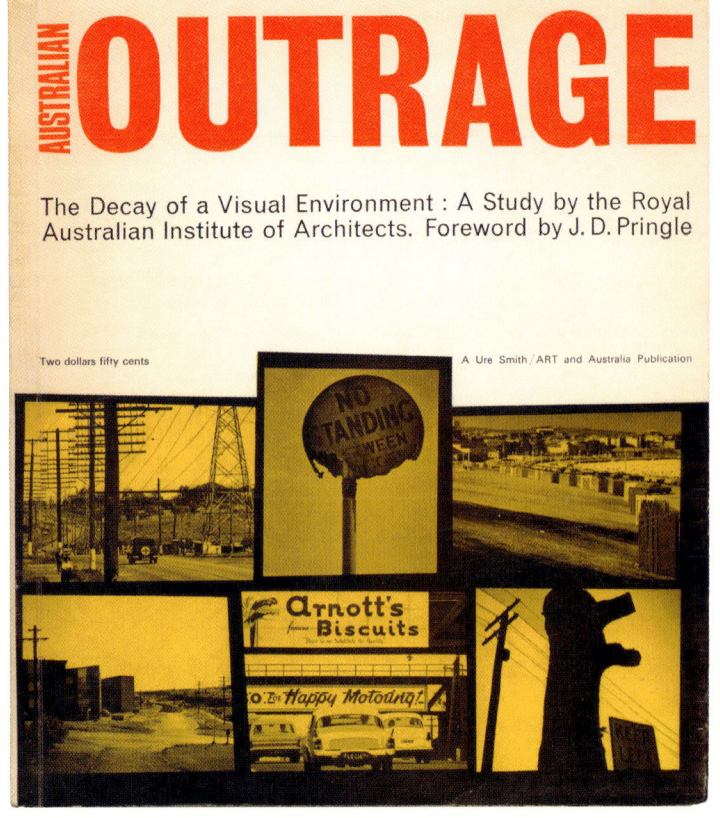

Better Outdoor Living | 1965

Beryl Guertner, founding editor in 1948 of
Australian House and Garden, was an influential
taste-maker. Amongst her many books, few
more accurately captured the age than *Gregory's
Australian Guide to Better Outdoor Living*
(Sydney, 1965). Let the author explain: 'There
is a powerful difference between an average
backyard and the garden which is planned as a
proper outdoor room. When you press a pattern
of smooth river stones into a section of terrace
paving; when you build a pergola; when you can
lie back in a shaded sun lounge on a hot summer's
day, then you are really living outdoors.' *Sic transit
gloria mundi*.

Naturalness with order | 1966

This expressive plan from Betty Maloney and Jean Walker's *Designing Australian Bush Gardens* (Sydney, 1966) was spread over ten pages of their small-format paperback. Not only were startled readers expected to dissect the book to assemble the composite plan but they were instructed to commence their garden by eliminating lawn and letting a 'soft restful carpet of fallen leaves and bark eliminate your weeding'. To a generation brought up on suburban neatness this was like flirting with the devil. Yet Walker's drawings had a sensual immediacy, bringing the plants to life and allowing the reader literally to use them as working drawings.

10ʟ $1
DESIGNING AUSTRALIAN
BUSH GARDENS
BY BETTY MALONEY AND JEAN WALKER

Pebble gardens | 1967

The tradition of rock gardens and rockeries
sat well with Australia's harsh climates, the
alpines of European gardens being exchanged
for succulents and other drought-tolerant
plants. Yet nothing could prepare suburbia
for the pebble garden mania of the mid-1960s.
Just as bush gardens had promised weed-free
gardening, so pebble gardens beckoned a
low-maintenance future. An unmistakable
signature was the proud unfurling of black
polythene sheets, soon tucked snugly into
besser-block bed ends. Lawn was banished
and a severely diluted Japanese aesthetic
brought contentment to Australia's courts
and crescents.

173

Pa carked here | 1968

The long airless wait was too much. The cult of the automobile, now shamelessly yoked to the halls of commerce, had claimed its victim. While Myer called to the fairer sex with siren-like allure, the faithful old husband had expired, bewildered and unable to cope with the modernity of the drive-in shopping centre. The trees between the parking bays were mere saplings without shade, and urban planning had not yet popularised the ramped multi-storey model. The asphalt wasteland, chequered with outsize herringbone treads, stood mute as the latest manifestation of the urban garden—a park for cars.

Design with Nature | 1969

The rise in ecological awareness and its translation into landscape design was fused in Ian McHarg's seminal text *Design with Nature* (New York, 1969). 'The World is a Capsule' he mused, as human footprints were being implanted on the moon. The study of ecology had grown throughout the twentieth century, but it was Rachel Carson's explosive best-seller *Silent Spring* (1962) that had thrown the ecological cat amongst the pesticide pigeons. McHarg freely acknowledged his debt to Carson and rode the environmental momentum to create an international landscape design movement.

TOWN OF PORTLAND

Best Kept Native Garden

This is to certify that

of

has been granted the Award of the Town of Portland

for the best kept Garden of Australian Native Plants

for the year 19

In Witness Whereof the Common Seal of the Mayor,

Councillors and Burgesses was hereunto affixed in the

presence of

....
MAYOR

....
COUNCILLOR

....
TOWN CLERK

Keeping nature at bay | 1970

Optimistic claims by early proponents of the Australian bush garden fuelled hopes for a maintenance-free garden. Yet within a few short years, as exotic weeds pushed aside more capricious natives, many home gardeners dismissed the bush garden as nothing more than a fad, and returned to the folds of convention. The bush garden also invoked the spectre of wildly informal and unconventional garden designs, often the product of radical environmental thinking. Perhaps it was the spectre of such unkempt qualities that prompted Portland Council to award a prize for the town's 'Best Kept Native Garden'.

Very Important Plant | 1971

Author and artist Ted Greenwood was a passionate educator and committed environmentalist. In *V.I.P. Very Important Plant* (Sydney, 1971), he drew on these twin enthusiasms to produce a children's book of insight and elegance. His message of nature and nurture brought the miracle of plant life to his young audience through coloured drawings of deceptive simplicity. The book is a joy, with the large format and vitality of the original drawings bringing an even greater appreciation of Greenwood's wish for people and plants to share their environment.

EARTH GARDEN

No. 1 $1

Earth Garden | 1972

Black sheep featured prominently in the early issues of *Earth
Garden*, the Balmain-published magazine of Irene and Keith Smith.
The unconscious irony probably went unnoticed as earthy types
in hand-knits forged a new ethic of 'natural living and growing'.
As the pace of environmentalism quickened, *Earth Garden*
captured a new and disparate audience, drawn together by an
earnest enthusiasm for ecological and organic imperatives.

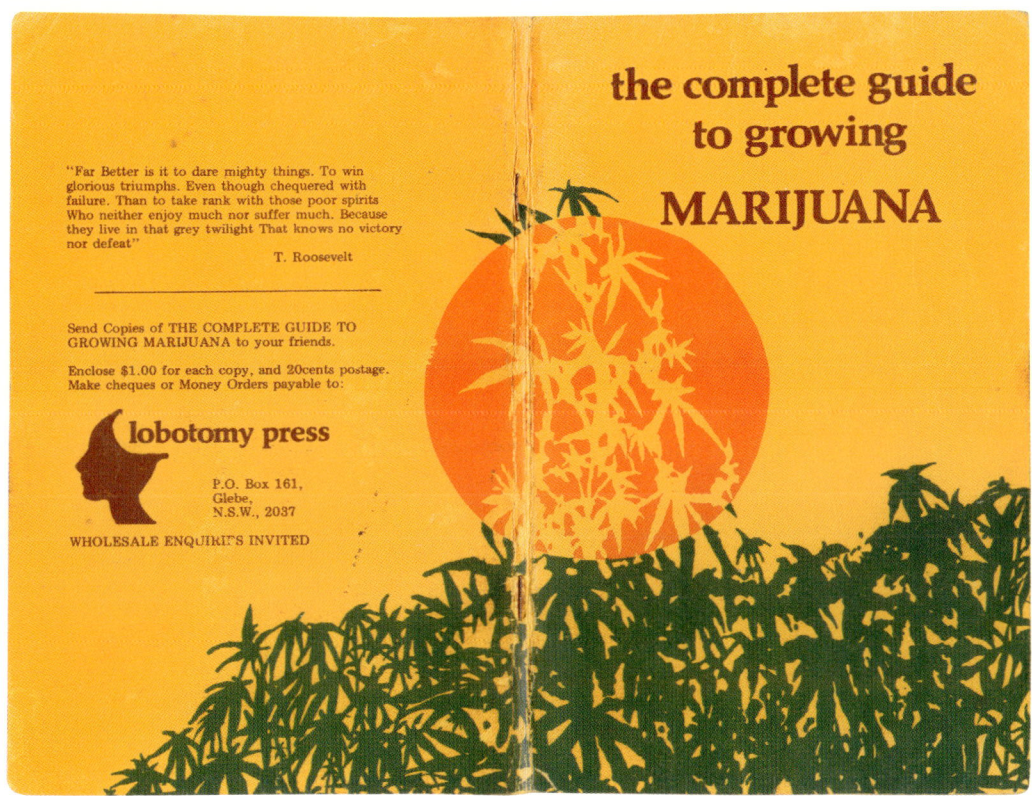

'Let the Earth Bring Forth Grass' | 1973

Hydroponics blossomed in the 1970s with the increasing popularity of *Cannabis sativa* (marijuana),
grown indoors to avoid prying eyes. The literature of gardening received an unexpected boost, as novice
hands came to grips with this complex horticultural process. The term 'hydroponics' had been coined in
the early 1930s but drew on much earlier traditions of soil-less culture. *The Complete Guide to Growing
Marijuana*, first published in San Diego, California, in 1970, was adapted for the Australian market by
Sydney's Lobotomy Press in 1973. Opening whimsically with a biblical quote from the book of Genesis,
it ended more pragmatically with a crop log to record the season's harvest.

Eureka | 1974

Cyril and Cecil knew a thing or two about citrus. For gardening journalists, ailing lemon trees accounted for more column inches, radio airtime or television transmission than any other horticultural problem. Sagacious advice, dispensed with patient regularity, usually brought disappointment to the lemon-tree constituency, yet this broad mass learned from experience. Collar rot and black aphis aside, popular horticultural journalism—from weekly newspapers to magazines, radio and television—has been the lifeblood of gardening in Australia, bringing ideas and enlightenment to the great mass of home gardeners. Its presenters have taken the mantle of modern-day Archimedes in the antipodes.

'Rocky' Stones | 1975

Ellis Stones—'Rocky' to his friends—died in 1975 after four decades of achievement in the field of landscape construction and design. He worked from an intuitive love of the natural environment, sculpting timber, stones and plants into designed landscapes of great sensitivity. 'It is a rare thing this gift for placing stones', wrote Edna Walling, 'and strange that a man possessing it should bear the name Stones.' His collaboration during the 1960s with Merchant Builders, whose housing projects set new standards of design excellence in the notoriously shabby speculative market, produced landscapes of economy and equipoise.

Wildflower Diary | 1976

Winifred Waddell, founder of the Native Plants Preservation Society of Victoria in 1952, was a tireless campaigner for her cause. Following a long career in teaching, she used public education to promote the Australian flora. Waddell's *Wildflower Diary* (1976) drew together articles published in the children's section of Melbourne's *Age* newspaper in 1960–64. More generally, her advocacy was directed towards the preservation of native bushland and the establishment of wildflower sanctuaries. Waddell's conservation message found parallels in the work of the Society for Growing Australian Plants, formed in 1957.

Tiny utopias | 1977

Expansive suburban ideals met an abrupt challenge in the 1970s as inner-city terrace housing became the preferred address for busy professional people. Gardeners had only limited space and time, and wished to maximise both. Tiny gentrified balconies and backyards in Parkville and Paddington soon overflowed with potted plants, hanging baskets and makeshift vegetable plots. Unsurprisingly, *The Tiny Utopia* (subtitled 'A Minimum Effort Maximum Effect Garden Book') was published by the *Terrace Times* newspaper in Balmain, spiritual heartland of Sydney's tiny utopians.

Permaculture | 1978

Between the earnest early 1970s enthusiasm of *Earth Garden* and the popular dilution of organic gardening for a mass market in the 1990s stands permaculture. Texts by Bill Mollison and David Holmgren, commencing in 1978 with *Permaculture One*, propounded a revolutionary system of perennial agriculture. Combining landscape design, plants and animals in a complementary union, permaculture was designed to capitalise on high yields from low energy inputs. From modest Tasmanian origins, permaculture is now an international movement.

Converting the Wilderness | 1979

The stuff of garden history lies in many repositories. Libraries, art galleries, museums and even garden sheds hold the documents of our gardening past. Just as importantly, many gardens survive to represent a taxonomy of different types and styles. The excitement of linking these documentary and physical streams was beautifully demonstrated in the national touring exhibition *Converting the Wilderness* (1979–80), for which curator Howard Tanner balanced colonial paintings with contemporary black and white photographs by Richard Stringer. A significant legacy of the exhibition was the launch of the Australian Garden History Society, which has carried forward the work of Australia's pioneer garden historians.

WHITEFELLA
DREAMING
(1980s–1990s)

The turbulent knotted figure of the scheme centripetally absorbs . . . disparate geographic and metaphoric centres, interlocking them at the heart of the project, as if to suggest that Australia's introspective contradictions are the paths along which its maturity and extroverted global citizenship are dependent.

Room 4.1.3, *Garden of Australian Dreams*, 2000 <www.room413.com.au>

AS the 1980s commenced, there was a collective longing by Australian horticultural tastemakers for European gardens and plants. Perhaps it was the gradual realisation that bush gardens were not maintenance-free. Or that floriculture depicted in European books and magazines had an undeniable and seemingly irresistible allure. This rejection of the environmental awakening of the previous two decades had profound effects on Australian gardens.

Suddenly the cottage garden was all the rage. Specialist nurseries seemed to spring up almost overnight, supplying a dizzying array of flowering plants, principally perennials but also including many long-cherished annuals. Establishing and maintaining long, billowy borders required considerable horticultural

expertise, and a new round of publishing filled the gap. The gardener's craft was re-established, fracturing its yoke to the rote needs of public parks and gardens. Garden visiting was popularised, giving a vicarious thrill for many, but often at the expense of independent thought.

This cottage garden revival also went hand in hand with a new awareness of Australian's historic gardens, and the need to rejuvenate these by complementing older and hardier tree and shrub plantings with the ephemeral delights of the flower garden. Picket fences, wire arbours, trellised summerhouses, and other accoutrements of the cottage garden raged out of control. Decoration proceeded well ahead of need or propriety. This often rendered the integrity of historic gardens at greater risk than if they had lain unidentified. Too often, authenticity was sacrificed at the expense of aesthetics. The Englishness of the herbaceous border teased with subtle charms, though, and plants that glowed under soft northern light and misty rain were often cruelly exposed down under—wet dreams for a dry country.

Just as suddenly as the cottage garden crossed from connoisseurship to commonplace, so the meteoric rise of television gardening beguiled the home gardener. The tag of lazy gardener was initially used in jest, but soon television programmes promising instantaneous transformations of homes and gardens were available at the push of a button. The arts of transplantation, roll-out and brush-on soon replaced climatic awareness, regionalism and inherited culture awareness. Much was promised but little was provided—style triumphed over substance.

Town planners and traffic engineers, too, were glued to their screens, still dreaming expansively about freeways and caring little for public transport. The suburban backyard, once treated as leftover space, was by now a hotly contested political and cultural site. The suburban garden and its vernacular joys—airbrushed to perfection by Howard Arkley—was also a site of debate. Much derided, this pocket of individual fantasy was challenged by urban consolidation. How could you have your cake and eat it?

The sensitivity of the suburban family home was epitomised by the debate over Aboriginal land rights. The Mabo decision of 1992 finally exposed the fallacy that Australia's land had belonged to no one before the arrival of Europeans. Responses to invasion and colonisation—depending on individual views of priority—provided a touchstone for middle Australia. Above all, the family freehold stood as a symbol of political power, a sacred site often invoked when Euro-centric notions of ownership were being debated. These complex and often conflicting notions of the land lay at the heart of a major new garden for the new millennium, the Garden of Australian Dreams at the National Museum of Australia.

The underhand chop | 1980

While the 1980s saw the rise of Landcare and a burgeoning interest in environmental history, it is ironic that 1980 marked the publication of James Preston's book *Racing Axemen: A History of Competitive Woodchopping* in Australia. As a sport, wood chopping provides thrilling action for its devotees, yet as a microcosm of environmental attitudes it has ominous overtones. In a decade when trees and politics collided, *Racing Axemen* illustrates a perfect metaphor for conflict over old-growth logging: the underhand chop.

The Underhand Chop

And to steal a line from the old Bard:

THERE IS SOMETHING ROTTEN IN THE GARDEN STATE.

We are in the grip of a long term economic and social blight with unemployment now greater in relative terms than anywhere else in Australia; our manufacturing industry is in decline; our youth increasingly leave the state to find employment elsewhere; our energy reserves are being exploited and squandered to serve the needs of multinational capital; and our social services such as transport are rapidly uprooted and thrown on the compost heap.

During all of this, the compost keeper, Dick Hamlet, sits upon his model of a glass pyramid casino muttering "Ian Smith or not Ian Smith - that is the question".

She's cactus, mate | 1981

Garden and plant analogies have long formed part of the Australian vernacular. We might go bananas, be up a gum tree, come up smelling of roses, or even—beyond the black stump—encounter a bananabender. 'Beats watering the garden' they might say, with justifiable irony, when a flood has rendered their garden cactus. In the hands of the Communist Party of Australia, Victoria's 'Garden State' tag took a similar linguistic twist. Reporting to comrades in 1981, Philip Herington parodied Shakespeare by declaring that 'Something is Rotten in the Garden State'. 'Compost Keeper Hamlet' (Premier Rupert Hamer)—who had only recently revived the Garden State title to promote the state's image—was assailed by Herington's ideological desire to 'Weed the Liberals from the Garden State'.

Medalling at Neerim | 1982

The shed may be corrugated iron with its strapping exposed, yet the concentration and rigour of the judges are worthy of an Olympic venue. Agricultural shows have been the lifeblood of Australia's rural communities since the mid-nineteenth century. The competitive aspect has been an important part of this annual ritual—as it is here at Neerim, in Gippsland—yet agricultural shows now have a much wider role in bringing rural and urban communities together in times of change.

The Garden
State presents:
Fitzroy | 1983

Outraged by the poor state of
playgrounds and the high traffic
pollution in the inner Melbourne
suburb of Fitzroy, one woman
artist from the Jillposters collective
was moved to design this poster
and risk the fines associated with
illegally billing it. Victoria may
have prided itself as the 'Garden
State', but Melbourne's inner
suburbs bore the brunt of the
pollution caused by leafy outer
suburbanites making their way
into the city.

Gardening by remote control | 1984

'Burke's Backyard', first broadcast on Sydney radio in 1984, marked the advent of 'infotainment' for the home-maker. Whereas gardening had previously been the subject of dedicated programmes, presenter Don Burke successfully linked house and garden with an informative yet entertaining approach. A year previously, Burke's book *The Lazy Gardener* had brought his relaxed style to the gardening public. Meldrum's cartoon on the book's cover depicted the author—ensconced in a hammock—gardening by remote control. Remote controls were soon directed by viewers in startling numbers to the highly successful transfer in 1987 of 'Burke's Backyard' to the national television screen.

Co-operatives | 1985

The anti-elitist decade of the 1970s saw the emergence of alternative lifestyles and the rise of collectivism. Funding and government support in the 1980s meant that community groups could establish volunteer-run organic food co-operatives. The driving philosophy behind such food 'co-ops' was the belief that it was everybody's right to participate in the shaping of the world in which they lived. Fruit and vegetable co-operatives, such as the one in Collingwood, an inner-city suburb of Melbourne, supported and promoted natural, chemical-free horticulture and the reduction of packaging.

Displaced Objects | 1986

This portrait of the artist's mother, Amelia Marczak, is from Chris Barry's series 'Displaced Objects I'. Having arrived in Australia from post-war Europe in 1950, Marczak worked in factories all her life. Her life-weary face is echoed and complemented by the complexity and textures of the surrounding roses. This poignant tribute is also rich in floral symbolism for those who can unlock its meanings.

Vegetal voyeurism | 1987

Who could resist a peek at Dame Elisabeth's white dahlias, or Jamie's latest courtyard, or anything at all by Paul? The tradition of visiting private gardens—as a mark of rank or friendship, or through organised openings—has existed for centuries. The advent of Australia's Open Garden Scheme, established in Victoria in 1987, has consolidated this pleasurable activity as part of our garden-making rituals. Today, the limits of curiosity and appreciation are being constantly raised as an increasingly greater range of gardens becomes open for admiration and emulation.

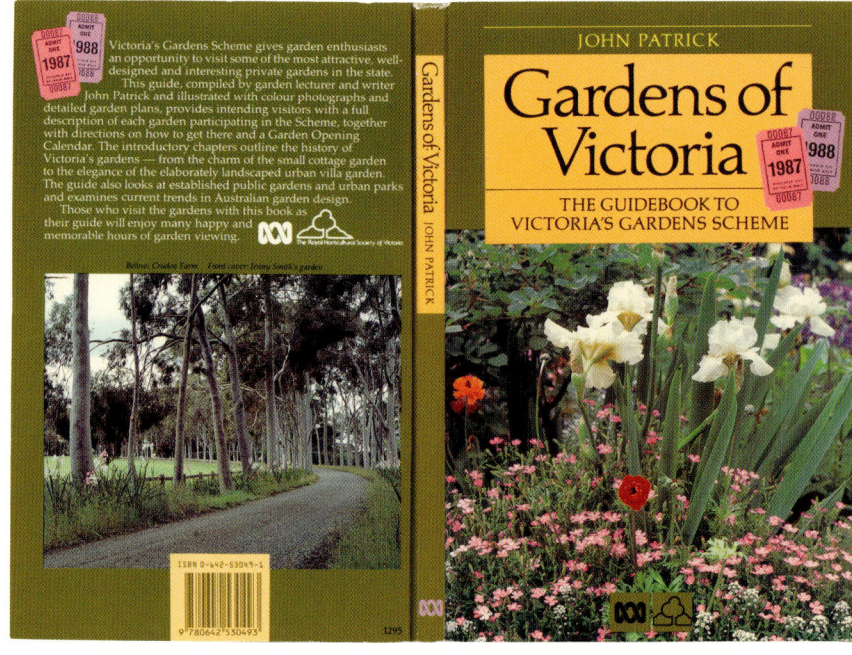

Horticultural 'isms and 'ologies | 1988

Whilst feng shui and its application to garden design achieved cult status in the 1990s, biodynamism captured the mood of the 1980s. This *1988 Astro Calendar of the Antipodes: Biodynamic moon planting guide & planetary rhythms* remains a powerful if ephemeral reminder of an age when horticultural cosmology ruled. (In fact, this was something of a second coming—almanacs and ephemeris had guided Australia's early agriculturists, who undertook much work in cool moonlit nights.) What, though, did the moon planters and rhythmic planetarians think of astro-turf?

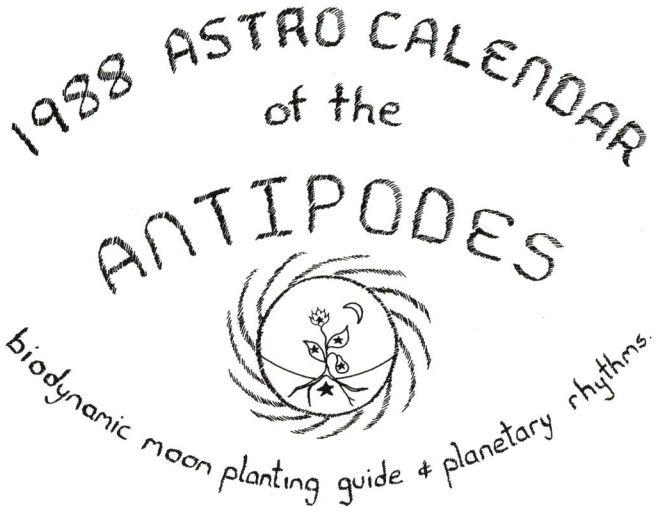

192

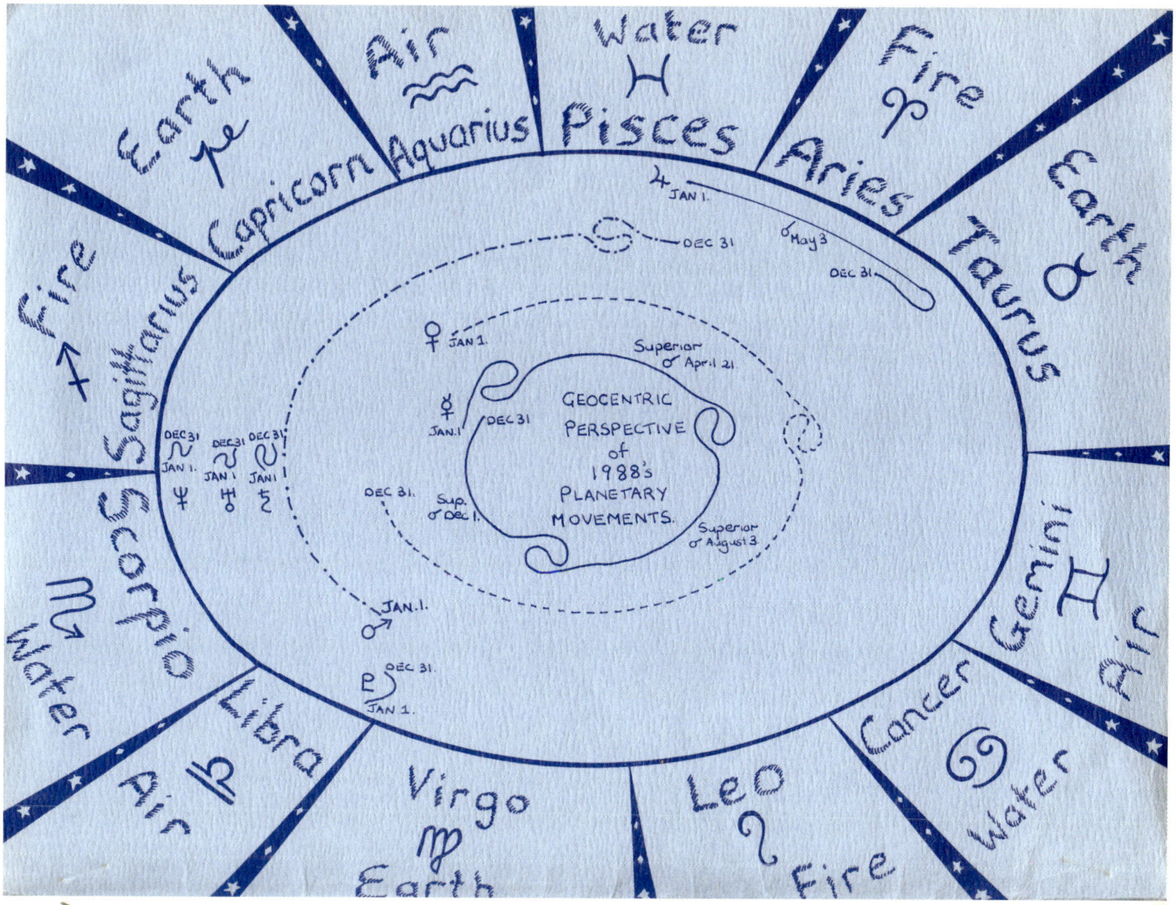

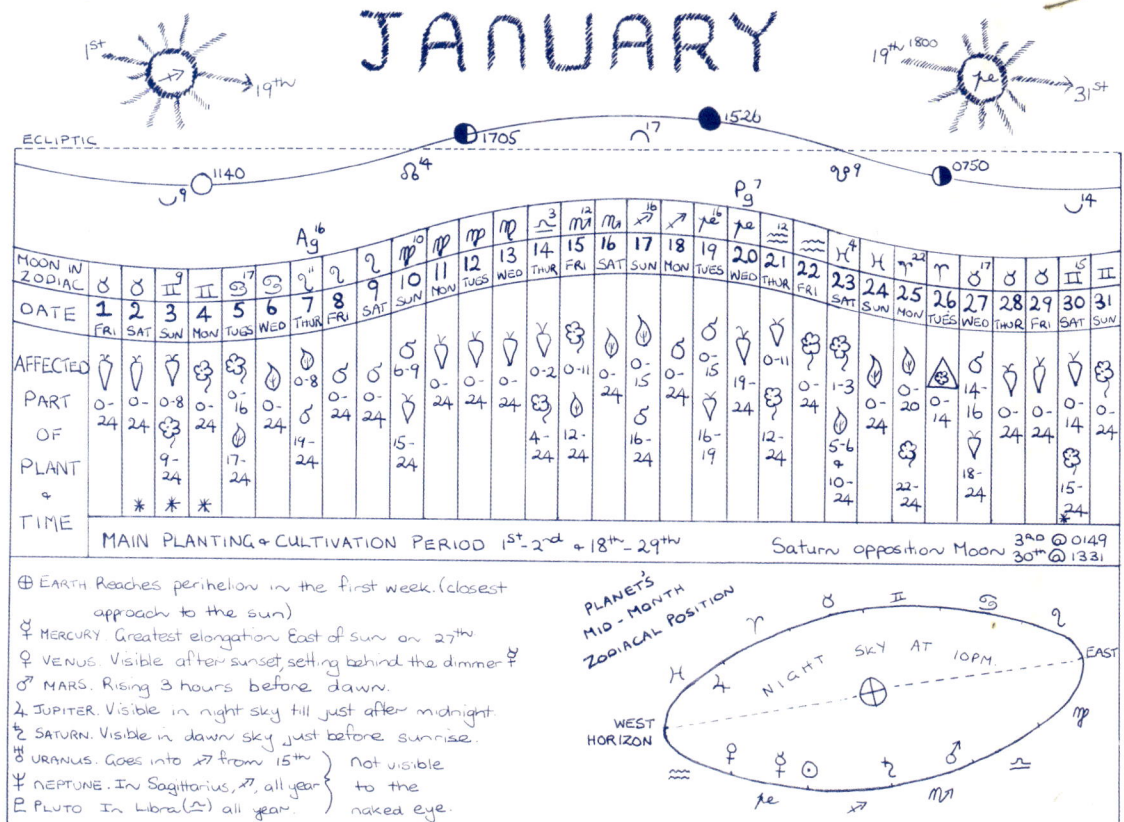

JANUARY

GEOCENTRIC PERSPECTIVE of 1988's PLANETARY MOVEMENTS.

Earth — Air — Water — Fire — Earth — Fire — Water — Air — Earth — Water

Capricorn · Aquarius · Pisces · Aries · Taurus · Gemini · Cancer · Leo · Virgo · Libra · Scorpio · Sagittarius

---

ECLIPTIC

MOON IN ZODIAC																														
DATE	1 FRI	2 SAT	3 SUN	4 MON	5 TUES	6 WED	7 THUR	8 FRI	9 SAT	10 SUN	11 MON	12 TUES	13 WED	14 THUR	15 FRI	16 SAT	17 SUN	18 MON	19 TUES	20 WED	21 THUR	22 FRI	23 SAT	24 SUN	25 MON	26 TUES	27 WED	28 THUR	29 FRI	30 SAT	31 SUN

AFFECTED PART OF PLANT & TIME

MAIN PLANTING & CULTIVATION PERIOD 1st–2nd & 18th–29th   Saturn opposition Moon 3rd @ 0149 / 30th @ 1331

⊕ EARTH Reaches perihelion in the first week. (closest approach to the sun)

☿ MERCURY. Greatest elongation East of sun on 27th

♀ VENUS. Visible after sunset, setting behind the dimmer ☿

♂ MARS. Rising 3 hours before dawn.

♃ JUPITER. Visible in night sky till just after midnight.

♄ SATURN. Visible in dawn sky just before sunrise.

♅ URANUS. Goes into ♐ from 15th) not visible

♆ NEPTUNE. In Sagittarius, ♐, all year) to the

♇ PLUTO In Libra (♎) all year) naked eye.

PLANET'S MID-MONTH ZODIACAL POSITION

NIGHT SKY AT 10PM

WEST HORIZON — EAST

Toorak backyard | 1989

'After the races, at home in the garden, a Toorak husband is punished by his wife because she was ignored by the social columnists.' Here Michael Leunig celebrates the sanctity of the Australian backyard as a place for private passions and domestic rituals. Such endearing depictions of closely observed behavioural eccentricities have become a much-loved feature of Leunig's work. Astute observers will notice parallels with that other Toorak matron of the turf, Mrs Pussington-Bigge, through whom Michael Leunig reveals essential truths about those from the eastern suburbs of Australian major capitals.

After the races, at home in the garden, a TOORAK husband is punished by his wife because she was ignored by the social columnists.

Perennial favourites | 1990

The 1980s and 1990s saw a peak of interest in perennial plants for the domestic garden. Lush swathes of colour in a seasonal succession—emulating the voluptuous herbaceous borders popularised in Edwardian times by Gertrude Jekyll—became a mark of horticultural excellence. In the Australian highlands this style still holds sway. For many elsewhere, though, the English look soon became one of disillusionment, as expensive plants succumbed to drought and neglect. Inventive minds adapted perennial planting schemes to suit prevailing climatic conditions, paving the way for a renewed interest in waterwise gardening.

Liberation from motor mowers | 1991

Those with weak arms know the frustration of wanting the lawn mowed, but being thwarted because they cannot summon the strength to start the motor mower. How liberating, then, is the hand mower. No more nagging, begging or cajoling to get a stronger member of the household to do it. Clipped lawn when you want it! Ruth Maddison's photographic series, *Women over 60*, challenges the conventional view of older women as housebound and dependent on their husbands and children. Here Fleur Finnie, aged 72, tends her garden with independence and pride.

Fleur Finnie, 72

It's annoying that my memory for names and faces is beginning to fail. And I walk more slowly—but I still do plenty of walking. I do the garden here at the flats, and I mow the lawn. I have to rug up because I feel the cold.

I'm a member of 108 organisations concerned with peace, social justice, conservation, health care of children, and care of animals. I'm a presenter of Race is Our Business on 3CR. I look after children in three families so their parents can get an evening out.

I go camping with the Down to Earth Confest at Christmas. I used to sleep on an inflatable mattress, then I changed to a collapsable bed. Now I sleep on the front seat of the car with a porta-potty on the floor beside me.

Terra nullius | 1992

The 1992 *Mabo* judgement—which led to the Commonwealth *Native Title Act 1993*—established that native title to land could be recognised by the common law of Australia. This acknowledged that Australia had not been *terra nullius* ('land belonging to no one') prior to European invasion, but that humans had occupied and managed this land for countless generations. The suburban back garden was an unwitting side player in this drama. This politically sensitive space was (incorrectly) represented by a coalition of the ill-informed, the prejudiced and the politically opportunistic as threatened by land rights claims. In Peter Nicholson's *Age* cartoon, Premier Kennett is depicted defending the sanctity of the backyard while Prime Minister Keating attempts to promote a wider view from outside the cosseted safety of its fence.

Suburban metaphor | 1993

Artist Howard Arkley explored the apparently banal rituals of suburban decoration—the path, the rows of mass-planted flowers, the patterns of the bricks—not to satirise the suburbs but to present them as metaphors for the Australian way of life. He rejected as romantic and unrealistic presentations of 'the bush' as the definitive Australian experience. Arkley's lurid colours were juxtaposed with mesmeric and often subliminal patterns, creating a familiar yet disconcerting representation of suburbia.

'England's Rose' | 1994

In life—as in death—Diana, Princess of Wales, was inextricably linked with floral symbolism. 'England's Rose' evoked her unmistakable aura of beauty and fragility. The pixillated princess of the poster cleverly transforms this symbolism into a splendid mid-1990s homage by using a photographic matrix of roses and other floral favourites. With the naming of *Rosa* 'Diana, Princess of Wales' (Jackson & Perkins, 1998) came a transubstantiation for the new age: 'Its ivory petals are overlaid with a clear pink blush, and its large, elegantly shaped buds open into graceful, full flowers with a sweet fragrance. It produces long stems perfect for cutting.'

Impending extinction | 1995

This photograph, from the series 'Disappearing Victoria', celebrates an innocent world once enlivened by milk bars, beauty salons and drive-ins. The photographer, Warren Kirk, has captured an Australian vernacular facing impending extinction. In this suburban image the proud garden owner has only blue and purple pots, taking us beyond the bounds of conventional taste. Kirk's photographs have a gentle artlessness that masks the care taken in the selection of his subject. His disarming images persuade us to believe that the extreme is the commonplace.

'You should see his back garden' | 1996

Posters send out powerful messages. We rarely associate such imagery with botanic gardens, yet few campaigns can have evoked such cultural complexities as this strident London Underground advertisement for the Royal Botanic Gardens, Kew. At first glance the portrayal of this Aboriginal man recalls the noble savage of the eighteenth century. The conquerors speak on his behalf—victors in armed struggles rarely forego that pleasure. Yet on a second glance, the back garden in question is given value by the intriguing juxtaposition of European and Indigenous perceptions. Qualities that were disparaged by early European explorers now seem to be recognised as part of a rich environment, managed for countless generations by its Indigenous custodians.

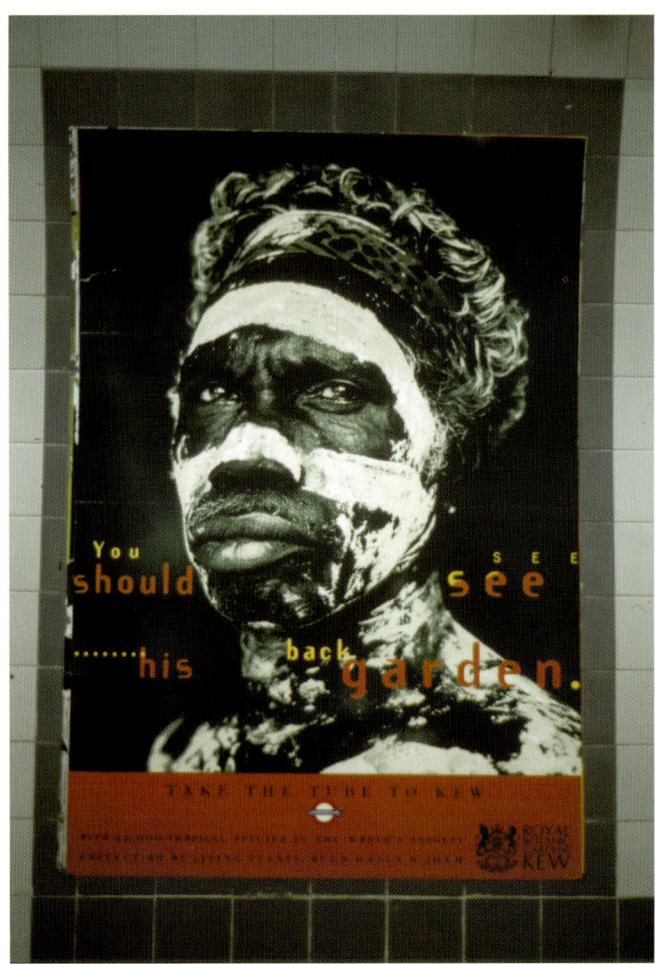

Garden of Australian Dreams | 1997

Perhaps the most challenging Australian garden of recent years is found in the courtyard of the National Museum of Australia in Canberra. The Garden of Australian Dreams is arguably the most thought-provoking example of nationalism in an Australian garden, or perhaps in any nation's realm of gardens. It was, indeed, intended by its designers to be 'a nationally symbolic microcosm'. Using opposite pairings (virtual : real, local : global, indigenous : exotic, academic : popular, natural : artificial, original : copy, celebratory : melancholic), the designers have created a rich fusion of layered fabric and meanings. Thus the grids of cartographers, surveyors and town planners are superimposed with conventional garden elements in a startling and unsettling mix.

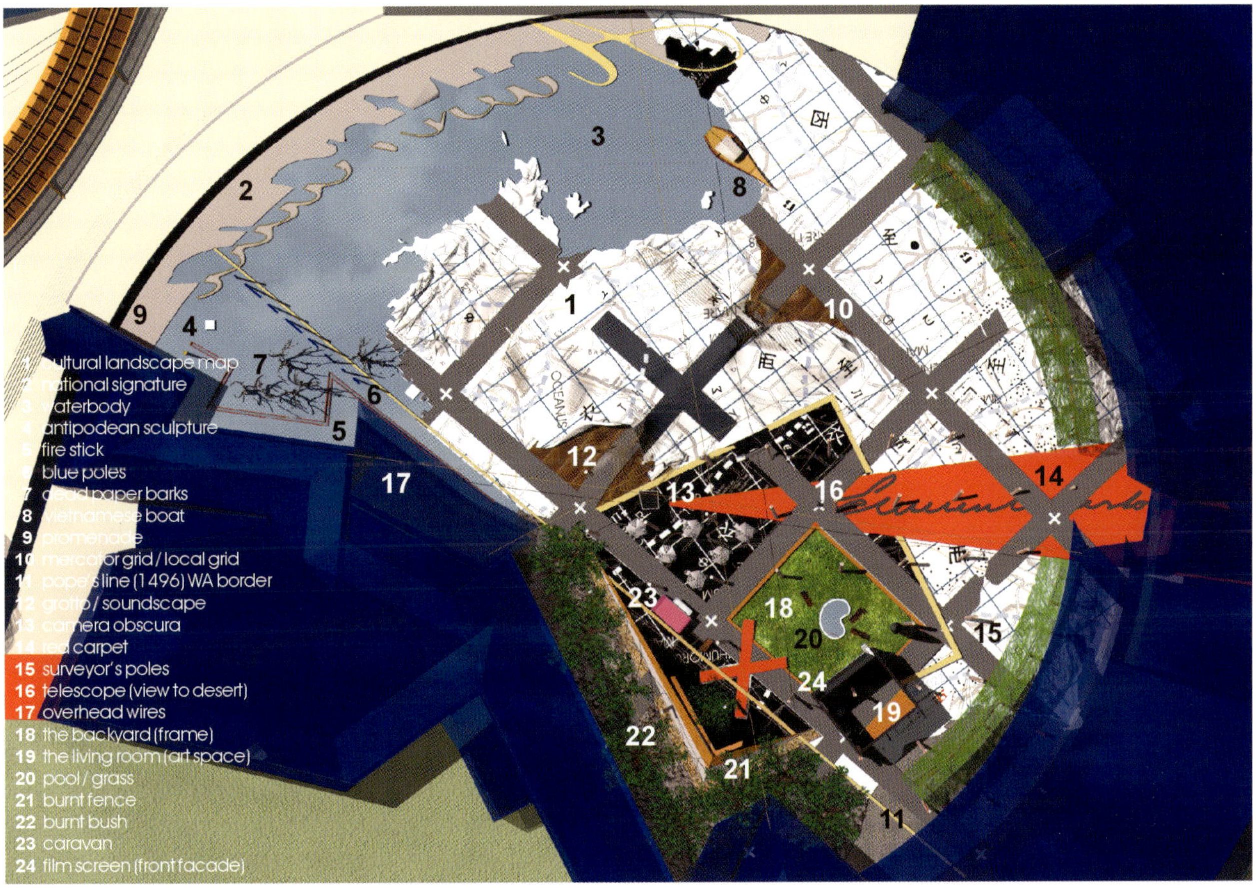

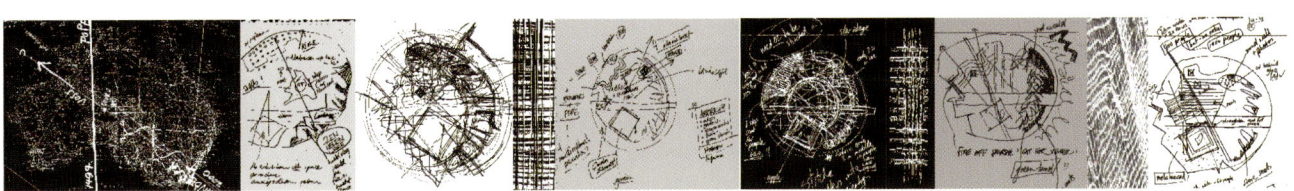

1. cultural landscape map
2. national signature
3. waterbody
4. antipodean sculpture
5. fire stick
6. blue poles
7. dead paper barks
8. vietnamese boat
9. promenade
10. mercator grid / local grid
11. pope's line (1496) WA border
12. grotto / soundscape
13. camera obscura
14. tea carpet
15. surveyor's poles
16. telescope (view to desert)
17. overhead wires
18. the backyard (frame)
19. the living room (art space)
20. pool / grass
21. burnt fence
22. burnt bush
23. caravan
24. film screen (front facade)

Wedding party | 1998

Inner city parks and gardens have long
been the scene for elaborate wedding party
gatherings. Here, in Kristin Headlam's
painting, Melbourne's Carlton Gardens
create a palatial backdrop for the bride
to play out her role as *Princess for a Day*.
Public parks are ordered spaces, designed for
the use and enjoyment of all. Often, however,
our love and sense of ownership of public
spaces see their use as though they were
private places, designed for the playing out
of intimate rituals.

Puckapunyal Safe Haven | 1999

Christobo Carvahlo, aged 12, from Taibese, Dili, here waters the vegetable garden at the Puckapunyal Safe Haven in Victoria. Lifted to safety from the violence in East Timor, the boy brings a universal message of hope through the redemptive power of gardening. Although only weeks into a residence of uncertain duration, the creation of a vegetable garden is here shown as a high priority in place-making, an act of humbling humanity in the face of widespread indifference to Carvahlo's plight.

GARDENING IN THE REPUBLICAN MANNER

(2000–)

> REPUBLIC . . . *A state in which the supreme power rests in the people and their elected representatives or officers, as opposed to one governed by a king or similar ruler; a commonwealth.*
> REPUBLICAN . . . *Of or belonging to a republic . . .*
>
> (*Shorter Oxford English Dictionary*, 1972)

JUST as the nineteenth century ended with debate over federation of the Australian colonies, so the twentieth ended with public engagement over the need for and nature of any future republic. The referendum setback for advocates of an Australian republic is now history—but what of future debate? Will there be such a thing as a Republican style of gardening, as there was a Federation style of architecture and gardening in the early 1900s? And if so, what form would this take?

The nature of a republic is that of power resting with the people and their elected leaders. It also implies a certain degree of equality among its members. Thus far, the aptness of a republican analogy to gardening is plausible, for there has been a major shift recently in the revaluing of public sentiment.

The social value of gardens, especially of public parks and gardens, is now commonly recognised, and often forms a determinant in future planning for these civic places. While some tiers of government may still view public land as potential development sites, opportunities for determined indifference to unified voices of concern may soon be a thing of the past. Who would now alter an urban square or a botanic garden without first consulting relevant communities of interest? The very nature of republicanism is that of belonging to the community.

People would figure strongly in any Republican garden style. The needs, aspirations and pleasures of people have influenced garden history in profound ways, yet at times the individual has been subordinated by the state. Think of the totalitarian aspects of grand formal gardens and landscapes, or the social consequences of the English landscape garden, where whole villages were swept aside, recalled so poignantly in 1770 by Oliver Goldsmith's poem 'The Deserted Village'. But we see signs of hope in the revaluing of social aspects of gardens—community gardens, gardens for therapy and rehabilitation, bush-food gardens as a focus for reconciliation with the land and its Indigenous peoples. This aspect of Republican gardening would require encouragement but little modification.

Perhaps a defining moment for Republican gardening has already come with the dramatically changed attitudes of water utilities. The pendulum has swung from the promotion of abundance to advocacy for conservation, and the good of the country has been placed ahead of private wants. So far, water has been a bastion against privatisation but vigilance is necessary. Wise counsel may be required for this life-sustaining necessity to be kept above fiscal temptation of the Crown and her representatives. Water already forms a major issue for twenty-first century environmentalism. Aridity, salinity and run-off are now key planks in debate over the environment. If environmentalism can be viewed as a national imperative—as it increasingly is—then nationalism is as likely to result in a new public park taking the form of a wetland than a rose-bordered lawn, or even a bush garden.

Attitudes to fence and boundaries will be a key to any Republican garden style. The formal grid, which swept across Australia with such imperial abandon, generated numerous fences and boundaries. But in many manifestations, these have had negative, melancholy or defensive qualities. Think of the rabbit-proof fence and the recent film of that name. Environmental musicians Jon Rose and Hollis Taylor, in their recent performance 'Bowing Fences', performed literally by using cello bows on the taut wires of fences. During their travels they pondered the metaphysical and political notions of boundaries. They wanted to play the security fence surrounding Pine Gap defence installation but were denied access. 'We'd love to play Woomera', they commented of the former-nuclear-facility-turned-detention-centre. 'That is some fence.'

Whimsy in the garden | 2000

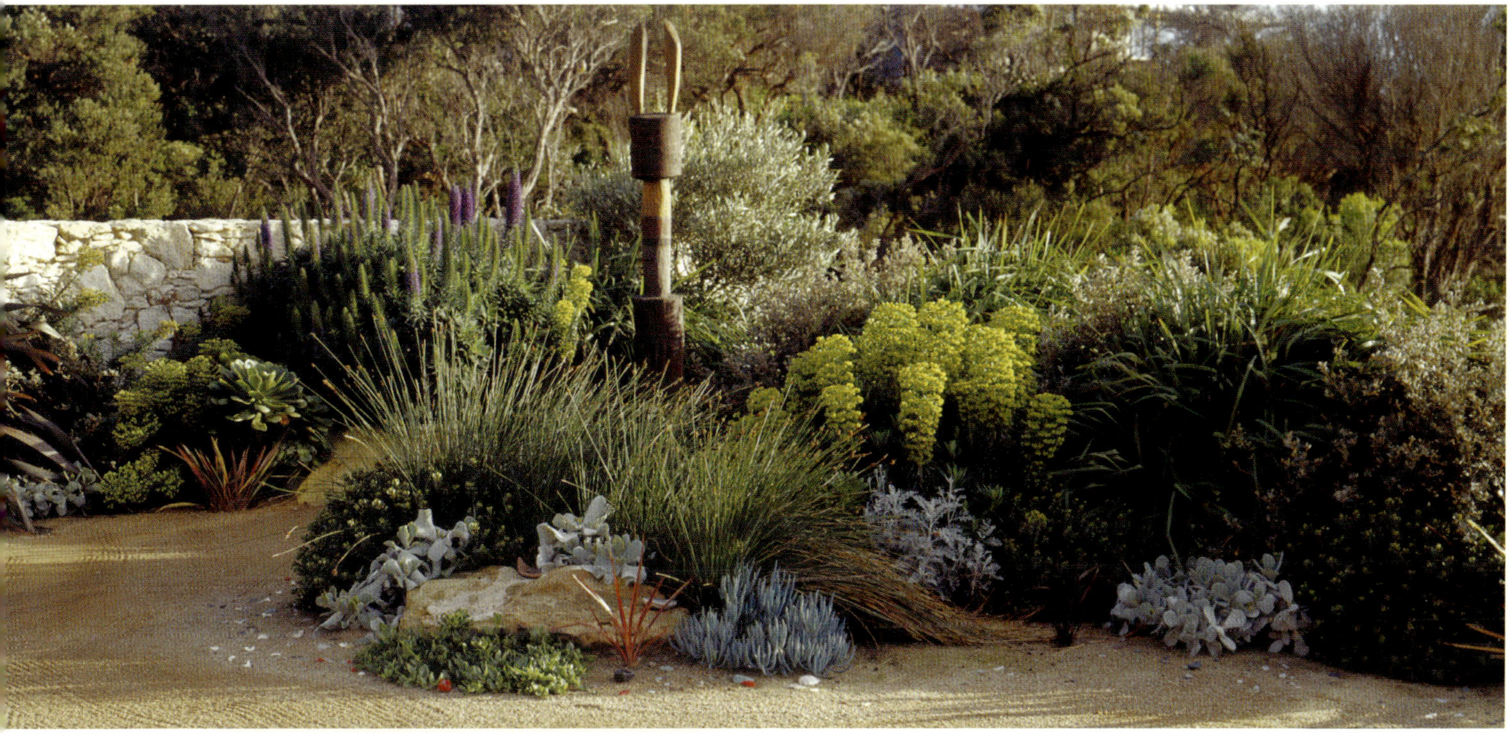

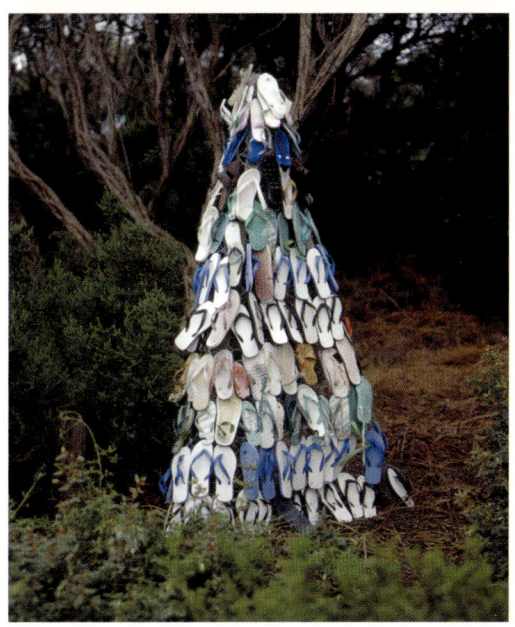

There is reason for optimism amongst Australian gardeners. Fresh ideas often spring from adversity—extremes of climate have, for instance, generated many horticultural responses. Fiona Brockhoff's Mornington Peninsula garden draws on its exposed seaside setting for inspiration. Elegant fusions of architectural forms with inventive plant combinations provide a clear sense of place. Yet in all of this, the garden does not take itself too seriously. Plants jostle for space with whimsical conceits. A thong tree, born of restless beachcombing, provides a striking specimen of uncertain taxonomy yet clearly indigenous origins. The art of the garden is alive.

Terror incognita | 2001

The bombing of New York's World Trade Center in 2001 unleashed far-reaching consequences. Here John Spooner combines garden imagery with those fateful moments to expose an Australian paradox. As a nation we seek to punish the perpetrators of such terror, yet we repel the very people we are intent on liberating. Published in Melbourne's *Age* newspaper to commemorate the first anniversary of the bombing—with our troops in Afghanistan but not yet Iraq—Australia looks out anxiously from within its white picket fence into an unknown and uncertain future. The well-armed gnome and his furry friend guard sacred domestic treasures. The garden has again become the *Hortus conclusus*, or enclosed garden of the ancients.

Heritage of the future | 2002

New outer suburbs carved out of rural paddocks are creating a rich lode of gardening—and architectural—heritage for future generations. This is as it has always been in Australian cities. It is just the time delay between development and veneration that is narrowing. Of course this elapse only exists for those on the outside, beyond contemporary taste. To insiders, these new outer urban gardens replete with roll-out turf and pop-up sprinklers are the Gardenesque delights of their heart's desire.

Victoria–Not the Place for G.E. | 2003

Graphically linking Victoria's 'Garden State' and 'The Place to Be' number-plate mottos, this poster targets the genetic engineering of food crops. Such environmental campaigns highlight the inherent weakness of trials involving genetically modified canola. Conducted with indecent haste and assessed in splendid isolation, they will determine outcomes that may not become apparent for centuries. How does a paddock of canola stay within the puny artificial boundary of fences? ask its opponents. Do crop trials mysteriously remain outside a food chain dependent on the smallest insects and micro-organisms? But the horticultural and agricultural industries are powerful. Doubtless money will talk.

'After the Fire' | 2004

Artist John Wolseley draws inspiration from the environment, its ceaseless rhythms and cycles swirling through scribbled notes and across paper. The duration of this movement is of crucial importance to his work—as it is for gardeners. In this recent lithograph entitled 'After the Fire' (2004), Wolseley quotes the English poet-artist William Blake: 'The fresh earth beams forth ten thousand thousand springs of Life'. The message is a timeless one. After the fire, epicormic shoots sprout from blackened trunks, seeds again swirl, and the cycles of nature continue performing their ceaseless regenerative rituals.

thousand springs of Life' (Blake)   John Wolseley
                                                        2004

GUIDE TO SOURCES

Perhaps the most enjoyable part of any project is the initial thrill of discovery. A great joy in the preparation of this book, and the exhibition on which it is based, has been the privilege of free access to the collections of the State Library of Victoria. The initial focus was to examine as many works as possible in the field of botany (Dewey catalogue numbers 580–588), horticulture (630–635), and landscape gardening (712–718). This revealed an unexpected richness of books and other works in diverse formats from the smallest pamphlet to the largest elephant folio. This joy of discovery is available to anyone via the electronic catalogue of the State Library of Victoria, and other major libraries. Those items selected for inclusion in this book are listed at the end of this Guide.

What the catalogue cannot adequately reveal is the richness of the State Library of Victoria's manuscript and pictorial holdings. Seldom are these are individual works, or items with discrete titles, capable of easy cataloguing. Each document or image reveals fresh information to the viewer, and generic labelling is seldom possible. To aid those who seek further detailed information on Australian gardens and gardening, the following list provides a guide to the major collections of potential interest.

COLLECTIONS

Australian Garden History Society

The Australian Garden History Society was established in 1980. It is administered by a National Management Committee, with branches responsible for activities at a state and territory level. Its mission is to 'be the leader in concern for and conservation of significant cultural landscapes and gardens through committed, relevant and sustainable actions'.

Scope | Minutes and other records of the National Management Committee (1980–) and Victorian Branch (1983–) are being progressively transferred to the State Library of Victoria
Extent | one box
Australian Manuscripts Collection, MS 11978

Bateman, Edward La Trobe

Edward La Trobe Bateman (1816–97), ornamental gardener, artist, and designer, was active in Australia during 1852–69. His love of the Australian flora is evident in many of his designs.

Scope | Plan of Wooriwyrite Station belonging to Thomas Shaw Junior, showing the site of a proposed house and grounds as laid out by Bateman; enlarged but undated plan of proposed house and gardens as laid out by Bateman; drawings of Jolimont and its gardens by Bateman
Extent | one plan; two volumes; collection of drawings
Gift of Mrs Shea-Simonds and Captain Charles La Trobe, via Mr G. M. Prendergast, 1924
Australian Manuscripts Collection, MS 10182 and MS 12248; Pictures Collection, H 98.135/1–22

Brown, Elizabeth

Collection of 144 colour transparencies by photographer Elizabeth Brown documenting the gardens at Belmont, Mooleric, Trawalla, Turkeith and Wombat Park.

Purchased 2000; works commissioned by the State Library of Victoria under the Garden History Archive joint initiative of the Library and the Australian Garden History Society (Victorian Branch)
Pictures Collection, H 2001.15/1–144

Davis, Mervyn

Mervyn Twynam Davis (1917–85), landscape architect, noted for her large-scale institutional designs, was a founder of the Australian Institute of Landscape Architects.

Scope | Collection of landscape and garden designs by Davis for 44 private and commercial commissions, 1960–79
Extent | 68 garden plans, 710 slides
Gift of Miss Mervyn Davis, 1980
Pictures Collection, H 42446–492 (LTAD 48); H 42449/1–710

Ford, Gordon

Gordon Craig Ford (1918–99), landscape designer, was a pioneer in the 1950s of the Australian bush garden movement. His philosophies are demonstrated in Gordon Ford: The Natural Australian Garden *(1999).*

Scope | Collection of garden plans by Ford, *c*.1954–99
Extent | 153 garden plans
Gift of Mrs Gwen Ford, 2001
Pictures Collection, H 2001.309/1–153 (LTAD 101)

Galbraith, Jean

Jean Galbraith (1906–99), botanist, naturalist, writer and gardener, made a major contribution to the popular appreciation of Australian flora. Her life is detailed in Anne Latreille's book Kindred Spirits *(1999).*

Scope | Correspondence and writings of Galbraith, including stories, verse and magazine articles, many concerning nature and its conservation; miscellaneous diaries, notebooks and exercise books, 1900–90; drafts of *A Gardener's Year* (published 1987)
Extent | 15 boxes
Gift of Miss Jean Galbraith, 1988; the balance was donated after Galbraith's death through her estate
Australian Manuscripts Collection, MS 12637

Gibson, Emily

Emily Matilda ('Millie') Gibson (1887–1974), horticultural journalist, lecturer, and landscape designer, was a pioneer of industrial landscape design in Australia. The majority of her designs were created for architects Stevenson and Turner.

Scope | Garden designs by Gibson, *c.*1920–40
Extent | Approximately 20 drawings of garden designs
Gift of Stevenson and Turner, 1994
Pictures Collection, Stevenson and Turner Collection, LTAD 110

Glass, Peter

Peter Glass (1917–97), artist, conservationist, and landscape architect, worked in the 1950s with influential environmental designer Alistair Knox, and from the 1960s practised independently and with Gordon Ford creating gardens in a natural style.

Scope | Collection of garden plans by Glass, *c.*1960–90; papers relating to Glass's career as a landscape architect, including sketch book and certificate of membership from Australian Institute of Landscape Architects
Extent | Approximately 250 garden plans; one box of papers
Gift of Mrs Cecile Glass, 1999
Pictures Collection, PA 99/4; Australian Manuscripts Collection, PA 99/87

Guilfoyle, William

William Robert Guilfoyle (1840–1912), landscape designer, was director of Melbourne Botanic Gardens from 1873 until 1909. He was responsible for the design of these and many other Victorian gardens.

Scope | Letter, 4 May 1875, to Dr Bleasdale, attached to 'rough draft of plan for the laying out of grounds in front of Public Library, by Director of Botanical Gardens'; papers related to Guilfoyle showing his involvement in Ramsay family properties
Extent | Plan, letter, and sketches
Australian Manuscripts Collection, MS 11133; Andrew Mitchell Ramsay papers, MS 11021; Pictures Collection, H 5474

Hammond, Eric

Eric Herbert Hammond (1898–1992), established Victoria's leading landscape contracting business in 1922 and was active for sixty years. He constructed many gardens for Edna Walling.

Scope | Company journals of E. H. Hammond, 1934–83; banner
Extent | 12 volumes; one banner
Australian Manuscripts Collection, PA 02/06

Hill, Ian

Collection of fifteen black and white photographs by photographer Ian Hill (b.1962) documenting the garden at Claremont, Newtown, Vic.

Commissioned 1999; works commissioned by the State Library of Victoria under the Garden History Archive joint initiative of the Library and the Australian Garden History Society (Victorian Branch)
Pictures Collection, H 99.216/1–15

Isaac, Cyril Everett

Cyril Everett Isaac (1884–1965), educator, horticulturist, parliamentarian and conservationist, was active in the school gardening movement in Victoria and a founder of the 'Save the Forests Campaign'.

Scope | Papers of C. E. Isaac, 1910–65, comprising biographical notes, printed speeches, seed catalogues, newspaper clippings and other printed material; diary of a fact-finding tour of Canada, the U.K. and the U.S.A. undertaken in 1956; material related to Victorian State Schools' Horticultural Society and Natural Resources Conservation League of Victoria
Extent | three boxes
Australian Manuscripts Collection, MS 12733

Lang, Thomas

Thomas Lang (1815–96), was amongst Victoria's leading nursery proprietors and seed merchants in the nineteenth century, following his early success in this field on the Ballarat goldfields.

Scope | Records of plants received into Lang's Ballarat nursery, 1856–67
Extent | one manuscript volume
Australian Manuscripts Collection, MS 10976

Pool, Lyn

Collection of thirty colour transparencies by photographer Lyn Pool (b.1963) documenting the restoration and condition of the gardens at Turkeith and Mooleric, Mount Gellibrand, Vic., both designed by William Guilfoyle

Commissioned 2002; works commissioned by the State Library of Victoria under the Garden History Archive joint initiative of the Library and the Australian Garden History Society (Victorian Branch)
Pictures Collection, H 2003.37/1–30

Sangster, William

William Sangster (1831–1910), landscape gardener and nursery proprietor, a partner in the well-known firm of Taylor and Sangster, was amongst Victoria's leading landscape designers in the nineteenth century.

Scope | Three notebooks, 1852–1933, containing gardening notes, journals describing activities at Como and Mount Pleasant, South Yarra, and at Taylor & Sangster's nursery at Mount Macedon, lists of plants and seeds, and poems; photographs, including portraits; a family register, 1856–90; prize certificates issued by the Horticultural Society of Victoria, 1860–65 and others undated; a pass to the Melbourne International Exhibition, 1880; share certificates for the Metropolitan Bank Limited, 1887–97; a certificate of right of burial in the St Kilda General Cemetery, 1894; published catalogue of choice plants, 1912; a bankbook, 1920–25; and a probate document re the estate of Andrew Coles Brock Sangster, 1925
Extent | one box
Australian Manuscripts Collection, MS 13350

Shepherd, William Henry

William Henry Shepherd was a fruit tree nurseryman in Somerville on Victoria's Mornington Peninsula. His father, William Andrew Shepherd, worked for a time at the Melbourne Botanic Gardens.

Scope | Diaries of William Henry Shepherd, 1884–1900; also loose sheets including memoranda, lists of food, letters, and brief family tree dated 30 March 1992
Extent | 18 volumes
Australian Manuscripts Collection, PA 01/19 and MS 9011

Stones, Ellis

Ellis ('Rocky') Stones (1895–1975), landscape designer, commenced his career in the mid-1930s constructing gardens for Edna Walling. He widely recognised for his designs using a natural style, published in his book Australian Garden Design *(1971).*

Scope | Garden plans, photographs and papers by and relating to Stones, c.1959–70
Extent | Approximately 300 garden plans, 4 photographic albums, and 3 boxes of papers
Gift of Ellis Stones's estate, 1991
Pictures Collection, LTAD 35 and PA/2004/4

Tindale, Ruth

Plant enthusiast Ruth Tindale and her husband George lived in the Dandenong Ranges, and their garden at Sherbrooke, Vic., is now open to the public as the George Tindale Memorial Garden.

Scope | Papers, 1920–75; Australian and overseas seed and plant catalogues and price lists, 1927–2001, including manuscript notes, lists and annotations
Extent | 4 boxes
Australian Manuscripts Collection, PA 02/105 and MS 13382

Victorian Horticultural Improvement Society

The Victorian Horticultural Improvement Society, established in 1859, catered for working gardeners, drawing a distinction between itself and the (Royal) Victorian Horticultural Society, its more elite rival.

Scope | Records and minutes of meetings of the Society held between 1859 and 1911; essay book containing transcripts of talks given at Society meetings
Extent | 5 volumes
Australian Manuscripts Collection, MS 12521

Walling, Edna

Edna Walling (1895–1973), landscape designer, conservationist, writer and photographer, was amongst Australia's best-known garden designers. Her legacy of gardens, writings, plans, and photographs continues to inspire many gardeners.

Scope | Papers, landscape designs and photographs by Walling, c.1935–60
Extent | Approximately 4000 photographs, 300 garden plans and numerous manuscript boxes
Gift of Mrs Barbara Barnes, 1993–99; Gift of Mrs V. M. Burston, 1993–94; Gift of Mr Glen Wilson, 1991 and 2001; Gift of Ms Mervyn Davis, 1978 and 1980 (the latter with Miss Daphne Pearson); Gift of Mr Peter Watts, 1992; Gift of Mrs. C. M. Howell, 1979
Australian Manuscripts Collection, PA 01/106, MS 10725, MS 408, and MS 13048; Pictures Collection H 97.150/1–2344, H 2001.180/1–483, H 2001.247/1–75, H 98.120/1–580, H 99.120/1–600, H 96.150/1–994, H 93.146/1–110 (photographs); H 97.270/1–154 (LTAD 86), H 2001.240/1–5 (LTAD 86), H 40465–40613 (LTAD 47), H 42826–42827 (LTAD 79) (garden plans)

Wilson, Glen

Glen Wordsworth Wilson (b.1927), landscape designer, is a leading advocate for designs that respond to the Australian environment. His design philosophy is detailed in Landscaping with Australian Plants *(1975).*

Scope | Collection of garden plans by Wilson, c.1957–2000
Extent | 188 garden plans
Gift of Mr Glen Wilson, 2003
Pictures Collection, H 2003.11/1–188 (LTAD 10

All items from State Library of Victoria unless otherwise indicated

p.ii   George Brookshaw, *Pomona Britannica, or a Collection of the Most Esteemed Fruits at present cultivated in this country*, the author, London, 1804–12 (detail of plate 20).

p.vi   H. A. James, *Handbook of Australian Horticulture*, Part 12, Turner and Henderson, Sydney, 1892. Private collection.

p.viii James Maddock, *The Florist's Directory: A Treatise on the Culture of Flowers*, new edition (by Samuel Curtis), John Harding, London, 1810.

p.1   Humphry Repton, *Observations on the Theory and Practice of Landscape Gardening . . .* , J. Taylor, London, 1802–05.

p.3   Buda gardener, Walter Cross, clipping the cypress hedge, *c.* 1920 (detail). Photograph courtesy Buda Historic Home and Garden, Castlemaine, Vic.

[1800]   Henry Godfrey, *November 1st / 43 Loubras*, 1843. Watercolour. Pictures Collection, State Library of Victoria, H 90.53/1.

1801   James Grant, *The Narrative of a Voyage of Discovery, Performed in His Majesty's Vessel the Lady Nelson . . . in the years 1800, 1801 and 1802, to New South Wales*, T. Egerton, London, 1803.

1802   *Descriptions Pittoresques de Jardins du Goût le Plus Moderne. Ornées de XXVIII planches*, Voss et Compagnie, Leipzig, 1802.

1803   James Fleming, *A Journal to and from King Island, &c., &c, &c.* 1803. Journal. State Records, New South Wales, SZ994.

1804   Jacques-Julien Houtou de Labillardière, *Novæ Hollandiæ Plantarum Specimen*, Dominæ Huzard, Paris, 1804–06.

1805   Humphry Repton, *Observations on the Theory and Practice of Landscape Gardening . . .* , J. Taylor, London, 1802–05.

1806   J.C. Loudon, *A Treatise on Forming, Improving, and Managing Country Residences . . .* , Longman, Hurst, Rees & Orme, London, 1806.

1807   Robert John Thornton, *New Illustration of the Sexual System of Carolus Von Linnaeus . . . and the Temple of Flora, or Garden of Nature, being Picturesque, Botanical, Coloured Plates, of Select Plants, Illustrative of the same*, Printed, for the Publisher, by T. Bensley, London, 1799–1807.

1808   William Gilpin *Remarks on Forest Scenery, and Other Woodland Views, Relative Chiefly to Picturesque Beauty . . .* , 3rd ed., T. Cadell & W. Davies, London, 1808. Private collection.

1809   *Curtis's Botanical Magazine; or Flower-Garden Displayed: in which The most Ornamental Foreign Plants, Cultivated in the Open Ground, the Green-House, and the Stove, are accurately represented in their natural colours . . .* , volume XXXI, Sherwood, Neely, & Jones, London, 1810.

1810   James Maddock, *The Florist's Directory: A Treatise on the Culture of Flowers*, new edition (by Samuel Curtis), John Harding, London, 1810.

1811   John Cushing, *The Exotic Gardener; In which the Management of the Hot-House, Green-House and Conservatory, is Fully and Clearly Delineated According to Modern Practice . . .* , Graisberry & Campbell, Dublin, 1811. Richard Clough collection, Sydney.

1812   George Brookshaw, *Pomona Britannica, or a Collection of the Most Esteemed Fruits at present cultivated in this country. . .* , the author, London, 1804–12.

1813   Aimé Bonpland, *Description des plantes rares cultivées à Malmaison et à Navarre*, P. Didot l'ainé, Paris, 1812–17.

1814   Walter Nicol, *The Gardener's Kalendar; or, Monthly Directory of Operations in Every Branch of Horticulture*, 3rd ed., Printed by David Willison, Edinburgh, for Archibald Constable and Company, Edinburgh; Longman, Hurst, Rees, Orme & Brown, London; John Cumming, Dublin, 1814. Private collection.

1815   Sydenham Edwards, *The Botanical Register: Consisting of Coloured Figures of Exotic Plants, Cultivated in British Gardens; with their History and Mode of Treatment*, volume 1, James Ridgway, London, 1815.

1816   Colleen Morris, *Middle Garden, Royal Botanic Gardens, Sydney*, colour transparency, 2004. Courtesy of the photographer.

1817   Conrad Loddiges & Sons, *The Botanical Cabinet Consisting of Coloured Delineations of Plants from all Countries, with a short Account of each, directions for Management &c. &c.*, volume 1, John & Arthur Arch, John Hatchard, C. Loddiges & Sons, and G. Cooke, London, 1817.

1818   A. Risso & A. Poiteau, *Histoire Naturelle des Orangers*, Mme Hérissant le Doux et des Musées Royaux, Paris, 1818.

1819   William Roxburgh, *Plants of the Coast of Coromandel, Selected from Drawings and Descriptions presented to the Hon. Court of Directors of the East India Company. Published, by their order, under the direction of the Right Honourable Sir Joseph Banks*, Printed by W. Bulmer & Co., for G. & W. Nicol, 1795–1819.

1820   J. J. Bernhardi & H. L. W. Völker (eds), *Christian Reichardt's . . . Land- und Garten-Schatz in fünf Theilen . . .* , 6th ed., in der keyserschen Buchhandlung, Erfurt, 1820.

1821   William Cobbett, *The American Gardener; or A Treatise on the Situation, Soil, Fencing and Laying-Out of Gardens; on the Making and Managing of Hot-Beds and Green-Houses; and on the Propagation and Cultivation of the several sorts of Vegetables, Herbs, Fruits and Flowers*, stereotype edition, C. Clement, London, 1821. Monash University Rare Books Collection.

1822   Maria Jackson, *The Florist's Manual, or, Hints for the Construction of a Gay Flower-Garden . . .* , 2nd ed., Henry Colburn, London, 1822. Private collection.

1823 Henry Phillips, *Sylva Florifera: The Shrubbery Historically and Botanically Treated, with Observations on the Formation of Ornamental Plantations, and Picturesque Scenery*, Longman, Hurst, Rees, Orme, & Brown, London, 1823.

—J.C. Loudon, *An Encyclopaedia of Gardening; comprising the theory and practice of horticulture, floriculture, arboriculture, and landscape-gardening, including all the latest improvements . . .* , revised edition, Longman, Rees, Orme, Brown, Green & Longman, London, 1834.

1824 *Australasian Pocket Almanack, for the Year of Our Lord*, 1824, R. Howe, Government Printer, Sydney, 1824.

1825 John Shute Duncan, *Botano-Theology, An Arranged Compendium, Chiefly from Smith, Keith, and Thomson*, Sold by J. Parker, Oxford; J. Murray, and C. & J. Rivington, London, 1825.

—Gilbert White, *The Natural History and Antiquities of Selborne*, new ed., Nathaniel Cooke, London, 1853 (detail).

1826 J.C. Loudon (conductor), *The Gardener's Magazine and Register of Rural & Domestic Improvement*, Longman, Rees, Orme, Brown, & Green, London, 1826–44.

1827 Robert Sweet, *Flora Australasica; or A Selection of Handsome, or Curious Plants, natives of New Holland, and the South Sea Islands*, James Ridgway, London, 1827–8.

1828 Carl Ludwig Blume, *Flora Javæ nec non insularum adjacentium*, J. Frank, Bruxelles, 1828–51.

1829 Richard Stringer, *Killymoon, Tasmania*, 1982. Photograph. Courtesy of the photographer.

—Edward Kemp, *How to Lay Out a Garden: intended as a General Guide in Choosing, Forming, or Improving an Estate, (from a quarter of an acre to a hundred acres in extent) with reference to both design to execution*, 3rd ed., Bradbury & Evans, London, 1864.

1830 'Specification of Edward [sic] Budding. Machine for Mowing Lawns &c. A. D. 1830, No. 5990' in *Specifications of Patents: Old Law*, volume CCXVII, 1830, Great Seal Patent Office, London, 1853.

—J.C. Loudon, *An Encyclopaedia of Gardening; comprising the theory and practice of horticulture, floriculture, arboriculture, and landscape-gardening, including all the latest improvements . . .* , revised edition, Longman, Rees, Orme, Brown, Green & Longman, London, 1834.

1831 Nathaniel Wallich, *Plantae Asiaticae Rariores; or Descriptions and Figures of a select number of unpublished East Indian plants*, Treuttel & Würtz, Treuttel Jun. & Richter, London; Treuttel & Würtz, Paris; Treuttel & Würtz, Strasburgh, 1830–2.

1832 Aylmer Bourke Lambert, *A Description of the Genus Pinus, with Directions relative to cultivation and Remarks on the uses of the several species: also Descriptions of many of the new species of the family of Coniferæ*, Messrs Weddell, London, 1832.

—J.C. Loudon, *Arboretum et Fruticetum Britannicum; or The Trees and Shrubs of Britain, Native and Foreign, Hardy and Half-Hardy, Pictorially and Botanically Delineated, and Scientifically and Popularly Described . . .* , 2nd ed., the author, London, 1844.

1833 Ray Joyce, *Panshanger, Tasmania*, 2003. Colour transparency. Courtesy of the photographer.

1834 Edward Henty, *Journal: Portland Bay*, 1834–9. Australian Manuscripts Collection, State Library of Victoria, MS 118A.

1835 Wilbraham Frederick Evelyn Liardet, *J. P. Fawkner's first house*, 1875. Watercolour, ink and pencil. Pictures Collection, State Library of Victoria, H 28250/1.

1836 Thomas Mawe & John Abercrombie, *Every Man his Own Gardener. The Complete Gardener, or Gardener's Calendar of Work to be done in the Kitchen, Fruit, Flower, Forcing Garden, &c. for every month of the year . . .* , revised edition, T. Tegg & Son, London; Griffin & Co., Glasgow; Tegg, Wise, & Tegg, Dublin; also James & Samuel Augustus Tegg, Sydney, Australia, 1836. Private collection.

1837 Richard Stringer, *Beaufront, Ross, Tasmania*, 1982. Photograph. Courtesy of Howard Tanner.

—Charles McIntosh, *The New Improved Practical Gardener, and Modern Horticulturist . . .* , Thomas Kelly, London, 1847 (detail).

1838 J.C. Loudon, *The Suburban Gardener and Villa Companion . . . intended for the instruction of those who know little of gardening and rural affairs, and more particularly for the use of ladies*, printed for the author and sold by Orme, Brown, Green, & Longmans, London; and W. Black, Edinburgh, 1838.

1839 Charles Frederick Leroux, *[Four-roomed cottage in Lonsdale Street, Melbourne] To be sold by auction by Mr James Hill on the Premises on Saturday July 20th 1839*. Ink and watercolour. Pictures Collection, State Library of Victoria, H 881.

1840 Nathaniel Wallich, *Report of Superintendent of Hon'ble Company's Botanic Garden, Calcutta*, printed by G.H. Huttmann, Bengal Military Orphan Press, Calcutta, 1840.

1841 Daniel Halfpenny, *Journal*, 1840–47. Australian Manuscripts Collection, State Library of Victoria, MS 13300.

1842 Edward Wilson, *He digs, but finds it hot, and And refreshes himself with a little watermelon*, c.1842–78. Watercolour, ink and pencil. Pictures Collection, State Library of Victoria, H 97.136/7–8.

1843 *Banksia cone in vase*, c.1850–70. Photograph. Royal Botanic Society Archives, courtesy of City of Westminster Library, London.

—Robert Marnock, *Plan of Royal Botanic Society's Garden, Regent's Park, London*, c.1840. Watercolour over engraved plan. Royal Botanic Society Archives, courtesy of City of Westminster Library, London.

1844 Wilbraham Frederick Evelyn Liardet, *Superintendent La Trobe's house*, 1875. Watercolour, ink and pencil. Pictures Collection, State Library of Victoria, H 28250/20.

1845 Sarah Susanna Bunbury, *Garden plan accompanying letter to Richard Hanmer Bunbury*, 27 July 1845. Bunbury Family Correspondence, Australian Manuscripts Collection, State Library of Victoria, PA 98/14.

1846 Long Ditton United Gardeners and Land Stewards' Mutual Instruction Society, *Address presented to Frederick John Plumridge for his services as secretary of the Society*, 13 January 1846. Gilt on fabric. Plumridge family collection, Melbourne.

1847 *Copy Invoice of Plants, Seeds, &c., Liverpool, 5 March 1847*. Invoice (detail). John Pascoe Fawkner papers, Australian Manuscripts Collection, State Library of Victoria, MS 13018.

1848 Wilbraham Frederick Evelyn Liardet, *Bishop Perry's residence*, 1875. Watercolour, ink and pencil. Pictures Collection, State Library of Victoria, H 28250/21.

1849 Great Britain. Ordnance Survey Office, *Suffolk Sheet IV S.W. / Norfolk Sheet XC S.W [Detail of Somerleyton Park]*, Ordnance Survey Plan, Ordnance Survey Office, Southampton, 1885. Maps Collection, State Library of Victoria.

—George Brunning, autographed address from book endpaper, 1864. Private collection.

1850 Daniel Bunce, *The Australian Manual of Horticulture*, 2nd ed., John Hunter, Melbourne, 1850.

1851 George Lawson, *The Royal Water-Lily of South America, and the Water-Lilies of our Own Land: Their History and Cultivation*, James Hogg, Edinburgh; R. Groombridge & Sons, London, 1851.

1852 Charles H. J. Smith, *Parks and Pleasure Grounds; or, Practical Notes on Country Residences, Villas, Public Parks and Gardens*, Reeve & Co., London, 1852.

—'Plan of the Gloucestershire Zoological, Botanical and Horticultural Gardens in the Park, Cheltenham' (detail), *Griffith's History of Cheltenham and its Vicinity . . .* , 3rd ed., Longman, Hurst, & Co., London, 1838. Private collection.

1853 *Township plan of Hamilton*, c.1853 (detail). Watercolour. Southern Grampians City Council.

1854 *The Colonial Gardener, being A Guide to the Routine of Gardening in Australia; with A Catalogue of Select Kitchen, Garden and Flower Seeds, as sold by Smith, Adamson and Co. . . .* , Goodhugh & Trembath, Melbourne, 1854.

1855 *The Rural Magazine, A Monthly Journal of Farming, Gardening, Botany, and Domestic Economy*, George Robertson, Melbourne, 1855.

1856 Shirley Hibberd, *Rustic Adornments for Homes of Taste, and Recreations for Town Folk, in the Study and Imitation of Nature*, 2nd ed., Groombridge & Sons, London, 1857.

1857 James Bonwick, *How Does a Tree Grow? or Botany for Young Australians*, James J. Blundell & Co., Melbourne; Sands & Kenny, Sydney, 1857.

1858 Lynette Zeeng, *Glenara, Bulla*, c. 2000. Colour transparency. Courtesy of the photographer.

1859 Charles Norton, *The front garden of Gwyllehurst the residence of John Gill Esq. Melbourne Victoria—with vista showing Hobson's Bay*, 1859. Watercolour. Pictures Collection, State Library of Victoria, H 88.21/68.

1860 *Prize certificate awarded to John Brown, Como*, 3 March 1860. William Sangster papers, Australian Manuscripts Collection, State Library of Victoria, MS 13350.

1861 F. H. von Kittlitz, *Twenty-four Views of the Vegetation of the Coasts and Islands of the Pacific with explanatory descriptions taken during the exploring voyage of the Russian corvette 'Senjawin' under the command of Capt. Lütke in the years 1827, 1828, & 1829 . . . Translated from the German and edited by Berthold Seemann*, Longman, Green, Longman, & Roberts, London, 1861.

1862 T. C. March, *Fruit and Flower Decoration: with some remarks on The treatment of town gardens, terraces, &c.; and with many illustrations of colour and contrast applicable to both subjects*, Harrison, London, 1862. John Viska collection, Perth.

1863 Victorian Horticultural Improvement Society, *Essay Book*, 1859–63 (detail). Australian Manuscripts Collection, State Library of Victoria, MS 12521.

1864 Richard Wendel and Troedel & Co., *Grand United Order of Free Gardeners of Australasia*, c.1864–1900. Certificate. Pictures Collection, State Library of Victoria, Troedel collection, volume 27.

1865 *Plan of the Government House Reserve, Botanic Gardens and its Domain, indicating the principal plantations. Drawn under the direction of Dr F. Mueller by E. B. Heyne* (detail), in Ferdinand Mueller, *Annual Report of the Government Botanist and Director of the Botanic Garden*, Victorian Parliamentary Papers, 1864–65/72.

1866 Jong Ah Sing, *The Case*, 1866–72. Australian Manuscripts Collection, State Library of Victoria, MS 12994.

1867 Henry Gritten, *Melbourne from the Botanic Gardens in 1867*, 1867. Oil on academy board. Pictures Collection, State Library of Victoria, H 298.

1868 *Plans of Flower Gardens, Beds, Borders, Roseries, and Aquariums; Accompanied by rules and directions for their formation, descriptions of the suitable plants, their arrangement and culture . . . by Contributors to the 'Journal of Horticulture'*, Journal of Horticulture and Cottage Gardener Office, London, 1868.

1869 W. Robinson, *The Parks, Promenades & Gardens of Paris described and considered in relation to the wants of our own cities and of public and private gardens*, John Murray, London, 1869.

1870 J. Weidenmann, *Beautifying Country Houses: A Handbook of Landscape Gardening. Illustrated by Plans of Places already Improved*, Orange Judd & Company, New York, 1870.

1871 *A Descriptive Catalogue of Fruit Trees [for] 1871–2, Cultivated for Sale by John Smith and Son, Riddell's Creek*, Clarson, Massina, & Co., Melbourne, 1871.

1872 Joseph Sayce, 'Report of Curator of Government House Domain, with photo-lithographed design and notes explanatory thereof', in Department of Lands and Agriculture, Victoria, *Report of the Secretary for Agriculture; to which is added the Report of the Inspector-General of Gardens, Parks, and Reserves*, 1 June 1873, John Ferres, Government Printer, Melbourne, 1873.

1873 Nicholas J. Caire, *Garden at Derriweit, Mount Macedon*, *c*.1873–82. Albumen silver photograph. Pictures Collection, State Library of Victoria, H 89.48/3.

1874 James Bateman, *A Monograph of Odontoglossum*, Reeve & Co. London, 1864–74.

—James Bateman, *The Orchidaceae of Mexico & Guatemala*, the author, London, 1837–43.

1875 F.W. Burbidge, *Domestic Floriculture, Window-gardening and Floral Decorations, being Practical directions for the propagation, culture, and arrangement of plants and flowers as domestic ornaments*, 2nd ed., William Blackwood & Sons, Edinburgh and London, 1875.

1876 Ferd. von Mueller, [Edmund Goeze (trans)], *Auswahl von aussertropischen Pflanzen, vorzüglich geeignet für industrielle Kulturen und zur Naturalisation, mit Angabe ihrer Heimathsländer und Nutzanwendung*, Theodore Fischer, Kassel and Berlin, 1883.

—Troedel & Co., *Baron Ferd. von Mueller K.C.M.G., M.D., Ph.D., F.R.S*, *c*.1880. Lithograph. Pictures Collection, State Library of Victoria, H 5057.

1877 Richard Aitken, *Palm House, Adelaide Botanic Garden*, 1982. Colour transparency. Courtesy of the photographer.

1878 Motoyoshi Ono, *Poisonous Plants. I. Collection*, Suye-hiro-cho, Kanda, Tokio, 1878.

1879 Richard Aitken, *Fortuna, Bendigo, Vic.*, 1985. Colour negative. Courtesy of the photographer.

1880 *The Famous Parks and Gardens of the World, Described and Illustrated*, T. Nelson & Sons, London, Edinburgh, and New York, 1880.

1881 William Guilfoyle, *[Plan of] Borough of Hamilton Public Garden*, 18 October 1881 (detail). Ink and watercolour. Hamilton Art Gallery, Southern Grampians Shire Council collection.

1882 *Rippon Lea, Elsternwick, Vic.*, *c*.1974–6. Colour transparency. Courtesy of National Trust of Australia (Victoria).

—Fredk. Manson Bailey, *The Fern World of Australia, with homes of the Queensland species*, Gordon & Gotch, Brisbane, 1881. Private collection.

1883 *Rippon Lea Elsternwick The property of the Honble F.T. Sargood. Esq., Scale 33 Feet to [an?] Inch, Reference: Soil pipes Red, Rain pipes Green, Fertilising pipes Brown, Agricultural pipes Yellow*, *c*.1883. Ink and watercolour. Sargood papers, University of Melbourne Archives.

1884 William Tibbits, *The Rest, Nelson Street, Abbotsford, Residence of Richard Goldsborough*, 1884. Watercolour. Pictures Collection, State Library of Victoria, H 6711.

1885 John Crombie Brown, *Forests and Forestry in Poland, Lithuania, The Ukraine, and the Baltic Provinces of Russia . . .* , Oliver & Boyd, Edinburgh; Simpkin, Marshall, & Co. and William Rider & Son, London; Dawson Brothers, Montreal, 1885.

1886 Frank J. Scott, *The Art of Beautifying Suburban Home Grounds of Small Extent . . .* , new edition, John B. Alden, New York, 1886.

1887 Ellis Rowan (attrib.), 'Sydney Wild Flowers', *Australian Town and Country Journal*, *c*.1888–92, supplement to Christmas edition. Chromolithograph. Private collection.

1888 Charles B. Walker, *Elevated view of a Victorian villa, showing brick residence with slate roof and two bay windows and garden layout*, *c*.1888. Albumen silver photograph. Pictures Collection, State Library of Victoria, H 81.111.

1889 Edward J. Wickson, *The Californian Fruits and How to Grow Them . . .* , Dewey & Co., San Francisco, 1889.

1890 Vilmorin-Andrieux & Cie, *Catalogue General, Printemps 1890*, Vilmorin-Andrieux & Cie, Paris, 1890.

1891 Josiah Conder, *The Flowers of Japan and the Art of Floral Arrangement*, Hakubunsha, Tokio; Kelly & Walsh, Limited, Yokohama, Shanghai, Hongkong, and Singapore, 1891.

1892 H.A. James, *Handbook of Australian Horticulture*, Turner & Henderson, Sydney, 1892.

1893 David Alexander Crichton, *The Australasian Fruit Culturist . . .* , Minerva Printing Works, Melbourne, 1893.

1894 Wilf Henty, *Bush scene, fern & male, Beech Forest, Vic.*, *c*.1901–40. Glass negative. Pictures Collection, State Library of Victoria, H 2002.106/19.

1895 A. Despeissis, *The Handbook of Horticulture & Viticulture of Western Australia*, Bureau of Agriculture, Perth, 1895.

1896 *The Wombat: A Quarterly Record of the Work of the Gordon College Museum and Kindred Associations*, Geelong, April 1896. McLaren Collection–Natural History, Baillieu Library, The University of Melbourne.

1897 W. Elliott, *Cole's Australasian Gardening and Domestic Floriculture*, E.W. Cole, Melbourne, 1897.

1898 Thomas Harlin & Mabel Gertrude Harlin, *Aspects of Nature: Selections from Milton, Cowper, Wordsworth, Shelley, Lowell, Ruskin*, Melville, Mullen & Slade, Melbourne, 1898.

1899 Melbourne and Metropolitan Board of Works, *Detail Plan of Abbotsford*, 1899. Lithographed plan, 160 feet = 1 inch (detail). Maps Collection, State Library of Victoria.

1900 Unknown photographer, *Men putting in poles in the hop garden (at Coranderrk?)*, *c*.1900. Inscribed on verso: 'Barak in centre looking on.' Photograph. Pictures Collection, State Library of Victoria, H 141252.

1901 A.E. Cole, *The Bouquet: Australian Flower Garden Handbook*, E.W. Cole, Melbourne, *c*.1914.

1902 Viscountess [Frances] Wolseley, *In a College Garden*, John Murray, London, 1916.

1903 C. Bogue-Luffmann, *The Principles of Gardening for Australia*, The Book Lovers' Library, Melbourne, 1903.

1904 J. H. Maiden, *The Forest Flora of New South Wales*, Wiliam Applegate Gullick, Government Printer, Sydney, 1904–24.

1905 A. R. Sennett, *Garden Cities in Theory and Practice: Being an amplification of a paper on The Potentialities of Applied Science in a Garden City read before Section F of the British Association*, Bemrose & Sons Ltd, London, 1905.

1906 'A National Rose Idea', *Journal of Horticulture of Australasia*, The Horticultural Publishing Press of Australasia, Melbourne, 1 (2), August 1906.

1907 *A Short Guide for Intending Emigrants to Victoria, the Garden State of Australia*, Issued by direction of the Minister of Lands, Melbourne, 1907.

1908 Gertrude Jekyll, *Children and Gardens*, Country Life Ltd and George Newnes, Ltd, London; Charles Scribner's Sons, New York, 1908.

1909 *Handbook or Descriptive Guide to the Botanic Gardens, Melbourne, with Plans, Views, etc.*, J. Kemp Government Printer, Melbourne, 1908.

1910 Butler and Bradshaw, *The Garden of Clive Baillieu Esq. Residence, Toorak*, 1910. Ink and pencil on linen. Melbourne University Architectural Collection, State Library of Victoria, WD HOU.144/3.

1911 Unknown photographer, *Hotel Canberra under construction*, c.1926 Photograph. Private collection.

1912 'Young Australia and his flower', *Australasian*, 14 December 1912, supplement. Private collection.

—Wattle Day badge, c.1915–20. Private collection.

1913 Hugh Michael O'Rorke, *Portrait of child dressed as an elderly woman, knitting as she walks in a garden*, c.1910–20. Glass negative. Pictures Collection, State Library of Victoria, H 99.224/174.

1914 Sears' Studio, *Basil Watson's aeroplane in the garden of his parents' house at Brighton, Vic.*, c.1916–17. Gelatin silver photograph. Pictures Collection, State Library of Victoria, H 39292.

1915 Richard T. Baker, *The Australian Flora in Applied Art. Part 1. The Waratah*, Department of Public Instruction, Technical Education Branch, Sydney, 1915.

1916 *Young Gardeners' League*, 1916. Certificate. Pictures Collection, State Library of Victoria, H 98.165/13.

1917 *Official Volume of Proceedings of the First Australian Town Planning and Housing Conference and Exhibition. Adelaide (South Australia) October 17th to 24th, 1917*, South Australian Executive on behalf of the State Executives of the Australian Town Planning Conference and Exhibitions, Adelaide, 1918.

1918 Thomas Patterson, *Reminiscences of an Amateur Carnation Enthusiast: A Paper read before the monthly meeting of the Carnation, Dahlia, and Sweet Pea Society of Victoria on the evening of Wednesday, March 27, 1918, at the Society's Rooms, Little Collins Street, Melbourne*, the Committee, Melbourne, 1918. McLaren Collection–Natural History, Baillieu Library, The University of Melbourne.

1919 Lynette Zeeng, *Maranoa Gardens, Balwyn, Vic.*, c.2000. Colour transparency. Courtesy of the photographer.

1920 Russell Grimwade, *An Anthography of the Eucalypts*, Angus & Robertson Ltd., Sydney, 1920.

1921 John Sulman, *An Introduction to the Study of Town Planing in Australia*, William Applegate Gullick, Government Printer, Sydney, 1921.

1922 A. E. Cole ('Bouquet'), *Half-hours in the Bush-house*, Angus & Robertson Ltd., Sydney, 1922.

1923 Algernon Darge, *Garden, trellis, tennis courts, and club house on south side of Bryant and May factory, Richmond, Vic.*, c.1925. Gelatin silver photograph. Pictures Collection, State Library of Victoria, H 92.401/143.

1924 *Australian Home Builder*, Edgar H. Baillie for The Herald and Weekly Times Limited, Melbourne, 8 September 1924.

1925 J. C. Shepherd & G. A. Jellicoe, *Italian Gardens of the Renaissance*, Ernest Benn Limited, London, 1925.

1926 Edward Edgar Pescott, *Gardening in Australia: A practical guide to laying out and cultivating gardens, lawns, hedges, patios; diseases and insect pests; propagation and reproduction of plants; soil preparation, etc.*, Whitcombe & Tombs Limited, Melbourne, 1926.

1927 Reg. A. A. Stoneham, *The Sun-raysed Waltz*, C. D. De Garis, Mildura, Vic., c.1925–30. Private collection.

1928 Mildred Stapley Byne & Arthur Byne, *Spanish Gardens and Patios*, J. B. Lippincott Company, Philadelphia & London; The Architectural Record, New York, [2nd impression], 1928.

1929 Hugh Ferriss, *The Metropolis of Tomorrow*, Ives Washburn, New York, 1929.

1930 Richard Aitken, *Dahlias and umbrellas, Ballarat, Vic.*, 1994. Colour transparency. Courtesy of the photographer.

1931 Edward Edgar Pescott, *Wild Flowers of Australia*, Shell Company of Australia, Melbourne, 1929.

1932 Posters Pty Ltd., *Yates' Reliable Seeds*, c.1930–32. Colour lithograph. Pictures Collection, State Library of Victoria, H 97.252/9.

1933 Charles Barrett & Edward E. Pescott, *New Way Gardening*, E. H. Baillie for United Press, Melbourne, 1933.

1934 *Tarnagulla Presbyterian Church Flower Show and Centenary Fair, Prize Schedule, 4 October 1934*, T. Page & Son, Printers, Quambatook, Ultima, and Manangatang, 1934. Poster. Private collection.

1935 Le Corbusier, *La Ville Radieuse: Eléments d'une doctrine d'urbanisme pour l'équipement de la civilisation machiniste*, Éditions de l'Architecture d'Aujourd'hui, Paris, 1935.

1936 James Northfield, *Melbourne: The Garden Capital of Victoria, Australia. Take a 'Kodak'*, 1936. Colour lithograph. Pictures Collection, State Library of Victoria, H 94.62.

1937 Edna Walling, *Garden Plan for Mrs Theo. Beggs 'Eurambeen', Beaufort, Victoria*, 1937. Watercolour, pen. ink and wash. Edna Walling Collection, State Library of Victoria, H 42827.

1938 *The Garden Year with Mr Bear*, Arthur Yates & Co., Sydney, 1938.

1939 Jean Galbraith, *Garden in a Valley*, Horticultural Press Pty Ltd, Melbourne, 1939.

1940 Thistle Y. Harris (ed.), *The Arbor Day Book: A Collection of Songs, Poems, and Plays suitable for presentation on Arbor Day*, Australian Forest League (New South Wales Section) Schools Branch, Sydney, 1940. Private collection.

1941 Edna Walling, *Red Cross Ballet on stage at 'Sonning'*, *c*.1941–4. Gelatin silver photograph. Edna Walling Collection, State Library of Victoria H 98.120/1

1942 Owen Bothers and Department of Agriculture, Victoria, *Dig for Victory: Grow your own Vegetables*, *c*.1942. Poster. Private collection.

—*Wartime Vegetable Growing at Home*, Victorian Department of Agriculture, Government Printer, Melbourne, 1942. Private collection.

1943 *Yates' Seed Book of What & When to Sow*, Arthur Yates & Co. Pty Ltd, Sydney, *c*.1943–44. Private collection.

1944 John Littlewood, 'Australia Day, 1994?', *Salt*, Australian Army Education Service, Melbourne, 7 (10), 17 January 1944. Private collection.

1945 Walter Bunning, *Homes in the Sun: The Past, Present, and Future of Australian Housing*, W. J. Nesbit, Sydney, 1945. Private collection.

1946 Elyne Mitchell, *Soil and Civilisation*, Angus & Robertson Ltd, Sydney, 1946. Private collection.

1947 Victorian Railways, *Garden Silhouette, No. 1 . . .* , 1947. Glass negative. Pictures Collection, State Library of Victoria, H 91.330/981.

1948 Rose Stereograph Company, *Fletcher Jones, Pleasant Hill, Warrnambool, Vic.*, *c*.1950–60. Glass negative. Pictures Collection, State Library of Victoria, H 32492/4806.

1949 W. A. Comeadow, *The Australian Horticultural Judge's Handbook for Judges and Exhibitors: Dahlias, Gladiolus, Chrysanthemums and other Cut Flowers, Floral Art, Vegetables*, Royal Horticultural Society of Victoria, Melbourne, *c*.1949. Private collection.

1950 Richard Aitken, *Suburban garden, Melbourne*, 1994. Colour transparency. Courtesy of the photographer.

1951 Herbert Young, 'Those urgent summer jobs', *Australian House and Garden*, K. G. Murray, Sydney, November 1951.

1952 Edna Walling, Red *Gums (E. camaldulensis)*, *c*.1930–60. Gelatin silver photograph. Edna Walling Collection, State Library of Victoria, H 98.120/345.

1953 *Ballarat Royal Visit Begonia Festival March 5th to March 15th, 1954*, Ballaarat Begonia Festival Committee, Ballarat, Vic., 1954. Private collection.

—*Ballarat Begonia Festival March 1 to 11 1957*, Ballaarat Begonia Festival Committee, Ballarat, Vic., 1957. Private collection.

1954 Nucolorvue Productions Pty Ltd, *Mosaic Imperial Crown, at the Shell House, Ballarat, Victoria*, *c*.1960–70. Postcard. Private collection.

1955 Commonwealth of Australia, *Australia Patent Specifications*, Patent specification 8770/55, no. 212130, Commonwealth Government Printer, Canberra, 1958.

1956 *The Queensland Garden Annual*, 3rd ed., Consolidated Publications Pty Ltd, Brisbane, *c*.1956. Private collection.

1957 *Notre Dame Abbey, Tarrawarra, Vic. On Way to Work*, *c*.1957. Postcard. Helen Doyle collection, Melbourne.

—B. A. Santamaria, *The Earth Our Mother*, Araluen Publishing Co., Melbourne, 1945. Private collection.

1958 Unknown photographer, *This tree, Eltham's oldest ~ rests in anger. ~ Slaughtered by S.E.C. 31.7.58*, 1958. Photograph. Peter Glass papers, Australian Manuscripts Collection, State Library of Victoria, MS PA99/87.

—*Build Among Our Trees Not Over Them*, Eltham Tree Preservation Society, Eltham, Vic., *c*.1958. Peter Glass papers, Australian Manuscripts Collection, State Library of Victoria, MS PA99/87.

1959 *Catalogue of Ogden Garden Products*, Ogden Industries Pty Ltd, Huntingdale, Vic., *c*.1959. Private collection.

1960 *Yates Garden Guide for Australian Home Gardeners*, Arthur Yates & Co. Pty Ltd, Sydney, 27th ed., *c*.1960. Private collection.

1961 Unknown photographer, *German immigrants in the backyard of the house rented by Helene and Josef Sandl, 1961*. *c*.1991, Gelatine silver photograph. Pictures Collection, State Library of Victoria, H 92.425/48.

1962 A. D. J. E. Slater, *Plan of rose garden*, *c*.1960–62. Ink drawing. Private collection.

—*Rose label*, *c*.1960. Private collection.

1963 Glen Wilson, *Garden design for Dr & Mrs Douglas Duffy, Mount Martha*, 1963. Ink drawing on letterhead. Pictures Collection, State Library of Victoria, H 2003.11/27.

1964 Donald Gazzard (ed.), *Australian Outrage. The Decay of the Visual Environment: A Study by the Royal Australian Institute of Architects*, Ure Smith, Sydney, 1966.

1965 Beryl Guertner (compiler), *Gregory's Australian Guide to Better Outdoor Living*, Gregory's Guides and Maps Pty Ltd., Sydney, *c*.1965.

—Gordon Cullen, 'Monstera deliciosa', in Margaret E. Jones & H. F. Clark, *Indoor Plants and Gardens*, The Architectural Press, London, 1952.

1966 Betty Maloney & Jean Walker, *Designing Bush Gardens*, Horwitz Publications Inc. Pty Ltd, Sydney, 1966.

1967 G. Moore & Paul Wycherley, *Pebble Gardens*, Southdown Press, Melbourne, *c*.1967.

1968 John Button (ed.), *Look Here! Considering the Australian Environment*, F. W. Cheshire, Melbourne, 1968.

1969 Ian McHarg, *Design with Nature*, The Natural History Press (American Museum of Natural History), New York, 1969.

1970 Town of Portland, *Best Kept Native Garden*, *c*.1970. Certificate. Private collection.

1971 Ted Greenwood, *V. I. P. Very Important Plant*, original illustrations (subsequently published by Angus & Robertson, Sydney, 1971). Pictures Collection, State Library of Victoria, PA 2004/11.

1972 *Earth Garden*, Keith Vincent Smith and Irene Smith, Balmain, NSW, no.1, 1972.

1973 *The Complete Guide to Growing Marijuana*, Lobotomy Press, Glebe, NSW, 1973. Private collection.

1974 *Your Garden*, Herald Gravure Printers, Hawthorn, Vic., 27 (7), July 1974.

1975 Ellis Stones (attrib.), *Merchant Builders' housing*, c.1971. Colour transparency. Ellis Stones Collection, Pictures Collection, State Library of Victoria, PA 2004/4.

1976 Elizabeth Cochrane, 'Common Fringe-lily', frontis to Winifred Waddell, *Wildflower Diary*, Native Plants Preservation Society of Victoria, Melbourne, 1976.

1977 Frances Kelly & Pauline Clements, *The Tiny Utopia for the Australian Gardener with Limited Space and Limited Time*, The Terrace Times, Balmain, NSW, 1977.

1978 Bill (B.C.) Mollison & David Holmgren, *Permaculture 1: A Perennial Agricultural System for Human Settlements*, Corgi Books, Melbourne, 1978.

1979 Richard Stringer, *Ard Choille, Mount Macedon*, 1978. Photograph. Courtesy of Howard Tanner.

1980 James Preston, *Racing Axemen: A History of Competitive Woodchopping in Australia*, Craftsman Press, Hawthorn, Vic., 1980.

1981 Philip Herington, *Something is Rotten in the Garden State: Report to Victorian State Conference April 1981* (detail), Melbourne, 1981.

1982 Merryle Anne Johnson, *Judging Jams – Neerim Show*, 1982. Type C photographs. Pictures Collection, State Library of Victoria, H 93.182/58-9.

—*Australian Home Beautiful*, Sun-News Pictorial, Melbourne, February 1954.

1983 Jillposters, *The Garden State, Fitzroy Presents: Choking to Death in Fitzroy*, 1983, Poster. Pictures Collection, State Library of Victoria, H 89.281/184.

1984 Don Burke, *The Lazy Gardener*, Horwitz Grahame Books Pty Ltd, Cammeray, NSW, 1983. Private collection.

1985 Greg Smith, *Organic Fruit and Vegetable Co-operative, Collingwood*, c.1985. Poster. Pictures Collection, State Library of Victoria, H 97.55/20.

1986 Chris Barry, *Mother*, from the series 'Displaced Objects', 1986. Cibachrome photograph. Pictures Collection, State Library of Victoria, H91.291/1.

1987 John Patrick, *Gardens of Victoria: The Guidebook to Victoria's Open Gardens Scheme*, ABC Enterprises, Sydney, 1987.

1988 *1988 Astro Calendar of the Antipodes: Biodynamic Moon Planting Guide & Planetary Rhythms*, Brian Keats & Susan Pearson, Bowraville, NSW, 1987. Private collection.

1989 Michael Leunig, *After the races, at home in the garden, a Toorak husband is punished by his wife because she was ignored by the social columnists*, 1989. Pen, ink and watercolour. Pictures Collection, State Library of Victoria, H 2000.80/110.

1990 Leigh Clapp, *Gravel path, Lambley Nursery borders, Ascot, Vic.*, 1996. Colour transparency. Courtesy of the photographer.

1991 Ruth Maddison, *Fleur Finnie, 72*, 1991. Gelatin silver photograph. Pictures Collection, State Library of Victoria, H 97.76/4.

1992 Peter Nicholson, *Mabo*, 1993. Ink and wash. Pictures Collection, State Library of Victoria, H 96.148/26.

1993 Howard Arkley, *Family Home Suburban Exterior*, 1993. Acrylic on canvas. Monash University Museum of Art. © The Estate of Howard Arkley, courtesy of Kalli Rolfe Contemporary Art.

1994 *England's Rose*, c.1994. Poster. Private collection.

1995 Warren Kirk, *Western Suburbs*, c.1995. Cibachrome photograph. Pictures Collection, State Library of Victoria, H 98.99/20.

1996 Richard Aitken, Poster *'You should see his back garden' created by Royal Botanic Gardens, Kew, for London Underground*, 1996. Colour transparency. Courtesy of the photographer.

1997 Room 4.1.3 (Vladimir Sitta and Richard Weller), *Garden of Australian Dreams competition design*, 1997. Digital image. Courtesy of Room 4.1.3.

1998 Kristin Headlam, *Public Park: Wedding party*, 1998. Oil on canvas. Pictures Collection, State Library of Victoria. H 2001.185.

1999 Ross Bird, *Christobo Carvahlo, aged 12, from Taibese, Dili, watering the vegetable garden at Puckapunyal Safe Haven*, 1999. Gelatin silver photograph. Pictures Collection, State Library of Victoria, H 2000.198/38.

2000 Simon Griffiths, *Brockhoff garden, Mornington Peninsula, Vic.*, c. 2000. Colour transparencies. Courtesy of the photographer.

2001 John Spooner, September 11 dust cloud looming over Australian front yard, cartoon published in the *Age*, 7 September 2002.

2002 Ian Harrison Hill, *Park in 'The Grove' on St Georges Avenue, Caroline Springs*, 2002. Gelatin silver photograph. Pictures Collection, State Library of Victoria, H 2002.118/14.

2003 Anonymous, *Canola: Victoria - Not the place for G. E.*, 2003. Silkscreen print. Pictures Collection, State Library of Victoria, H 2004.23.

2004 John Wolseley, *After the Fire, I, — 'The fresh earth beams forth ten thousand thousand springs of Life' — Blake*. 2004. Lithograph. Private collection.

p.226 *Home and Garden Beautiful*, B. R. Gowan & Co, Melbourne, December 1915.

INDEX

Bold numbers indicate illustrations

THE MIEGUNYAH PRESS

This book was designed and typeset by Ruth Grüner
The text was set in 10½ point Granjon with 2 points of leading
The text is printed on 130 gsm matt art

This book was edited by Clare Coney

Five thousand copies of this edition were printed
by Imago Productions